Gendered Vulnerability

Gendered Vulnerability examines the factors that make women particularly electorally vulnerable. For instance, female candidates get less and lower quality coverage from the media; they face stronger political opponents; and they receive less support from their political parties. Beyond these purely electoral factors, women face persistent gender biases throughout society that make it more difficult for them to succeed and also lead them to doubt their abilities and qualifications. These factors combine to convince women that they must work harder to win elections, a result that Jeffrey Lazarus and Amy Steigerwalt term "gendered vulnerability." Since women feel constant pressure to make sure they can win reelection, they devote more of their time and energy to winning their constituents' favor. For example, women secure more federal spending for their districts and states than men do; women devote more time and energy to constituent services; women introduce more bills and resolutions; and women's policy positions are more responsive to what their voters want. Lazarus and Steigerwalt examine a dozen different facets of legislative behavior, and find that across them all, female members simply do a better job of representing their constituents than male members.

Jeffrey Lazarus is an Associate Professor of Political Science at Georgia State University.

Amy Steigerwalt is an Associate Professor of Political Science at Georgia State University.

LEGISLATIVE POLITICS & POLICY MAKING

Series Editors

RECENT TITLES IN THE SERIES:

The Jeffords Switch: Changing Majority Status and Causal Processes in the U.S. Senate
CHRIS DEN HARTOG AND NATHAN W. MONROE

The Committee: A Study of Policy, Power, Politics, and Obama's Historic Legislative Agenda on Capitol Hill
BRYAN W. MARSHALL AND BRUCE C. WOLPE

The Whips: Building Party Coalitions in Congress
C. LAWRENCE EVANS

Indecision in American Legislatures
JEFFREY J. HARDEN AND JUSTIN H. KIRKLAND

Electoral Incentives in Congress
JAMIE L. CARSON AND JOEL SIEVERT

Gendered Vulnerability: How Women Work Harder to Stay in Office
JEFFREY LAZARUS AND AMY STEIGERWALT

Politics over Process: Partisan Conflict and Post-Passage Processes in the U.S. Congress
HONG MIN PARK, STEVEN S. SMITH, AND RYAN J. VANDER WIELEN

On Parliamentary War: Partisan Conflict and Procedural Change in the U.S. Senate
JAMES I. WALLNER

The Rise of the Representative: Lawmakers and Constituents in Colonial America
PEVERILL SQUIRE

Implementing Term Limits: The Case of the Michigan Legislature
MARJORIE SARBAUGH-THOMPSON AND LYKE THOMPSON

The Modern Legislative Veto: Macropolitical Conflict and the Legacy of Chadha
MICHAEL J. BERRY

Leadership Organizations in the House of Representatives: Party Participation and Partisan Politics
SCOTT R. MEINKE

For a complete list of titles in this series, please see www.press.umich.edu.

GENDERED VULNERABILITY

How Women Work Harder to Stay in Office

Jeffrey Lazarus and Amy Steigerwalt

University of Michigan Press
Ann Arbor

First paperback edition 2019

Published in the United States of America by the
University of Michigan Press
Manufactured in the United States of America
⊗ Printed on acid-free paper

First published in paperback August 2019

A CIP catalog record for this book is available from the British Library.

Library of Congress Cataloging-in-Publication data has been applied for.

ISBN: 978-0-472-13071-9 (hardcover : alk. paper)
ISBN: 978-0-472-12359-9 (e-book)
ISBN: 978-0-472-03758-2 (pbk. : alk. paper)

For Roberta, Ellen, Rachel, Alison, Jessica,
and all the women in my life
—Jeff

For my son, Gavin
—Amy

Contents

Acknowledgments

The origins of this book lie in an article we published together in 2009 about how earmarks are distributed differently among members in the House and Senate. In conducting our analysis for that article, we discovered that one senator in particular, Olympia Snowe, received so many earmarks that she was throwing off our results—none of our models made any sense unless we excluded her from the analysis. After taking a second look, we noticed that Snowe was not the only woman who had a lot of earmarks—many of the women of the Senate were at or near the top of the list. This lead us to wonder why, and what else women did more of than men in Congress. And it turned out that no matter what we looked at or how many different activities we examined, we always seemed to get the same answer—women in Congress do more of it. The result, nearly 10 years later, after a lot of data collection, analysis, and theorizing, is this book.

Over those 10 years, we have received assistance from more people than we can probably remember. We would like to thank Jessica Burke, Richard Gardiner, Jeff Glas, Lindsey Herbel, Elizabeth Karampolis, Deniz Ozbas, Natalie Rogol, Anastasia Vishnevskaya, Brian Webb, Alexandra Wishart, and Camille Wolpe, for the thankless task of research assistance. Craig Goodman and David C. W. Parker generously shared their data with us. We would like to thank Janet Martin, David C. W. Parker, Beth Reingold, Michelle Swers, participants at the Emory University Roundtable Discussion, and anonymous reviewers for helpful comments and suggestions. The authors also thank Meredith Norwich, David Cannon, Janet Box-Steffensmeier, and members of the editorial board at the University of Michigan Press for helping us bring this project to completion. Finally, we acknowledge and appreciate the financial assistance of the Department of Political Science of Georgia State University.

ONE

Introduction

In 2010, politics was dominated by a national discussion of earmarks, spending projects that individual members of Congress could easily slip into bills for their constituents. At the time all the members of Congress making national headlines were men, often for the wrong reasons. Representative Jack Murtha (D-PA), for example, used his position on the House Appropriations Committee to dole out earmarks to his constituents, and help himself out in the process. He created an illegal pay-to-play scheme: if someone wanted an earmark from Murtha, they first had to hire a lobbying firm headed by Murtha's former staffer. Murtha was never charged; he died while under federal investigation. But Representative Randy "Duke" Cunningham (R-CA) was charged—and convicted and sent to jail—for accepting millions of dollars in bribes from constituents he procured earmarks for. Senator Ted Stevens (R-AK) was responsible for the "Bridge to Nowhere," perhaps the nation's single most notorious earmark, a proposed $300 million project to connect an island with fifty residents to a larger island. On the other side of the issue, Senator Jeff Flake (R-AZ) made waves by refusing to accept any earmarks at all. All of these members received copious national attention for the earmarks they brought home (or in Flake's case, did not) to their constituents.

But behind all the noise generated by congress*men's* earmarks, congress*women* were the real leaders in procuring spending for their district. Congress's most prodigious earmarker that year was not a high-profile member, but a relatively undistinguished (as these things go in Congress) Senate Democrat from Michigan, Debbie Stabenow. Stabenow brought home more earmarks (254) and more money via earmarks ($565 million) than any other member of Congress, House or Senate. She was an unlikely champion earmarker: she was not a member of the committee that doles out the earmarks (Appropriations), she was not a committee chair, and she was not especially senior (she had only served ten years at the time). But Stabenow is a woman, and it turns out that makes a big difference when it comes to members "bringing home the bacon."

In 2010 female members of Congress out-earmarked the men in virtually every respect. In the Senate, four of the top five were women: Stabenow, Maine's Olympia Snowe, Dianne Feinstein from California, and Patty Murray from Washington. (The sole man in the top five was Mississippi's Thad Cochran.) To be sure, not every female senator was among the top-ranking earmark winners. But on average, female senators got more earmarks and more money for their states than male senators did. In the House of Representatives, the top earmark procurers were mostly men, but across the entire chamber a similar story unfolded—on average, women got more earmarks and brought home more money than men. In fact, this is not just true for earmarks, and it is not limited to any single year. There are lots of different kinds of pork barrel spending, and if you look at any of them you'll see the same thing—female members of Congress get more pork for their constituents than the men do (Anzia and Berry 2011). We discuss this trend more comprehensively in chapter 6.

Overall, the aim of this book is to demonstrate that women's advantage in pork barrel spending is not unique to that aspect of legislative behavior. When it comes to interacting with constituents, we argue that women's tendency to outdo men is a wide-reaching phenomenon that pervades all aspects of legislative life. We examine more than a dozen different activities that members of Congress engage in that are in whole or part related to communicating with or delivering goods to constituents, from traveling to their district to introducing bills to gaining membership on committees. No matter the area of legislative activity, the underlying story is always the same: for any activity a member of Congress engages in that is designed to get the attention or win the affection of voters, female members simply *do it more*. As well, there are some types of legislative behavior that are more nuanced, and the story of constituent influence cannot be told just by counting. For instance, do members introduce bills that are designed to impress voters, or try to secure positions on committees that have jurisdiction over policy areas that are most salient to their constituents? Here again, we find that the actions of female members of Congress are more closely tied to what their voters care about than the actions of male members. Even though every member of Congress takes advantage of the perquisites of office to help themselves win reelection, women do it more often, in greater numbers, and with closer attention to what their constituents want. In short, the primary theme of this book is that female members of Congress pay more attention to their constituents than male members do, and we detail how this pattern unfolds in each of the various ways that members use their office to try to impress voters.

Why Are Women So Constituent Oriented?

We argue that congresswomen's disproportionately constituent-oriented behavior is a function of both social and electoral forces that shape women's behavior once in office. To explain these forces, we rely on previous literatures on peoples' attitudes toward women's competence in the workplace (and in politics specifically), on how women react to these attitudes, and on the unique electoral hurdles faced by female candidates for office. These previous studies suggest that (a) in part because of how others view them, female incumbents perceive themselves to be vulnerable in their positions as members of Congress even when traditional measures of electoral safety—such as the size of a member's war chest or the member's vote share the last time he or she ran for office—indicate they are safe; and (b) when women run for election or reelection, they actually do run in a more objectively difficult electoral environment. Combined, these two factors generate a sense of electoral urgency among female members of Congress that we label "gendered vulnerability."

The first theoretical pillar underlying gendered vulnerability is the outsized doubts that women tend to have about their own abilities. These doubts exist in virtually all walks of life, including politics. On one hand, women generally express less confidence in their abilities and qualifications than men. On the other hand, these doubts are many times mirrored by external actors, which reinforces their hold on women's self-image.

Turning to the political arena, former House member Pat Schroeder recounts in her autobiography that running for the House—her first foray into politics—was not even her own idea. Her husband suggested it to her after a meeting of a local Democratic Party committee, where her name came up as a possible candidate. She mulled it over and decided to run, but she did not expect to win. "I was certain my candidacy was a well-meaning and short-lived exercise in futility. I'd be a Dona Quixote!" (Schroeder 2003, 6). Lawless, Fox, and Baitinger (2014) use data from 2001 and 2011 to paint a consistent picture: regardless of their actual qualifications, women are much less likely than men to assess themselves as qualified to run for office, and much less likely to positively assess their chances of winning if they were to run. Representative Anne Northup, interviewed by the authors of this work, endorses this view:

> More men run, because I think there is a history or tradition where women sort of wait to be invited, and men pop right up and say—this is a sweeping generalization of course—but men tend to pop right up and say, "I'd like to run." They are not intimidated by the fact that somebody else may want to run. . . . And so women, in my experience, tend to want to be chosen to run. So every time there is an election, there are plenty of people that would like to run for office. Now they may or may not actually run a good campaign, and they may or may not have the confidence to raise the money and go out and campaign, but there are plenty of people that think that would be something they would like to do. And, more often the men step right forward, step right up.

Lawless, Fox, and Baitinger (2014) also find that women perceive their potential electoral environment as more treacherous than men, whether in terms of competition or possible gender-based biases. Similarly, Thomas and Wilcox (2014) report that 53 percent of female respondents perceive that women do not win elected office as often as men, while a striking 73 percent of women do not believe that women running for office raise as much money as male candidates. A recent Associated Press–NORC Center for Public Affairs Research poll conducted in August 2016 similarly reports that 60 percent of female respondents believe women have "some" or "a lot" fewer opportunities in politics than men (40 percent of men responded similarly). Regardless of whether these perceptions are empirically founded, women view the electoral landscape as a treacherous one that creates impediments for women based solely on their gender (see also Lawless and Hayes 2016).

Finally, women must address the doubts of others: Senator Amy Klobuchar relates, "From the day I publicly said I was considering [joining] the race, I had been repeatedly asked whether a woman could win a U.S. Senate seat in Minnesota; this is a question men simply are not asked" (Klobuchar 2015). In her interview with the authors, Representative Northup expressed the same doubts, despite her veteran status in the chamber: "I had a district where everybody thought I would lose every two years. I mean, I thought I was going to lose. There would be a day in October where I would say, 'How did I ever win all my elections?'"

The second pillar of gendered vulnerability is that when women do decide to run, there are a number of ways in which the electoral landscape presents hurdles for them that are greater than the hurdles men must face. Specifically, they face pervasive gender stereotypes that influence how others perceive their candidacies, they receive less and lower-quality media attention, and they must contend with more and more-qualified challengers. For example, in 1986 now-Senator Dianne Feinstein had this advice for female candidates and working women in general: "Do not cry. No matter what. If you've got to bite off your tongue or close your eyes so tight that nobody can see what's in them, do it. Because a man can cry and somehow that doesn't bother anybody. If a woman cries, it is an immediate, destructive thing that goes out and that everybody seems to remember" (Pogash 1986). More recently, an article congratulating Iowa senator Joni Ernst's 2014 election win highlighted the tenuous line female candidates must walk: "So how did she pull it off in a state that has so long resisted making women its top leaders? A weak opponent, a breakthrough ad in the hog barn that went viral, and a carefully cultivated image that female politicians from Hillary Rodham Clinton to Sarah Palin have struggled to translate into votes: Tough, strong, but nonthreatening" (Reston 2014).

Further, female candidates for office receive less media coverage than male candidates, and the coverage they do get is more likely to focus on character items, clothing, or horserace aspects of the campaign—anything other than the candidates' views, positions, and actions. The differences in coverage between male and female candidates have lessened in recent years, but they have not disappeared altogether, meaning that even a decade and a half into the twenty-first century, a popular media outlet can run an article on Congresswoman Nydia Velazquez's (D-NY) inauguration entitled "Fashionable Nydia Inaugurated with Love" (Fiala 2013), and another can repeatedly call Senator Elizabeth Warren "Granny" during her successful 2012 race against Scott Brown.[1]

Finally, female candidates for office face more and better-quality challengers than male candidates. When women run for office, they typically face a greater number of opponents (particularly in their primary election), and their opponents are better funded and are more likely to have held prior office than the opponents faced by men. A staffer we interviewed noted this: "In elections, women are viewed as more vulnerable. People are systematically not as threatened by women, so they're more likely to run against them. [My two male bosses] did all the same things and [my previous female boss] got two primary opponents, and they got zero."

Notably, both of these conditions—women's perceptions of their own vulnerability and the fact that they face more difficult electoral conditions—apply not only to female challengers but also to female incumbents. Thus, not only are female *candidates* conditioned to expect that they will have to work harder than males to win election, female *incumbents* likewise know that when they seek reelection they will face a much more challenging reelection environment than males simply by virtue of being female. Voter stereotypes, potentially biased media coverage, and the belief by many political elites that women make weak candidates do not go away once a woman has won office. Female candidates and elected officials are *both* socialized to view their position as inherently vulnerable, and thus susceptible to attack, regardless of their actual performance.

We show that the barriers women face reach beyond the electoral arena, and into the legislative arena. Women who have already won election and hold office must overcome their own self-doubts to run for reelection while simultaneously taking conscious steps to reassure constituents, party leaders, and colleagues that they are worthy; this is the crux of our notion of "gendered vulnerability." The question we ask is whether this gendered vulnerability influences women's actions not just during the campaign but also after the race has been won and female candidates become female officeholders. That women act differently than men while in office is well established—they tend to be more liberal on average, pay more attention to women's issues, and engage their colleagues in a more consensual manner. We move beyond these conceptions of gender differences to offer a theoretical argument that covers the broad spectrum of activities in which legislators engage: we argue that women's gendered vulnerability induces them to pay more attention to their constituents, and to act as better representatives for their constituents' interests and needs.

Are Even Safe Women Safe?

The two factors identified above—pervasive self-doubt and heightened electoral difficulty—influence all women regardless of how objectively "safe" they are in their elected offices. In this way, "gendered vulnerability" is distinct from traditional notions of electoral vulnerability—it is as much about the *perception* of electoral vulnerability as it is about any objective factor that might lead an officeholder to believe that she is vulnerable. Even when female incumbents hail from a district that is safe in the traditional sense, and even when they have won election numerous times previously, they still face the possibility of threats within their own party, questions about their abilities, and more challenges on their road to reelection than would be expected. Additionally, broader social forces lead women and their potential political opponents to believe that female officeholders are less qualified or must do more to prove that they belong or are successful, or both. As a result, gendered vulnerability affects all female members of Congress (potentially, all female elected officeholders) regardless of how safe their seats are according to more traditional measures of electoral safety. This leads female legislators to act as though they are vulnerable in the ways they carry out the duties of their office, even if traditional measures of electoral vulnerability suggest they are anything but. We showcase this phenomenon by drawing two comparisons of seemingly similar male and female members of Congress. These two comparisons illustrate that even though both the male and female member appear safe by traditional standards, only the male member actually was protected from attack. In both cases, the female member faced stiff electoral competition despite her seeming electoral safety. We suggest these two examples reflect the norm rather than the exception: overall, even seemingly electorally "safe" female incumbents must continually guard against attacks, even from members of one's own party.

We begin by comparing two Republican members of the House of Representatives from Illinois—Judy Biggert and John Shimkus. As summarized in table 1.1, both initially won office by winning multicandidate primaries, but their subsequent paths differed. Shimkus narrowly won election when he first ran in 1996. However, since then he has not faced a single primary challenger, and his only real general election challenge came postredistricting when he was pitted against another incumbent, Democrat David Phelps, in 2002. Alternatively, Biggert has consistently drawn both primary challengers and strong general election challengers. Even though she won her initial general election in 1992 comfortably with 69 percent of the vote, she faced a strong primary challenger in 1994. In 1996 she ran for the Republican nomination unopposed and again won the general election comfortably (71 percent). But this wide electoral margin did not protect her from facing five primary challengers in 1998. For the next three cycles she ran unopposed in the primaries, winning her general elections with 65 percent of the vote or more, but again faced primary challengers in 2006 and 2008. In 2008 she also faced her strongest Democratic challenger to date, business owner Scott Harper. Harper raised almost $650,000, an impressive sum for an inexperienced challenger going up against a safe incumbent, and garnered 44 percent of the vote. Harper challenged her again in 2010, and she won this second time with a convincing 63 percent of the vote. Ultimately, these electoral successes were not enough to shield her from defeat. In 2012 her district was redrawn, and the new 11th District was much more heavily Democratic. Former U.S. Representative Bill Foster won the Democratic primary, and eventually defeated Biggert 59–41.

Our second example compares Senators John McCain (R-AZ) and Barbara Mikulski (D-MD); their respective electoral histories are reported in table 1.2. Both ran for an open Senate seat in 1986 after serving multiple terms in the U.S. House (five and three, respectively), and both won their

TABLE 1.1. Comparative Electoral Fortunes of Representative Judy Biggert and John Shimkus, both Republicans from Illinois

	Judy Biggert		John Shimkus	
	Primary	General	Primary	General
1992	Biggert—38% J. McCarthy—25% T. Vandermyde—13% A. Clark—12% J. Curry—12%	Biggert—69% D. Briggs (D)—31%		
1994	Biggert—54% J. McCarthy—46%	Biggert—78.5% Chalberg (D)—21%		
1996	Unopposed	Biggert—71% Brockway (D)—29%	Won six-way primary	Shimkus—50% J. Hoffman (D)—50%
1998	Biggert—45% P. Roskam—40% D. Shestokas—5% M. Krzyston—5% A. Clark—4% W. Marksym—2%	Biggert—61% S. Hynes (D)—39%		Shimkus—61% R. Verticchio (D)—38%
2000	Unopposed	Biggert—66% T. Mason (D)— 34%	Unopposed	Shimkus—63% J. Cooper (D)—37%
2002	Unopposed	Biggert—70% T. Mason (D)—30%	Unopposed	Shimkus—55% D. Phelps—45%
2004	Only write-in challenge	Biggert—65% G. Andersen (D)—35%	Unopposed	Shimkus—69% T. Bagwell (D)—31%
2006	Biggert—80% B. Hart—20%	Biggert—58% J. Shannon (D)—42%	Unopposed	Shimkus—61% D. Stover (D)—39%
2008	Biggert—77% S. O'Kane—23%	Biggert—54% S. Harper (D)—44%	Unopposed	Shimkus—64% D. Davis (D)—33%
2010	unopposed	Biggert—63% S. Harper (D)—36.2%	Unopposed	Shimkus—71% T. Bagwell (D)—29%
2012	unopposed	Lost: Biggert—41% B. Foster (D)—59%	Unopposed	Shimkus—69% A. Michael (D)—31%

TABLE 1.2. Comparative Electoral Fortunes of Senators Barbara Mikulski and John McCain

	Barbara Mikulski		John McCain	
	Primary	General	Primary	General
1986 Open Seat	Mikulski—49.5% Rep. Michael Barnes—31.4% Gov. Harry Hughes—14.3% (+ 4 other candidates who received less than 2%)	Mikulski—60.5% L. Chavez (R)—39.5%		McCain—60.5% R. Kimball (D)—39.5%
1992 Reelection	Mikulski—76.8% Thomas Wheatley—6.4% Walter Boyd—5.4% Don Allensworth—4.0% Scott Britt—2.7% James White—2.5% B. Emerson Sweatt—2.3%	Mikulski—71% Alan Keyes (R)—29.0%	Uncontested	McCain—55.8% C. Sargent (D)—31.6% E. Mecham (I)—10.5%
1998 Reelection	Mikulski—84.4% Ann Mallory—10.4% Kauko Kokkonen—5.2%	Mikulski—70.5% R. Pierpont (R)—29.5%	Uncontested	McCain—68.8% E. Ranger (D)—27.2%
2004 Reelection	Mikulski—89.9% A. Robert Kaufman—7.1% Sydney Altman—3.1%	Mikulski—64.8% State Sen. E. J. Pipkin (R)—33.7%	Uncontested	McCain—76.7% S. Starky (D)—20.6%
2010 Reelection[1]	Mikulski—82.3% Christopher Garner—7.5% A. Jaworski—3.2% Blaine Taylor—2.28% (+ 3 additional candidates who received less than 2%)	Mikulski—62.2% Eric Wargotz (R)—35.8%	McCain—56.2% J. D. Hayworth—32.1% Jim Deakin—11.7%	McCain—59.3% Rodney Glassman (D)—34.6% David Nolan (LBT)—4.7%

races with approximately 61 percent of the vote. However, the two candidates were treated very differently when they each sought reelection in 1992: McCain was uncontested in the Republican primary and then won the general election with 63 percent of the two-party vote against a candidate who had breezed to victory in his own relatively uncontested primary. By contrast, Mikulski was challenged by six candidates in the Democratic primary while fifteen candidates competed in the Republican primary. Even with all of this competition, Mikulski retained her seat easily, winning the primary with 77 percent and the general election (against Republican Alan Keyes) with 71 percent of the vote. In 1998, McCain again faced no challengers in the primary and easily won the general election with 69 percent of the vote, but Mikulski once again faced considerable opposition—two Democrats challenged her in the primary and ten Republicans sought the Republican nomination. Nonetheless, Mikulski still won with margins (84 percent in the primary and 71 percent in the general) that suggested her opponents greatly overestimated her vulnerability. In 2004 McCain yet again reaped the benefits of his incumbency status, facing no primary challenger and easily defeating a relatively weak challenger in the general election. Mikulski, however, had to ward off two challengers in the Democratic primary—which she did in spectacular fashion by winning 90 percent of the vote—as well as a state senator in the general election.

While both Mikulski and McCain were elevated to the U.S. Senate after serving multiple terms in the House, and won the two-party vote by similar margins, McCain faced no primary challengers and relatively weak general election challengers in his next three electoral cycles. Comparatively, Mikulski continually faced opposition in both her primary and general elections, even after winning each of her elections with 70 percent of the vote or more. Only in 2010 did McCain face a primary challenger, and that likely had much to do with his unsuccessful run as the Republican presidential nominee in 2008. For Mikulski, the pattern remained the same in 2010, again facing multiple primary challengers and a relatively strong general election challenger, even though her previous win in the general election with 65 percent of the vote would normally put her seat squarely in the "safe" category.

These examples showcase a broader trend: female candidates and incumbents face heightened competition across the board (e.g., Lawless and Pearson 2008). Even those in safe seats who won their previous elections by wide margins face some kind of competition, seemingly due to the perception that women are simply more vulnerable to defeat. One of the staffers we interviewed noted that her female boss "was always approaching [her job like] she was vulnerable. Absolutely, she won by 69 percent but she always . . . I think that is how she approached legislation, too. She had to prove that she was the best." Stories like these also highlight the fact that female candidates have had to continuously worry about reelection and challenges—even from their own party—regardless of how one might objectively categorize their relative level of "safety" from electoral threats. Even sizable victories do not protect women against the perception—or the reality—of vulnerability, a vulnerability that attaches to women simply due to being women. As a result of this gendered vulnerability, even a dominant female politician must be ever vigilant against perceptions of diminished abilities and threats to her seat. Most important for the purposes of this study, it also implies that while in office she will act in ways that try to overcome this gendered vulnerability.

We argue that this gendered vulnerability induces female officeholders to work to mitigate the effects of potential electoral attacks by addressing the needs of their constituents and preparing for reelection. Women adhere more closely to the policy positions their voters prefer, spend more time on constituent-oriented activities and issues, and generally spend more time and effort on the activities of office that offer the highest electoral payoffs. Even though all officeholders use the resources of their offices to help win reelection, women are induced by several forces, including the structural disadvantages they face in their electoral environment, to do so more than men. And the path women choose leads them to devote more time and energy in office to their constituents than men.

The Electoral Connection

Before moving on, it is worth asking whether the things that members of Congress do while in office actually affect their chances of winning reelection. Because if the answer is no—if voters take no note of what their members do when deciding who to vote for—then there would be no point in female members of Congress even trying to use the perquisites of their office to try to overcome their electoral disadvantages (both real and perceived). All of that effort would be for naught, and there would be no use in even trying.

David Mayhew's (1974) seminal work imagines members of Congress as caring about nothing but winning reelection. Of course, in reality members have plenty of other concerns aside from winning reelection (most important, pursuing policy goals), but the conceit of the single-minded reelection seeker allowed Mayhew to explore the many ways in which members use their office to help themselves electorally. Since the publication of that work, scholars have further asked whether any of the things that members do with an eye toward winning reelection actually helps in that regard. Members can engage in all the reelection-oriented activities they want, but if voters don't notice them or don't care, all of that effort will have been wasted. So the question is, do voters respond to the things that members do? Do these activities actually help members? Generally, the answer has been yes—there are three types of legislative activity that voters appear to take into account when evaluating their members of Congress and deciding who to vote for come reelection time.

First and foremost, voters reward and punish members of Congress for the substantive policy positions they take while in office, particularly policy positions that members express in roll-call votes. Indeed, it would seem odd if voters didn't respond to members' roll-call voting, given the amount of care and effort members take to match their (publicly held) policy positions with those of the district (Kingdon 1989). Scholars have noted cases where members' vote shares when running for reelection are significantly related to how they voted on high-profile bills. These bills include the 2010 Affordable Care Act (Nyhan et al. 2012), President Clinton's 1993 budget bill (Heidom 1994), a selection of crime bills (Canes-Wrone, Minozzi, and Reveley 2011), and the 2008 Troubled Assets Relief Program (Green and Hudak 2009). More broadly, voters appear to punish members whose voting records are too overtly ideological (Canes-Wrone, Brady, and Cogan 2002; Erikson 1971; Erikson and Wright 2000; Ansolabehere, Snyder, and Stewart 2001), or too overtly partisan (Carson et al. 2010). Moreover, it seems that a policy position doesn't even have to be expressed in a roll-call vote for voters to notice it—there is also evidence that voters can reward and punish members for the bills they introduce (Parker and Goodman 2009) and the speeches they make on the chamber floor (Box Steffensmeier et al. 2003).

The second type of legislative activity that can affect members' fate when they seek reelection is pork barrel spending. Across the board, voters report more favorable opinions of Congress members who procure high levels of spending for their districts (Johannes and McAdams 1981a; McAdams and Johannes 1988; Stein and Bickers 1994; Alvarez and Schousen 1993; Pew Research Center 2010; Sellers 1997). More important for members, this individual-level support translates into success at the ballot box: members of Congress get higher vote percentages when they secure a large number of pork barrel projects for their districts—although here the effect seems to be limited to Democratic members of Congress (Levitt and

Snyder 1997; Alvarez and Saving 1997; Sellers 1997; Lazarus and Reilly 2010).

Third, voters appear to be responsive to casework—the work that Congress members and their staffs do to help individual voters who have problems when dealing with government bureaucracy. Here the record of scholarship is not quite as clear (we review the literature in chapter 3), but the most recent and methodologically advanced studies all suggest that when members of Congress do more casework, they are rewarded with higher levels of voter approval and better evaluations (Romero 2006; Parker and Goodman 2009, 2013; Cover and Brumburg 1982; Serra and Cover 1992).

Altogether, the evidence strongly suggests that members are, as Mayhew (1974) put it, "in a position as individuals to do [something] about" their own electoral prospects (17). Through the bills they vote for (or against), the pork barrel projects they procure, and the casework they perform, members can influence their constituents to be more likely to know who their members are, to evaluate their members more favorably, and to be more likely to vote for the member come election time. So it makes sense that members focus on reaching out to voters in these and other ways.

Studies also confirm that members pursue these activities in the hopes of shoring up their reelection chances, and that electorally vulnerable members do so more than those holding "safer" seats. For example, Lazarus (2009) finds that electoral vulnerability results in more earmarks for members of the majority party in the House, while Koger (2003) and Harward and Moffett (2010) both find electorally vulnerable members cosponsor more bills, and Goodman and Parker (2010) find an increased use of franked mail by more vulnerable members. We extend this literature to argue that, due to their perceptions of gendered vulnerability, women pursue a similar strategy. Moreover, since gendered vulnerability transcends traditional notions of electoral vulnerability and instead extends to all women due simply to their gender, we will thus see female members of Congress engaging in more of these electorally beneficial and constituent-oriented activities, and at higher levels, than their male colleagues. We thus offer a novel and comprehensive theory for understanding why gender differences in legislative behavior emerge, and how they manifest themselves in the myriad of activities legislators undertake while in office.

Chapter Outline

In chapter 2 we present our theory of "gendered vulnerability." We first provide an overview of the two distinct literatures that underlie the core assumptions of our theory: the literature highlighting the social forces that lead women to perceive that they are inherently more vulnerable to attack, and the literature showing that female candidates face a more treacherous electoral arena than males. We use the gender socialization literature to illuminate not only how women are more likely to doubt and question their own abilities but also how they must contend with a world that doubts them as well. We then show how the political arena reinforces these beliefs, serving as a type of crystallization process that indelibly influences how women act once in office. We argue there are three main electoral hurdles all women candidates, challengers and incumbents alike, face: pervasive gender stereotypes among both voters and party elites; a greater likelihood of facing more and better-quality challengers than their male counterparts; and media coverage that is both low quality and more focused on women's appearance and traits than their issue positions or quality. Further, even if these electoral impediments are diminishing over time, female politicians, and even potential politicians, continue to perceive them as still standing in their way to success.

We then argue that these forces create a sense of gendered vulnerability that induces female members to behave differently than their male colleagues once in office. We argue that the effect of gendered vulnerability reaches across all areas of legislative behavior, and all potential issues that legislators address, to produce clear differences in the actions undertaken and the outcomes produced by female and male legislators. Specifically, in order to overcome their gendered vulnerability, female officeholders, as compared to males, will concentrate more of their efforts on constituent-related activities and those that provide the highest reelection payoffs. Our theory moves beyond the traditional arguments concerning women legislators and substantive representation to argue that women, as a result of their gendered vulnerability, will serve as better substantive representatives of all of their constituents.

The next four chapters test the empirical hypotheses suggested by our theory of gendered vulnerability. Mayhew (1974) argues that legislators seeking reelection pursue credit-claiming activities that send the message to a legislator's constituents that the legislator is responsible as an individual for getting the government to do something desirable. Legislators also engage in position-taking activities by expressing their judgments on issues of interest. Credit-claiming and position-taking activities thus serve to help legislators advertise their efforts for their constituents back home and aid their reelection goals by highlighting legislators' attempts to address their constituents' needs (see also Fenno 1978a). Since female legislators must be concerned with overcoming their gendered vulnerability and proving their worth to the voters (as well as potential challengers), they are more likely than their male colleagues to directly seek to fulfill their constituents' needs and more likely to spend their time on those activities with position-taking and credit-claiming payoffs.

Throughout the book we examine the legislative behavior of members of the U.S. Congress in both the House and the Senate, primarily from the 103rd to 110th Congresses (1993–2005) using a variety of measures and metrics. The 103rd Congress was the first Congress after the 1992 elections, which brought a marked increase in the number of women in both chambers of Congress. Female representation in the Senate more than doubled (increasing from three to seven), and female representation in the House of Representatives increased by 60 percent (from thirty to forty-eight). We also enhance these findings with evidence from over twenty qualitative, in-depth interviews we conducted with current and former members of Congress, as well as former and current congressional staff, during the summer of 2013. Most of the staff we interviewed served during the period our data covers, as well as in more current periods, and the vast majority of them also worked for both male and female members, allowing us to draw upon their reflections of potential differences. Representative John Lewis (D-GA) has served in Congress since 1987, while former Representative Anne Northup (R-KY) served from 1997 to 2007 and later was a commissioner for the U.S. Consumer Product Safety Commission from 2009 to 2013. Unlike most studies of Congress, we do not focus on a single chamber. Rather, all of our investigations into legislative behavior cover both the House of Representatives and the Senate. In that way, we can both broadly understand core gender differences as well as capture how these differences may manifest themselves in distinct ways within each chamber.

Chapter 3 examines direct constituency services. Female members of Congress more heavily use the resources their offices provide to remind constituents of who represents them in Congress, to keep constituents appraised of their legislative activities, and to help constituents with the problems they face in dealing with government bureaucracy (this help is generally known as casework). We argue that gendered vulnerability leads women to want to keep their successes and achievements in the forefront of voters' minds, and to prioritize services that aid constituents. In particular, we examine members' use of the franking privilege (federally funded mail sent from members' offices directly to constituents), the assignment of staff to district offices (these staff are typically assigned to do casework), and members' travel to their districts to visit constituents personally. We find that female House members send more franked mail, while female senators assign more of their staff to the district than male members do.

Chapter 4 turns to one of Congress members' best tools for directly benefiting their constituencies: the procurement of pork barrel spending. Pork barrel spending brings federal money straight into a particular district and visibly aids constituents (both those hired at the initial construction phase if something is to be built, and those who later use whatever the money is spent on). Moreover, members of Congress can plausibly claim credit for these projects, since they so directly benefit the district. We expect that female legislators will procure more pork barrel spending for their districts than males. We test this hypothesis by examining two distinct types of pork-barrel spending: individual spending items written directly into spending bills (as discussed above, commonly known as earmarks) in the 110th Congress, and bureaucratic awards specifically coming out of the 2009 economic stimulus package. In both cases, we find that female legislators in both chambers procure more earmarks and more bureaucratic awards than their male colleagues. We also extend this analysis beyond simply the quantity of procurements to the substantive effect of the procurements. Again utilizing awards from the 2009 economic stimulus package, we posit and find that female legislators are more likely to successfully procure awards when their district's level of economic need is higher than males representing similar high-need districts. We thus find that not only do women overall procure more federal dollars for their districts but also that women are more likely to do so in a manner that reflects their constituents' needs.

Chapter 5 examines the ways in which members use the legislative process. We argue that many if not most bills that members introduce are not meant to be passed into law, but are meant to publicly advertise policy positions to voters—such bills are known in Washington as "messaging bills." Other legislative devices that members use to publicly take positions on issues include resolutions and cosponsorships. Our theory of gendered vulnerability predicts that female members work to prove to their constituents, their colleagues, and potential challengers that they are working hard for their districts in order to stave off potential doubts and attacks. Female members should therefore sponsor more bills and resolutions than male members, and cosponsor more as well. We find that female members of the House and Senate each sponsor more bills and resolutions, and cosponsor more as well, than their male colleagues. Female sponsors in both chambers also secure more cosponsors for their bills and see fewer of their bills become law, which we take as further indications that the bills that women introduce are more likely to be messaging bills targeted at showing their constituents that they are working actively to promote their interests and needs.

In chapter 6, we again look past the *amount* of legislative activity that members undertake and instead examine the substantive policy aspects of what they do. Not only do members need to prove they are active, but they also need to show that they are faithful representatives—and this is more true for members who are vulnerable, both traditionally and via gendered vulnerability. We show that women are more responsive to voters than male members in their legislative work in a number of different ways. First, we examine committee memberships. Membership on a standing committee allows members to work much more closely on issues within the committee's policy jurisdiction; many members seek seats on committees that hold jurisdiction over issues that their constituents care most about. Utilizing a Monte Carlo simulation procedure, we find that female members' committee assignments in both chambers more faithfully reflect the needs of their districts than those of male members. Next, we reexamine the bills members introduce, this time concentrating on the policy content of those bills. Similar to committee assignments, we find that the correlation between district characteristics and the bills that members introduce is higher for female members than for male members. Finally, we examine roll-call votes, and find a closer correspondence between voter preferences and roll-call ideology for females than for males.

We conclude in chapter 7 with a summary of our overall findings and a discussion of the broader implications of our theory of gendered vulnerability. In particular, we highlight the results of chapters 4 and 6, which indicate that gendered vulnerability induces female legislators—and, potentially, all female elected officials across the three branches of government as well as the local and state levels—to be more faithful representatives of their constituents than men. The normative implication of these findings is that electing women results in better substantive representation for *all* constituents. While numerous studies debate the link between descriptive and substantive representation in terms of whether women better represent women (see, e.g., Reingold 1992, 2000; Swers 2002; Vega and Firestone 1995), we argue that women work more faithfully to represent *all* of their constituents' interests and needs than men. In a way, our most important contribution to the existing literature on gender and legislative behavior is to broaden its focus on women's policy priorities to include issues that do not solely address the needs of women, but instead are salient to their voters, whoever they are. We argue that gendered vulnerability leads women legislators to more clearly pursue constituent-oriented work and policies across the panoply of potential issues in a way that is distinct from their male colleagues.

Our results thus also imply—barring a drastic change in the social and electoral forces confronting female candidates—that increasing the number of women in the U.S. Congress will directly benefit all Americans. As of 2017, 21 percent of senators are female, as are 19.1 percent of representatives. And, as of January 2017, the United States ranks 104th (out of 193 countries) in the world in terms of female representation in federal legislatures; nations in the top ten include Rwanda, Cuba, Iceland, Nicaragua, and Senegal (Inter-Parliamentary Union 2017). One set of arguments in favor of growing this number is the need for increased substantive representation of women and their interests, a group that makes up almost 51 percent of Americans. We add another strong argument: that female legislators improve the representation experienced by all of their constituents, female and male, young and old, rich and poor. Electing women thus ensures that our representative democracy functions at its highest level.

TWO

"Coya, Come Home"

Gendered Vulnerability and Women in Office

Coya Knutson was elected to the House of Representatives from Minnesota in 1954, joining only sixteen other female House members, and one female senator. Her legislative career got off to a promising start—in just her first two terms she created the first federal grants for cystic fibrosis research and established the first federal student loan program. Her career was cut short, however, when she lost her bid to win a third term because—in a move that seems unthinkable today—local leaders of her own party engineered her defeat. Knutson had never been entirely accepted by local party bosses, partly because she was a woman and partly because she had defeated a party-backed candidate to win her seat in the first place. But tensions between Knutson and the local chapter of the Democratic-Farmer-Labor Party (effectively, the Minnesota Democratic Party) erupted when she endorsed Estes Kefauver to be the Democratic nominee for president in 1956. The state and local DFL endorsed Adlai Stevenson, largely because he was likely to pick Minnesota's own Hubert Humphrey as his running mate. Kefauver ended up defeating Stevenson handily in the Minnesota presidential primary. DFL leaders were deeply embarrassed, and they targeted Knutson for revenge.

First, the state DFL refused to endorse Knutson in the 1958 House elections. According to state party rules at the time, candidates with the DFL's endorsement could have their names placed directly on the November ballot. Without the endorsement, Knutson would have to run in a contested primary election. She won the primary and with it the party's nomination, but the DFL was not deterred. Next, local party leaders started a rumor that Knutson, who was married, was having an affair with one of her staff members. Finally, they broke out the big guns: party leaders approached her husband, Andy Knutson, to help them derail her career. Andy was an alcoholic and physically abusive—Knutson moved to Washington, DC, rather than live there part time, to put distance between herself and Andy. By some accounts, Knutson regularly wore sunglasses to hide the bruises she received at Andy's hands. Despite—or perhaps because of—the abusive nature of the Knutsons' marriage, DFL leaders presented Andy with a letter that they had written in his name. The letter demanded that Coya Knutson retire from Congress and return to her rightful place in the family home. It painted her as a negligent mother and wife, unable to perform her family duties because of the time she spent in Washington as a member of Congress. It read, in part,

> Coya, I want you to tell the people of the 9th District this Sunday that you are through in politics. That you want to go home and make a home for your husband and son. As your husband I compel you to do this. I'm tired of being torn apart from my family. I'm sick and tired of having you run around with other men all the time and not your husband. I love you, honey. . . . Come back. Come back to our happy, happy home.

Andy signed the letter. He later claimed he was drunk at the time and would not have signed it sober, but the damage was still done. The "Coya Come Home" letter was printed in newspapers all over the country shortly before the 1958 election, briefly making Coya Knutson a national celebrity. The letter also sunk her reelection campaign. Knutson received overwhelmingly negative coverage in the press as a result of her supposedly home-wrecking ways, and lost her reelection bid that November by about 1,000 votes. And, further emphasizing the underlying implication that a woman simply did not belong in Congress, she lost to a Republican named Odin Langen, who ran on the slogan "A Big Man for a Man-sized Job" (National Public Radio 2014; Thomas 1996).

Thus, to summarize Knutson's remarkable and shocking story, a party organization worked to defeat an incumbent of their own party, and a promising one at that. They manipulated electoral rules, spread false rumors, and, when all else failed, colluded with her own abusive spouse to engineer her defeat.

The driving factor behind all of this, of course, is that Knutson was a woman. Not only was Knutson's gender a factor in *why* party leaders worked to engineer her defeat, but the fact that she was a woman also made it possible for them to do so. Female politicians are uniquely vulnerable to personal attacks based on the idea that their career somehow detracts from their ability to meet family obligations. There could be no "John Come Home" letter written by a wife, imploring a male member of Congress to come back home. Male members of Congress do important work, and if their families were left back in the district, that was a noble sacrifice the family had to make to support their breadwinning head of household. Questioning a male member of Congress for traveling across the country to do the work he was elected to do seems unthinkable. But when the member of Congress is female, her mere presence in Washington, DC, becomes an electoral liability, and can be used against her. It is a trap for female politicians—they are elected to do a job, but just doing the job puts them in electoral jeopardy.

Of course, the "Coya Come Home" letter was published sixty years ago, and things have changed in the intervening years. The idea of a woman with a professional career has gone from impossible to rare to not uncommon to normal. Instead of being 2 percent of Congress members, women now constitute 20 percent. It is almost as ridiculous to think of a modern female member of Congress being subjected to the humiliation of a "Nancy (Pelosi) Come Home" letter as it is to think of a modern male member of Congress being subjected to it.

And yet female members of Congress are still subject to public relations and electoral pressures that men simply do not have to worry about. There are numerous parallels between Coya Knutson's story and life for the modern woman politician. For instance, female candidates may not have the (complete) support of their own families: most notably, Bob Dole admitted in an interview in 1999 about Elizabeth Dole that he was strongly considering giving money to John McCain, her opponent for the 2000 Republican Party nomination, while also replying that "it is too early to tell" as to her chances against Al Gore in the general election (Berke 1999).

Female politicians today also still face scrutiny over how their careers affect their families. Female politicians at all levels are forced to field questions on the campaign trail relating to how their husbands feel about the fact they are running for office; whether they can still manage their families; how the campaign has affected their children; and any number of other topics about how their campaigns are affecting their family that no male candidates have to face. Senator Heidi Heitkamp (D-ND) ran for governor of North Dakota in 2000, and was routinely asked about the ages of her children; she famously replied, "They're the same age as my opponent's kids"; Senator Kelly Ayotte (R-NH) similarly received multiple questions in her 2010 Senate race about having enough time for her children (Grenell 2016). As recently as 2013, Barb Byrum, a Michigan state legislator who was considering a run for Michigan lieutenant governor, was asked by an influential Michigan political publication, *Michigan Information Research and Service Inc.*, whether her young children would not rather she stayed at home (Morris 2013). Similarly, in 2012 Illinois attorney general Lisa Madigan was considering a run for governor when she was asked by *Chicago Sun Times* reporters—three separate times—"whether she could serve as governor and still raise her kids the way she wants to." The article notes that, after her first answer, "they pressed further on whether she could simultaneously hold both jobs—governor and mom . . . remind[ing] [Madigan] that being governor is a lot more demanding than attorney general" (McCarthy 2012). And Representative Katherine Clark (D-MA) reported in 2016 that "[y]ou still run into, 'Well, how are you possibly gonna do this to your children?' Just questions male candidates don't get asked" (Terkel 2016).

Another parallel is that party organizations still often give less-than-full-throated support to their female nominees for office. For instance, fifteen years after the Coya Knutson episode, Patricia Schroeder got no support from local party groups when running in her first House election. Even after she won the primary, when it came time to address the Colorado Democratic Convention she was given thirty seconds to speak when every other Democratic House candidate was given several minutes (Schroeder 1999). Twenty years after that, when Barbara Boxer and Dianne Feinstein were the Democratic nominees for the two California Senate seats that were up for election in 1992, there was some concern that having two female candidates running at the same time would put the party at a disadvantage because voters might balk at the idea of two female (and no male) senators (Boxer 2016). Both women won.[1]

Women in the modern era are also the subject of false rumors, just as Coya Knutson was. Throughout the 1980s and 1990s, it was common for men running against women to plant rumors that they were having affairs, or were lesbians. Barbara Jordon (Rogers 1998), Ann Richards (Morris 1992), Susan Molinari (Molinari 1998), and Dianne Feinstein (Morris 1992) are just a few women who were the subject of whisper campaigns about their sexual orientation or sexual activities, or both. Carol Moseley Braun, the first black, female U.S. Senator, was accused by opponents during several of her elections of being a "welfare queen," a common stereotype for black women (Braun 1999). Even as recently as the 2016 presidential campaign, rumors surfaced that in the 1970s Hillary Clinton had a lesbian affair with Yoko Ono (DeCoskey 2016).

Perhaps nothing separates male and female politicians as widely as how much people talk about what they wear. Patricia Schroeder claims that one of the reasons Knutson ran afoul of local party bosses is that in between her legislative work "she also found time to dye her hair and buy some stylish clothes, which did not sit well with some of her constituents in a conservative Lutheran district" (Schroeder 1999, 128). To this day, women have to constantly worry about their clothes because they know that their dress will be mentioned in whatever press coverage they get. And if they make a sartorial mistake, the clothes themselves will become the focus of the story. In 1990, Susan Molinari caused an uproar when she delivered a speech on the House floor wearing a pantsuit. She got more national attention for the pantsuit than she got for any of the policy statements she made during the speech (or possibly during her entire career), despite the fact that by 1990 women had been wearing pants on the House floor for twenty years (Molinari 1998; Washington Post 2011). Molinari further recounted in her biography, "There I'd be, in a war zone in Bosnia, and some reporter—usually female—would comment on how I was dressed, then turn to my male colleagues for answers to questions of substance" (Molinari 1998, 7). And, in 2007, Hillary Clinton delivered a speech on the Senate floor wearing an ensemble that showed just a tiny hint of cleavage, and was widely denounced for it. An article in the *Washington Post* stated, "It is tempting to say that the cleavage stirs the same kind of discomfort that might be churned up after spotting Rudy Giuliani with his shirt unbuttoned just a smidge too far. No one wants to see that. But really, it was more like catching a man with his fly unzipped. Just look away!" (Givhan 2007).

As recently as 2017, a sizable group of female Democratic House members wore white to a presidential address at a joint session of Congress. The color was a political statement, as many women—politicians and citizens alike—had taken to wearing white during the 2016 presidential campaign to commemorate the original suffragettes, who wore white. These members' sartorial choice was a subtle protest against President Donald Trump, who would be addressing the joint session and was himself the subject of many gender-related controversies. The next day, fellow House member Kevin Cramer (R-ND) called the women "poorly dressed." He went on to say, "There is a disease associated with the notion that a bunch of women would wear bad-looking white pantsuits in solidarity with Hillary Clinton and her loss. You cannot get that weird" (McCaskill 2017a). Cramer later doubled down on his criticism of the women:

> What was ugly was their demonstration, their rudeness, their . . . all sit together and make vulgar—or make inappropriate hand gestures to the president of the United States while he's delivering a message to the joint session of Congress. . . . They groan and moan and hiss and then they rush out of the room as soon as the speech is over, ahead of the President, which violates just common sense and good manners.

Thus, while things have certainly changed, and the number of women in politics has risen since Coya Knutson served in the House, female politicians continue to face a set of gender-based pressures that men simply do not.

The above examples illustrate some of the reasons why Judy Biggert and Barbara Mikulski—our two examples from chapter 1—continuously faced difficult reelection races over the course of their careers. Female officeholders in general confront a "gendered vulnerability"—due to their gender, they are consistently subject to challenge by political opponents, and thus need to continually prove their worth, both to their colleagues and to their constituents. This gendered vulnerability is grounded in women's social identity as well as forces particular to the political arena. The result is that female legislators, no matter how objectively safe their districts may be, must mitigate legislative and especially electoral opposition in a way males simply do not. As we indicated in chapter 1, the main focus of this book is drawing out the behavioral implications of gendered vulnerability. In the following chapters, we explore the ways in which gendered vulnerability leads women to focus more attention on their constituents, to hew more closely to their constituents' priorities, and to undertake more activities with clear reelection benefits than men.

Before we do that, however, we provide a detailed account of the argument that gendered vulnerability exists in the first place. First, we provide an overview of the scholarly literatures that form the basis of our argument that women in office devote more time and attention to constituents than men do. These literatures include explanations of how and why women perceive their own abilities differently than men, and how social forces serve to reinforce these persistent self-doubts, as well as the factors that create a more treacherous electoral landscape for women. We argue these overarching social and electoral forces combine to create the perception that women, due simply to their gender, face a more precarious road to office and reelection than men. We then discuss what implications these conditions, and gendered vulnerability, have for female legislators. Finally, we present our argument regarding how female members act differently while in office due to their gendered vulnerability.

Gender and Its Implications

In *Ferraro: My Story*, Geraldine Ferraro, who eventually became the first female Vice Presidential nominee of a major party in 1984, talks about first entering Congress in 1979, when only seventeen women served in both chambers. The story is one that many women can relate to: "There were traps everywhere, even on the most insignificant details, and I made sure I fell into as few of them as possible. When I first went down to Washington, I overhead a male member say about a new female member: 'She walked off the floor of the House and couldn't even find her way to the ladies' room.' No one was ever going to be able to say that about me, I decided. So before I walked out of any door, I mentally walked to wherever I was going, mapping out my exact route. Silly, right? And totally inconsequential. But you have to look as if you know where you're going—and nothing is worse than looking as if you don't" (2004, 43). She later lamented that "for all that my female colleagues and I had achieved, we still had to do more, work harder, and produce more to be judged the same as men. . . . In the very male and highly competitive world of politics, however, the stakes were very high" (2004, 57). In an interview on March 6, 2017—some thirty-two years after Ferraro left office—current Senator Deb Fischer (R-NE) echoed these same sentiments: "Here in Washington, I would say that I feel I have to work harder than my male colleagues" (Brown 2017).

In interviews we conducted with current and former congressional staff in the summer of 2013, a similar refrain was continuously sounded: female legislators felt a need to prove themselves, and an overriding concern with being seen as ignorant or unprepared, that male legislators simply did not feel. As one staffer explained,

> I think that the senator I worked for, especially being that she began her career when there were very few women legislators, I think she always endeavored to be the best prepared, and so we as a staff had a duty and burden of making sure that she was the best prepared. In fact, a lot of the other members on the committees always would remark to us and to the senator how we were the one's coming in

> with the armloads of materials and they would come in with a folder. I think that my personal view of it was always that that came from a desire beginning especially early in her career, there were very few women to prove that she was an equal or could meet everyone's mettle. So I feel like it was the preparedness was a much higher priority than a lot of the senators who I witnessed . . . kind of a needing to prove that the women were able to do as much as the men.

Another had this observation: "I think that other members, especially men, not exactly don't care but they are kind of more arrogant and, maybe . . . confident in the way they make their decisions, while I think women, female members, they were always worried about what their colleagues thought, how they were going to bring it home, about what their message is."

Perhaps most notable was the number of times that staffers we interviewed noted that the female members, but not males, would worry about being perceived as unknowledgeable or unqualified. For example, one staffer explained, "Women are worried about giving the wrong answer. Men are not because people forget. Women want to not be seen as uninformed because of the more stringent lens they are viewed through to be seen as experts." Another drew this comparison between her previous bosses, one female and one male: "She's much more concerned with being caught off-guard or sounding uneducated. My old [male] boss, not sure if it was arrogance, but that did not bother him. If he was asked a question he did not know, he would answer something else and they would feel lucky to be with the congressman." A different staffer offered a similar conclusion: "The women are hard-working—definitely females who are incredibly, incredibly hard working; some men, too. But the intensity level among women is higher—the amount of information needed to be prepared . . . [Senator X] does not want to be wrong. But it is almost unnecessary [how much time she spends preparing] . . . 'If I'm asked, am I going to look stupid?' She didn't want to feel stupid, unprepared, or that she did not know. [The male member I worked for] did not see it the same way, he just didn't." Interviews with congressional staff conducted by Michele Swers (2013, 238) echo these same concerns:

> One Democratic staffer explained, "[O]ne thing that does stem from her being a woman is that she wants no appearance of her being wishy-washy. She does not want to give any ammunition to the assumption that women are indecisive." A Republican staffer said, "[Maine senators Susan] Collins and [Olympia] Snowe want to

> know every detail about what happened in a hearing on a bill before they go in. They engage in hyperpreparation. . . . Lots of details, and they study and read and come to the hearing knowing more than others. . . . [T]hey fear being blindsided and having their credibility or expertise questioned."

Ferraro's and Fischer's experiences and the results of our interviews point to a basic assumption underlying our argument: women believe that they must constantly work to prove themselves in a way men do not. We argue that this belief is a function of women's experiences and socialization, both in the political arena and beyond. At its crux, gender matters: people use it as a quick way to identify and sort people. And this sorting many times reflects both implicit and explicit attitudes linked to one's gender. Gender is what sociologists term a "status characteristic," and one that is (generally) easily identifiable. Attached to status characteristics are socially defined and shared "status beliefs" that reward (both in terms of worth and competence) those that hold certain status characteristics while devaluing those who do not (Correll and Ridgeway 2003). Importantly, these status beliefs apply broadly, and are internalized both by those who hold the status and those who do not. With respect to gender, studies overwhelmingly find that the status of "male" is rewarded, and the status of "female" diminished, by men and women alike (see, e.g., Auspurg, Hinz, and Sauer 2017; Foschi 1996). This social conditioning may then "bias the extent to which a woman, compared to a similar man, asserts herself in the situation, the attention she receives, her influence, the quality of her performances, the way she is evaluated, and her own and others' inferences about her abilities at the tasks that are central to the context" (Ridgeway and Correll 2004, 519). The result is that many women feel constant pressure to reaffirm their competence and their right to hold a certain position. We first assess the broad social conditioning and pressures facing women in general, and then turn to how they are reinforced in the electoral arena.

"Math Class Is Tough. Want to Go Shopping?": Gender and Social Conditioning

In 1992, Mattel introduced Teen Talk Barbie. It garnered almost instant controversy due to one of its programmed phrases: "Math class is tough. Want to go shopping?" To many, this language served to reinforce gender stereotypes that girls cannot do "hard" things like math and added another voice affirming girls' self-doubts about their own abilities. The reality is that all females, and perhaps especially female politicians, must confront long-standing gender stereotypes coupled with an undervaluing of traits typically associated with women and femininity. Character traits are often described as either "masculine" or "feminine," and they in turn reflect traditional notions of male and female roles in society (see, e.g., Conover and Gray 1983). Typical masculine traits include "assertive," "tough," "rational," and "self-confident," while typical feminine traits include "gentle," "sensitive," "emotional," and "talkative" (see, e.g., Deaux and Lewis 1984; Williams and Best 1990). Masculine traits are typically preferred over feminine traits in a diverse array of contexts (Broverman et al. 1972). The inherent linking of women with femininity and men with masculinity may further lead to a preference for men, but not women, exercising masculine traits. For example, Brescoll and Uhlmann (2008) find that men who express anger in a professional setting are rewarded while women are penalized; notably, this was true of both female and male evaluators.

Perhaps most unsettling, gender stereotyping persists strongly even today. Haines, Deaux, and Lofaro (2016) compared gender trait and role attitudes expressed in 1983 and 2014. They found little change in the degree to which respondents embraced gender stereotypes, whether with respect to traits, gender roles, or gendered expectations in terms of occupations, but rather "a surprising durability of basic stereotypes about women and men" (360). Even in 2014, women were judged to be more likely than men to "cry on occasion," cook, do chores, and be a "source of emotional support," while men were more likely to be the "financial provider," "head of household," and "responsible for household repairs" (see figure 2.1). Occupations were also viewed by respondents as highly gendered, with respondents viewing elementary school teachers, nurses, administrative assistants, and hairdressers as more likely to be women, while politicians, engineers, mechanics, and construction workers were more likely to be men.[2]

Studies suggest these still-prevalent gender stereotypes influence both external evaluations of women's job performance and capabilities, as well as women's evaluations of their *own* capabilities. For instance, studies in a wide variety of disciplines covering multiple venues find that the preference for more masculine traits results in a preference for male job candidates (see, e.g., Goldberg 1968; Gorman 2005). Foschi, Lai, and Sigerson (1994) had subjects review applicant files for engineering jobs; in each case they had to choose between a male and female applicant. They find that male subjects were less likely to rate female applicants positively, even when the female applicant was objectively superior; they did not find a similar result for female subjects. Foschi (1996) finds similar evidence of a "double stan-

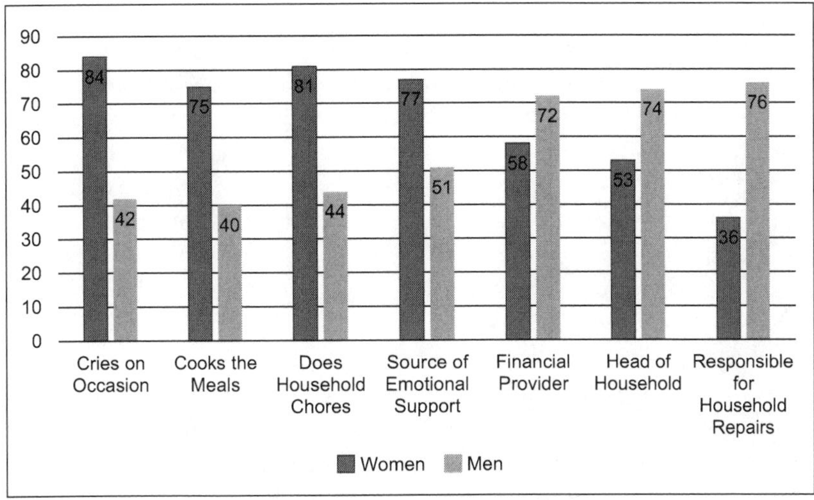

Figure 2.1. Gender stereotype beliefs in 2014

dard" in peer assessments, and specifically the fact that a higher standard for achieving competency was set for female partners as opposed to male partners. And a recent German experimental study finds that both male and female respondents appear to have internalized the status belief that men should be paid more than women, all else being equal (Auspurg, Hinz, and Sauer 2017). In other words, even when people perform similarly, the standards themselves vary across genders, thus resulting in women being evaluated more negatively. Notably, women are just as likely to hold and apply these differing gender evaluations.

Similarly, studies from a variety of professional contexts find that women's self-assessments are generally lower than those of men. For example, women assess their own ability to be an entrepreneur more negatively than men (Thebaud 2010). Female music students are significantly less likely than males to express confidence in their ability to do jazz improvisation, and significantly more likely to express anxiety about performing such musical tasks (Wehr-Flowers 2006). A study of engineering majors argues that "professional role confidence" is lacking in women as compared to men, thus contributing to the lack of women in engineering fields (Cech et al. 2011).

These lower self-assessments can also influence the choices women make. Women can internalize these stereotypes and thereby limit their own career choices (see, e.g., Correll 2001). Kay and Shipman (2014) provide a lengthy overview of the multiple ways in which women in all walks of life express less confidence in themselves and their abilities than men. The authors provide numerous anecdotes of how successful women, including themselves, tie their successes to luck or similar forces, rather than the belief that they simply possess the skill and abilities necessary to be accomplished. They summarize academic studies that confirm this confidence gap: females initiate salary negotiations less frequently than men and ask for less; women managers are less likely than men to express confidence in their job performance; women are less likely to both rate themselves as highly as their knowledge level or correctly assess how they performed on a test, with a tendency toward assuming they performed more negatively than they actually did; and so on (Kay and Shipman 2014). As Mendelberg and Karpowitz (2016) conclude, "the effect of women's status in group settings operates through their tendency to be regarded—and to regard themselves—as less capable, especially in tasks relating to politics" (54).

Moreover, it is not just women who have doubts about their own abilities—other, external actors judge women to be less qualified than men in professional settings as well. For instance, recent experiments that asked employers to judge prospective candidates' resumes suggest that identical resumes will be judged more poorly if the name at the top is female rather than male (Moss-Racusin et al. 2012; Reuben, Sapienza, and Zingales 2014). Other studies find that "agentic" or "masterful" women are more likely than men to be evaluated based on their social skills than on their abilities, and this in turn hurts them in terms of hiring (Phelan, Moss-Racusin, and Rudman 2008). A 2015 survey of academics in thirty different fields found that women were underrepresented in fields where members of those fields felt innate ability, or what they termed "field-specific ability," was necessary to be successful (Leslie et al. 2015). Consistent gender pay disparities can also reinforce these views: as Representative Chellie Pingree (D-ME) stated in 2012, "It is still shocking every time you're reminded of the incredible lack of pay equity between men and women, and this is just one more indication that it transcends every sector. I think women at the top think 'Oh my goodness, I'm making a million dollars, I have nothing to complain about,' but then they realize that the next guy's getting two million. I think that's a psychology that happens with women" (Lepore 2012). Further, women may even be penalized for trying to negotiate: Bowles, Babcock, and Lai (2007) find that female job applicants who attempt to negotiate their salary are more negatively evaluated than male applicants who do the same. Further, both female and male evaluators rated the female negotiators less positively, reinforcing that women themselves internalize and apply these differential status beliefs.

All of these forces combined result in women perceiving that they must overcome numerous hurdles in order to succeed in the workplace: *Women in the Workplace 2016*, a study produced by Leanin.Org and McKinsey & Company, surveyed 34,000 workers across the United States and found that women view the workplace as less fair if not outright hostile. Female employees are less likely than males to "agree" or "strongly agree" with the notion that "the best opportunities go to the most deserving employees" or that "they have the same opportunity for growth as their peers." Females are more likely, however, to conclude that "their gender will make it harder to get a raise, promotion, or chance to get ahead."

Gender Stereotypes in Office

Taken as a whole, the above studies suggest that women confront more doubts about their competence and skills than men, and are socialized to internalize such doubts and to have to work to overcome them. These same gender stereotypes and socializing forces—and the potential backlash for violating them—also carry over into the political arena. Fox and Lawless (2010, 2011) identify how this phenomenon operates in the political world by connecting women's doubts about their abilities to the persistent underrepresentation of women seeking public office. And, with respect to electoral politics, studies find that women consistently evaluate their skills and abilities more negatively than men (see Lawless and Fox 2010; Lawless and Hayes 2016).

The Citizen Political Ambition Study surveyed potential political candidates in 2001, 2008, and 2011.[3] As figure 2.2 shows, women consistently evaluate their qualifications to run for political office more negatively than men. While we see some improvements over the years—22 percent of women view themselves as 'very qualified" in 2011, as opposed to 14 percent in 2001—men are still much more likely to view themselves as "very qualified" (35 percent in 2011), while women are significantly more likely than men to view themselves as only "somewhat" or even "not at all" qualified to run for public office.

The social conditioning that leads women to internalize the notion that they lack the necessary qualifications or experience also results in women being more likely to doubt their ability to win election. This judgment then results in women resisting running for office in the first place: women

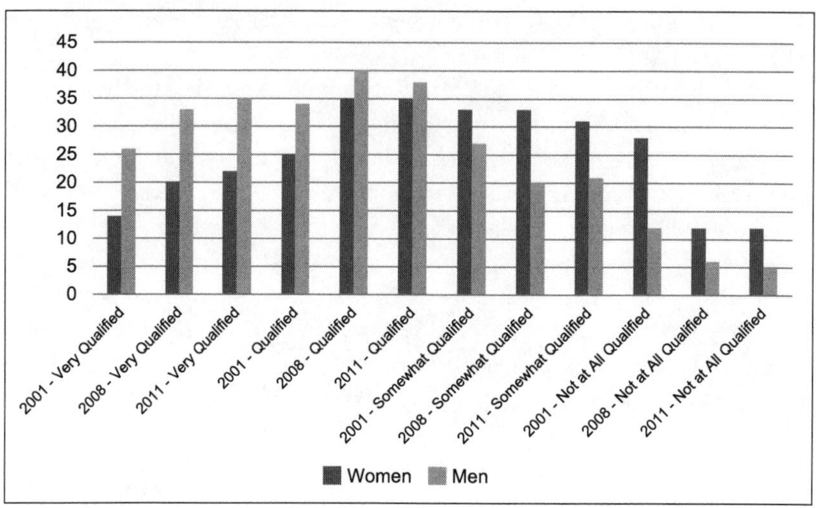

Figure 2.2. Perceptions of qualifications for political office

generally only pursue elected office if they have a high likelihood of winning; alternatively, men typically only need high ambition to run (Fulton et al. 2006). Carroll and Sanbonmatsu (2013) further argue that women are more likely to view the decision to run for office as a "relationally embedded decision . . . [that] is more likely to be influenced by the beliefs and reactions, both real and perceived, of other people and to involve considerations of how candidacy and office holding would affect the lives of others with whom the potential candidate has close relationships" (45).

Women are also more electorally risk averse than men, even if they rate their qualifications similarly; Kanthak and Woon (2015) suggest this aversion reflects concerns about competition and a potentially untrue/negative campaign. The Center for American Women and Politics 2008 Recruitment Study of state legislators reveals that women are more likely than men to view as "very important" factors such as financial resources, the realization that they are "just as capable" as current officeholders, assessments of one's ability to "handle any public scrutiny," and party support when determining whether to run for office (see figure 2.3).[4]

Even when efforts are made to gender-balance recruitment efforts, Republican women are only half as likely as men to respond to such recruitment efforts; the gap was lessened, but still significant, for Democratic women (Preece, Stoddard, and Fisher 2016). We suggest these results reaffirm the notion that women are socialized to doubt their ability to succeed

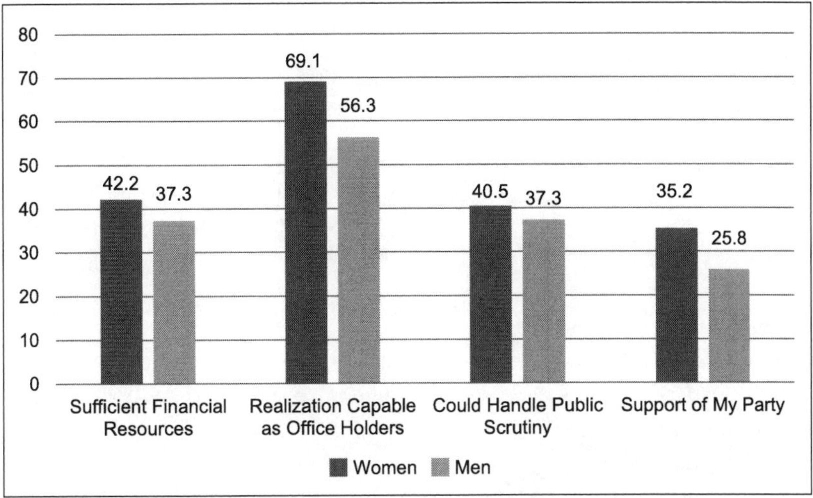

Figure 2.3. Assessments of importance of factors related to the decision to run for office

in the electoral sphere, or, at the very least, perceive that the road to electoral success is a rocky one.

Perceptions of bias may also cause women to refrain from running for office until they have achieved a certain level of quality as a candidate (Fulton 2010). As table 2.1 reports, women view the electoral arena as simply more competitive, and they also perceive that hurdles face them due simply to their sex. In both the 2008 and 2011 Citizen Political Ambition Study surveys, women were more likely than men to view their local and congressional elections as highly competitive, suggesting a barrier to entry into these races. Further, both men and women perceive that winning elections and raising money is harder for women; these perceptions are magnified for female respondents.

Similarly, a Pew Research Center Survey conducted November 12–21, 2014, found that 73 percent of women believe it is easier for men to get elected to high political offices (as do 58 percent of men). Almost half of women (47 percent, as compared to 28 percent of men) responded that "women are held to higher standards than men" is a major reason few women hold elected office, while 41 percent of women (and 31 percent of men) felt a major reason was "many Americans aren't ready to elect a woman to higher office." Perhaps most strikingly, current state legislators, as surveyed in the Center for American Women and Politics 2008

Recruitment Study, reflect more sex-specific views: 56 percent of women legislators surveyed reported that "it is harder for female candidates to raise money than male candidates," while only 9 percent of men said the same (Sanbonmatsu, Carroll, and Walsh 2009). Thus, even if the number of women in office is growing, and even if long-held stereotypes are easing, the reality is that women still strongly perceive that the electoral arena is less hospitable to females than males. And those currently holding office continue to hold these perceptions as well.

Responding to these perceptions and biases, the qualities that women emphasize in determining their own level of quality reflect "stereotypically feminine attributes and competencies—like communication, fidelity and selflessness—as if women were compensating for anticipated discrimination by developing attributes that under contemporary standards, are appropriately sex-typed" (Fulton 2010, 18). Senator Claire McCaskill confirms that even successful female politicians may view their own successes with a grain of salt: "Luck, timing, and opportunity all play a role in politics, and they sometimes seemed like three offensive linemen opening up a hole just for me" (McCaskill 2015).

For those who do choose to run and are ultimately elected, a new set of pressures emerges. Once in office, female officeholders must deal with

TABLE 2.1. Perceptions of the Electoral System

	2008 Survey		2011 Survey	
	Women	Men	Women	Men
In the area I live, local elections are highly competitive	57	47	55	39
In the area I live, congressional elections are highly competitive	61	48	62	50
It is more difficult for a woman to be elected to high-level public office than a man	87	76		
Women running for office win as often as similarly situated men	—	—	47	58
It is harder for a woman to raise money for a campaign than a man	64	38	—	—
Women running for office raise as much money as similarly situated men	—	—	27	40
Sample size	914	1,097	1,753	1,833

Note: All differences between men and women significant at $p<0.05$ or less.

Source: Citizen Political Ambition Study, conducted in 2008 and 2011 by Jennifer Lawless and Richard L. Fox. Data for table adapted from reports on each of these studies: Lawless and Fox (2008) and Lawless and Fox (2012). Slightly different questions were asked in the 2008 versus 2011 surveys with regard to respondents' perceptions of how women fare in the electoral arena and women's ability to raise campaign funds.

their own perceptions as well as those of their colleagues. Older studies suggest that male officeholders expressed overt bias to female officeholders, at least through the 1990s: for example, Susan Mezey's (1978) interviews with male legislators reveal that at least some believe female legislators are less effective because of their "hyperemotionalism" and "weakness" (498). Similarly, Deutchman's (1992) interviews suggest that male legislators provide ambiguous support for their female colleagues. Kathlene's (1994) examination of gender differences at committee hearings also reveals that rank-and-file men are more likely to scrutinize the bills proposed by females, regardless of the female sponsors' relative position of power in the chamber or on the committee. Thus, not only were female legislators more likely to receive pushback on their policy proposals, but positions of authority did not insulate them from this trend.

These studies are borne out in the personal accounts of female Congress members who served at the time. In 1972 Patricia Schroeder was assigned a seat on the Armed Services Committee. Committee chair F. Edward Hébert expressed his displeasure at having a female on his committee by assigning Schroeder and Representative Ron Dellums, an African American, a single chair to share between them. He stated "that women and blacks were worth only half of one regular Member" (Schroeder 1999, 41). Just a few years earlier, in 1969, when Shirley Chisholm arrived as the first African American woman elected to Congress, she was assigned a seat on the Agriculture Committee. Democratic Party leaders did not give this incongruous committee assignment to her despite her 100 percent urban New York City district—they did so *because* of that district (Chisholm 1970). Marjorie Seward Holt expressed how these and other incidents affect how women saw themselves and their place in Congress: "It's interesting to be a woman in that world. As long as you were quiet and moving slowly, nobody got upset. But as soon as you became pushy or strident, the men realized that you were threatening them. So you had to move carefully" (Guhne, 1992). An article published not long after Holt was elected summed up her views in the following manner: "She is not angry about her problems as a woman in politics. She merely accepts that a woman to succeed in any field traditionally male must work about ten times as hard" (Hutchinson 1973, 2–2).

While many of these overt biases have lessened over time, many of the women covered in our study were elected during these periods, and so these early socialization periods may still exert a substantial influence. More important, these biases have not disappeared altogether. Kanthak and Krause (2010) find that as the number of women in a legislature increases, male representatives give more money from their personal PACs to male colleagues and less to female colleagues, all else being equal; the implication is that being part of a larger minority, but not the majority, may not in fact aid a group's institutional support more broadly.

The experiences of more recent female officeholders further suggest it is still difficult to be a woman in office. Female members of Congress report overtly sexist stories, as well as those that speak to more subtle gender-based biases. For example, Representative Linda Sanchez recalls being propositioned by other members (Sanchez and Sanchez 2008), and her sister and fellow member of Congress Loretta Sanchez reports that life on the Hill is not easy for women: "Sexist, patronizing, and dismissive attitudes are a sad fact of life for women on the Hill. Without a doubt, there are certain members of Congress who still believe women don't belong there" (2008). Loretta Sanchez also withdrew from the Congressional Hispanic Caucus in 2007 after accusing the chairman of calling her a "whore"; other female caucus members raised similar concerns about sexist treatment (Hearn 2007). Senator Kirsten Gillibrand's 2015 book tells numerous stories about other senators commenting on her weight and appearance. A 2015 article about the women then serving in the Senate offered this summary: "Even today, the women of the Senate are confronted with a kind of floating, often subtle, but corrosive sexism, a sense of not belonging that is both pervasive and so counter to the narrative of real, if stubbornly slow progress that many are reluctant to acknowledge this persistent secret" (Mundy 2015).

Female politicians additionally confront a host of less well-defined biases and obstacles, from being excluded from certain types of professionally related social events, to being worried about social proprieties and double standards, to dealing with the greater restraints of political life on marriage and family life (see, e.g., Blair and Stanley 1991; Diamond 1977; Gehlen 1977; Kirkpatrick 1974; Mezey 1978). One former staffer we interviewed confirmed that those types of social barriers still exist: "It is harder to be a woman in the electoral situation and do the kind of glad-handing that the men can do, you know. In the political cycle, you know, they smoke cigars, they go to cigar bars, they smoke cigars, go to baseball games, and, you know, that sort of thing. It is harder for women, the opportunities aren't there. The women seem to be working while the men seem to be socializing." Furthermore, even a relatively recent study (Thomas 2002) finds that female state legislators shoulder a disproportionate amount of childcare and housework duties, furthering the so-called second shift working women often confront. At the very least, politics is still a male-dominated field: as former Representative Anne Northup noted in her interview,

"[L]et me say in defense of women, there are more men. You can go to any committee meeting and you're going to be outnumbered. There's no question that more lobbyists are men than women. . . . I went to a fundraiser this morning and there were maybe three out of thirty other people who were women. I am like, 'Oh God, even today at a fundraiser.'"

All of these forces, great and small alike, combine to reinforce the perception among female legislators that they must work to overcome the many "double binds" that still exist (see, e.g., Hall Jamieson 1995), while simultaneously proving that they are worthy of holding their positions. Even if, for example, 95 percent of Americans are now willing to vote for a "qualified woman" for president (Suffolk University/USA Today poll, September 2015), the perception of gendered vulnerability still remains today and exerts an important influence on female officeholders.[5] As Senator Claire McCaskill recently noted, "There have been many times in my career that I have had a probably subconscious fear that somebody was going to tap me on the shoulder and say, 'What are you doing here? You don't belong here'" (quoted in Mundy 2015).

In the next section, we develop these ideas in the context of electoral vulnerability. Women's beliefs—brought on both by internal factors and external stimuli—that they are less qualified, face more challenging obstacles, or both, help create a sense of vulnerability to challenge and attack that is exclusive to women, simply as a function of their gender; hence the concept of gendered vulnerability. The electoral process then reinforces this sense of vulnerability. We now turn to the ways in which elections serve as a type of crystallization process that buttresses the notion of gendered vulnerability among female legislators.

Gender and Elections

The electoral playing field is not even for male and female candidates for office. While the overt sexism that historically blocked women from active participation in public life (Baxter and Lansing 1980; Witt, Paget, and Matthews 1994) has lessened considerably, it has not gone away completely. Relative to male candidates, female candidates face several distinct disadvantages when running for office.[6] First, female candidates must contend with pervasive gender stereotyping. Second, female incumbents face both more and higher-quality challengers in primary and general elections. Finally, media coverage of female candidates is lower in both quality and quantity than media coverage of male candidates. Even though female candidates many times ultimately triumph—indeed, women win election at proportionally the same rate as men (Lawless and Pearson 2008)—these disadvantages create a more hostile election environment for female candidates. Further, since these electoral issues apply equally to female challengers and incumbents, the factors we identify ensure that, simply by virtue of their gender, women will face challenges when they run for reelection even if by objective assessments they are a "quality" candidate running for a "safe" seat.

The disadvantages women face on the campaign trail that we discuss below crystallize the gender-related socialization issues discussed above, reinforcing women's concerns about having to prove themselves and their worth. Even if the overt biases of the past are diminishing, female candidates and legislators—as well as prospective female candidates—view the electoral arena as one that is fraught with biases and pitfalls. Simply put, we argue that female legislators view themselves as inherently vulnerable to electoral attack or challenge because of their gender, and orient their activities in office accordingly. The end result of this process is that women will spend more time in office tending to their constituents.

Gender Stereotypes

> Women candidates have a difficult time striking a balance between looking attractive and looking competent. Their clothes should not be so memorable that they detract from their message. Male candidates rarely have to worry about their clothes on the campaign trail, but women don't have that luxury. . . . [W]omen usually have a much finer line to walk than men when it comes to how they dress on the campaign trail, and it is unfortunate but true that this affects their ability to get elected.
>
> —Barbara F. Vucanovich, R-NV (Vucanovich and Cafferata 2005)

> Help take Betty Sutton out of the House and put her back in the kitchen.
>
> —Medina County Republican Party (Ohio),
> Ohio, Spring 2010 newsletter

During the final debate of the 2016 presidential election, Donald Trump infamously commented that Hillary Clinton was "[s]uch a nasty woman." Representative Bryan Babin (R-TX) attempted to defend Trump's characterization of Clinton the next day: "I think sometimes a lady needs to be told when she's being nasty." In 2010, Senator Arlen Specter and Representative Michele Bachmann appeared together on the Dom Giordano radio show. During a heated exchange, Specter stated, "Now wait a minute. I'll stop and you can talk. I'll treat you like a lady. So act like one." Later in the show, Specter said, "Don't interrupt me. I didn't interrupt you. Act like a lady" (Roper 2010). And, in 2011, Representative Allen West (R-FL) appealed to the House Democratic leadership to rebuke Representative Debbie Wasserman Schultz for a speech she gave on a House floor, suggesting she was "vile," "unprofessional," and "not a lady" (Sonmez 2011).

In all three cases, female politicians were accused of being unladylike for simply acting as a politician. As these vignettes suggest, the broad gender stereotypes that affect women in general also manifest themselves in the electoral arena (see, e.g., Alexander and Anderson 1993; Herrnson, Lay, and Stokes 2003; Hedlund et al. 1979; Sapiro 1981a). Senator Barbara Boxer referenced these stereotypes when she argued that, in politics, "A man is assertive where a woman is aggressive. A man has spirit where a woman is loud" (Page 2016). Senator Barbara Mikulski retired in 2016 and in one of her final interviews prior to leaving office, she responded to claims that she is reputed as "being intimidating at times—making male colleagues cower": "I've heard this one before," she answered. "And I think that when women are persistent and insistent we're viewed as tough. Now, I view it as just being effective" (Bash and Crutchfield 2016).

The existing literature suggests that durable gender stereotypes, both positive and negative, play a strong role in voter decision making. Voters presume female candidates are more engaged and competent on issues with a "female" orientation, such as education, health care, and those addressing families and children (Dolan and Sanbonmatsu 2009; Fox 1997; Kahn 1996; Koch 1999; Lawless 2004a; Leeper 1991). Women are also viewed by voters as more compassionate and consensus-oriented (Burrell 1994). Sanbonmatsu (2002) finds that voters have "baseline" gender preferences, and some voters prefer female candidates while others prefer males; she also finds that female voters are more likely to want same-gender representation and to want to see an increase in female representation due to the lack of such representation currently in legislative bodies (see also Dolan and Sanbonmatsu 2009).

However, these stereotypes also influence voters in negative ways that likely outweigh the positives. Stereotypical perceptions of women candidates can also lead voters to perceive women as less well-suited to holding public office. For example, numerous studies find voters prefer candidates with "masculine" traits and "masculine" policy expertise (such as foreign policy and defense), which in turn leads to a continued preference for male candidates (see, e.g., Huddy and Terkildsen 1993; Lawless 2004a; Rosenwasser and Dean 1989; Rosenwasser and Seale 1988; Sanbonmatsu 2002). Huddy and Terkildsen (1993) find that citizens were more likely to view "good" politicians as possessing masculine, rather than feminine, traits, while Koenig et al.'s (2011) meta-analysis finds a consistent link between masculine and leader stereotypes. Huddy and Terkildsen (1993) also find that "male" policy issue experience, such as with the military and economic policy, were seen as necessary prerequisites for candidates seeking higher levels of office (see also Mueller 1986).

Dolan's 2010 study posits that gendered trait stereotypes may not play as large of a role as in previous eras, but gendered issue stereotypes do: voters are much more likely to support female candidates when they perceive them to be competent in dealing with "male" issues such as the economy and terrorism. The dilemma, however, is that these issues are still viewed as traditionally male and thus better suited to a male candidate. The pervasive view that female candidates and legislators are more liberal can also hurt at the polls: Koch (2002) finds that perceived liberalness can harm Democratic female candidates in congressional general elections—though perhaps aiding them in Democratic primaries (Lawless and Pearson 2008)—while Sanbonmatsu and Dolan (2009) find that such stereotypical views may harm potential female Republican candidates. Bauer (2015) further suggests that activating feminine stereotypes—even, ironically, by female candidates themselves in ads suggesting they are, for example, "compassionate"—negatively impacts female candidates at the ballot box. Moreover, not only do voters generally prefer candidates with "masculine" traits and policy expertise, but they are also more likely to ascribe these attributes to male candidates. In an experiment assessing hypothetical male and female presidential candidates, female candidates were more likely to be rated higher on "feminine" tasks than male candidates, and vice versa; these "feminine" tasks were also more likely to be viewed as less important than stereotypically "masculine" tasks (Rosenwasser and Seale 1988; see also Alexander and Anderson 1993). More recently, Lawless (2004) finds that voters increasingly prefer male presidential candidates in the post-September 11 world, in part because they are expected to hold more "masculine" traits and greater expertise on issues such as national security. Holman, Merolla, and Zechmeister (2016) find that terrorist threats activate a desire for masculine traits, but the effect varies across party: Republican women are unaffected, but Democratic women receive increasingly negative evaluations. Dolan and Sanbonmatsu (2009) similarly find that while voters generally wish to see more women elected officials, they also are more likely—both men and women—to believe the "best government" is majority male.

Women's relationship with stereotypically male traits is fraught. Schneider and Bos (2014) suggest there exists a "subtype" of stereotypes for female politicians, as distinct from stereotypes applied to women more generally: "In particular, female politicians were characterized not by possession of typically female traits but by their deficiency in masculine traits . . . traits essential to the politician role, such as educated, confident, determined, well-spoken, hardworking, intelligent, knowledgeable, leader, charismatic, and commands respect. The discrepancy between female politicians and male politicians in this analysis demonstrates that female politicians are simply not seen as having qualities requisite for the politician role in comparison to their male colleagues" (259). Bauer (2017) similarly finds that female politicians may benefit from counterstereotypic campaign messages (i.e., emphasizing masculine traits) but (a) they benefit little from traditional feminine strengths and (b) they risk backlash from opposite party voters. Female candidates can succeed, but they must tread a very narrow and precarious path to do so.

Some studies suggest perceptions of women candidates may be changing overall (see, e.g., Dolan 2014; Hayes 2011). However, other recent studies suggest gender biases may now simply manifest themselves in less overt yet just as important ways. Ditonto, Hamilton, and Redlawsk's (2014) experimental study reveals how gender stereotypes may influence the information voters seek about candidates, ultimately influencing their vote choices. In two studies, one conducted in the 1990s and the other in 2010, respondents were presented with the opportunity to, as in a campaign, find out information about the candidates before casting a "vote." The studies focused on what information each respondent sought about the candidates. In both eras, respondents were more likely to seek out information related to competence if the candidate was female. This heightened attention to female candidates' competence suggests voters—and, notably, both male and female voters—continue to harbor doubts about female candidates' inherent fitness for office in a way they do not about males.

In a follow-up study, Ditonto (2017) finds that voters care much more about the competence of female candidates than that of males, and these concerns can even potentially trump partisan considerations. Specifically, she finds that negative information about competence harms women but not men; further, evidence of incompetence for female candidates can lead to voters preferring to support the male, out-party candidate (Ditonto 2017). Comparatively, males portrayed as incompetent emerge relatively unscathed. Relatedly, Mo (2015) experimentally assesses respondents' implicit and explicit gender attitudes and the effects of these attitudes on vote choice. In both cases, negative attitudes lead to a lower likelihood of supporting the female candidate. Implicit gender biases, however, are potentially overcome with information that the female candidate is highly qualified.

These studies thus reaffirm the linchpin of gendered vulnerability: while women can succeed electorally, they face an environment where they are inherently more vulnerable to attack—and more susceptible to successful attacks—simply due to their gender. As a result, successful female politicians must work harder to overcome inherent doubts about their abilities, and mitigate against any potential negative information, while their male opponents may emerge triumphant even in the face of evidence of incompetence.

Recent surveys of American voters also suggest that these issues remain a concern. While 95 percent of Americans said in 2015 they would vote for a "qualified woman," Ditonto's and Mo's studies suggest there is a higher bar to clear for women to be considered "qualified" than men. Further, other surveys that seek to probe more nuanced views of women in politics reveal more ambiguity than the Suffolk/USA Today poll suggests: an October 2015 Quinnipiac University poll found that only 73 percent of respondents were "entirely comfortable" with the idea of a woman president, while 16 percent admitted being only "somewhat uncomfortable" and 10 percent were either "somewhat" or "entirely" uncomfortable with this notion.[7] An August 2016 Associated Press–NORC survey also revealed that beliefs about women not being "tough enough" still remain for a sizable minority of Americans: 21 percent said a woman president would not be tough enough to "make the hard decisions a president has to make," while 27 percent believe a woman is not tough enough to "handle a military crisis" or "keep the country safe from terrorism."[8] And 48 percent of likely voters stated the United States is "not ready to elect two women as president and vice-president" as opposed to only 46 percent who said the United States is ready (Bloomberg poll, June 2016).[9]

Other types of gender stereotypes may also be at play in elections: for example, voters express less support for potential female candidates with young children (Hedlund et al. 1979). Physical appearance can also affect female candidates in stereotypical ways. Sigelman, Sigelman, and Fowler (1987) find that a more attractive female candidate is viewed as "nicer"; and, in turn, the nicer candidate receives greater support. During the 2014 congressional elections, a male New Hampshire state lawmaker suggested

Representative Ann McLane Kuster (D-NH) would likely lose reelection because she is "ugly as sin," while supporting her "truly attractive" opponent (Kaplan 2014). Campaign consultants note that women candidates must pay more attention to their physical appearance; Dittmar (2010, 27) recounts one instance where a set of campaign ads had to be reshot because a female gubernatorial candidate's attractiveness was overly distracting to focus group participants. Senator Amy Klobuchar candidly recounts being as worried about her looks as she was about policy preparedness when thinking about running for office: "But mastering farm, foreign, and forestry policy wasn't enough. There was something else I needed to upgrade before I would truly be prepared for a run for the United States Senate. That would be clothes and hair" (Klobuchar 2015).

Influential electoral gatekeepers may also reinforce these voter stereotypes: local party leaders and other recruitment agents often believe that females are less viable candidates than males, and are thus more likely to recruit male candidates (Burns, Schlozman, and Verba 2001; Carroll 1985, 1994; Diamond 1977; Sanbonmatsu 2002). Darcy and Schramm (1977) argue that the lack of women in the House in the late 1970s was due to women being predominantly recruited and nominated only in "the few, atypical, largely Democratic urban districts" (10). In past decades, many recruitment agents did not feel elected office was "appropriate" for women (Jennings and Thomas 1968). More recently, Niven (1998) finds that county party chairs are more likely to prefer candidate traits usually associated with men, such as being aggressive and competitive, and that the predominance of these sex stereotypes influence the recruitment of female candidates more generally. And Hennings and Urbatsch's (2015) examination of state gubernatorial races and state legislative leader races finds that parties shy away from putting more than one woman at the top of the ticket, suggesting that "too many women" is seen as a detriment to the party's success. This echoes concerns that California Democrats had in 1992 about Barbara Boxer and Dianne Feinstein simultaneously running for the state's two Senate seats.

Even successful, politically active women are less likely to receive encouragement and support for their potential candidacies (Fox and Lawless 2004; Niven 1998a, 1998b; Sanbonmatsu 2002). Figure 2.4 reports results again from the Citizen Political Ambition Study surveys in 2001, 2008, and 2011. In all years, women in these nationwide samples of potential candidates were less likely than men to report that they had been recruited to run for political office by party officials, elected officials, or nonelected political activists.

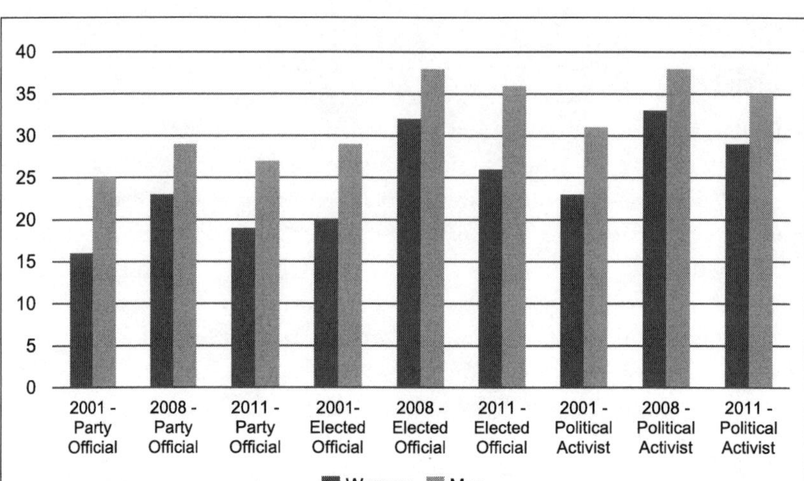

Figure 2.4. Encouragement to run for office by political actors

When female candidates are recruited, they tend to be recruited for challenger positions, rather than open-seat nominations (Bernstein 1986), or races where the party's chances of winning are lower, thus reinforcing the view of their relative nonviability (Crowder-Meyer 2013; Fox and Lawless 2005; Sanbonmatsu 2006). These trends may be even more pronounced in the South than in other regions of the country (Costantini 1990; Gertzog 1995; Norrander and Wilcox 1998). Finally, women's perception of bias by party elites leads to them questioning whether resources will be adequately devoted to their campaigns if they do agree to run, further undermining female candidate recruitment rates (Butler and Robinson Preece 2016).

Electoral Competition

The second electoral factor that may reinforce female legislators' perceptions of gendered vulnerability is that they are more likely to face electoral challengers than their male counterparts. In general, incumbents possess a strong advantage over potential challengers in terms of visibility and popularity, and these advantages translate into incumbents being more likely to win elections than challengers (see, e.g., Abramowitz 1975; Fiorina 1977; Mann and Wolfinger 1980; Mayhew 1974). As shown in figure 2.5 (data from Palmer and Simon 2010, 134), incumbents overwhelmingly win

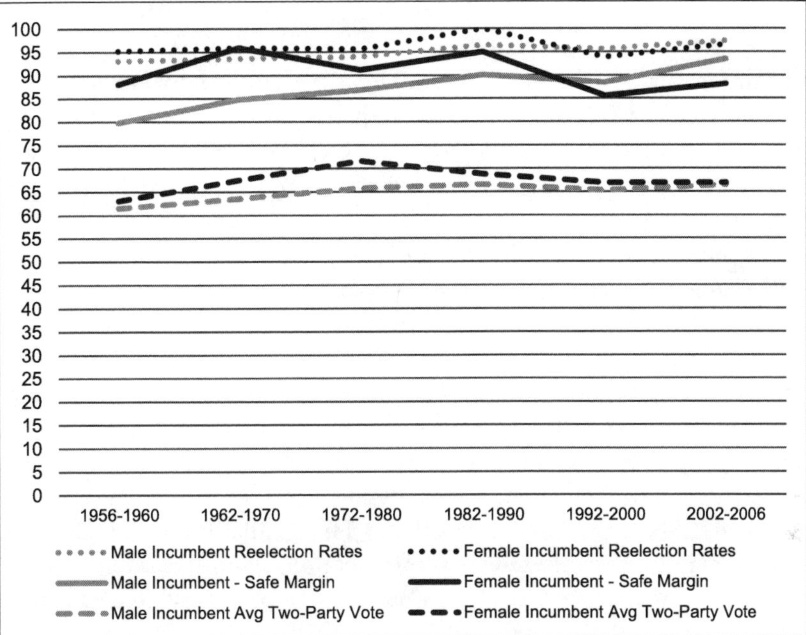

Figure 2.5. Reelection rates and margins of victory for male and female House incumbents, 1956–2006

reelection, and female incumbents consistently win at rates comparable to their male counterparts.

Challengers recognize these impediments and are thus typically more likely to run for office when the seat becomes open (Bond, Covington, and Fleisher 1985; Gaddie and Bullock 2000). It is not uncommon for incumbents to run unopposed in primary elections and face only token competition in general elections. For example, Boatright (2014, 173) reports that 72 percent of incumbents in U.S. House of Representatives races between 1970 and 2012 were unopposed in their primaries.

These accepted wisdoms, however, apply much more strongly when the incumbent is a male. Female candidates, including incumbents, are considered more vulnerable to attack than males due simply to their gender (Palmer and Simon 2010; Sanbonmatsu 2006), and therefore are much more likely to draw electoral opposition. Lawless and Pearson (2008) find that female candidates face increased primary competition relative to men regardless of whether they run as incumbents, challengers, or for an open seat. Examining all primaries between 1958 and 2004, they report that in Republican primaries with a woman, the mean number of candidates is 3.9; this drops to 2.2 in primaries without a female candidate. Similarly, when women run in a Democratic primary, the mean number of candidates is 4.3, as compared to only 2.5 in primaries with only male candidates (Lawless and Pearson 2008, 75). These differences imply that male candidates for office discount the effect a female challenger might have on their own chances for success.

Incumbency appears to do little to shield female candidates from perceptions of vulnerability, even within their own parties (Lawless and Pearson 2008; see also Palmer and Simon 2005, 2006). These findings are somewhat ironic given that female incumbents are actually more likely to hail from safe seats and to have won their last election with a larger share of the two-party vote than male incumbents. Looking again to figure 2.5, in all eras, the average two-party vote in the general election is actually higher for females than males; similarly, the percentage of female incumbents reelected by a "safe" margin is also comparable to that of males, if not higher. But these traditional measures of electoral safety do not apply similarly to males and females, particularly when challengers assess whether an incumbent is vulnerable: Palmer and Simon (2006, 149) report that between 1956 and 2006, 31.7 percent of female incumbents faced contested primaries, as compared to 29.0 percent of men: a slight but statistically significant difference. Female incumbents also face more general election challengers than male incumbents: while 16.2 percent of male incumbents from 1956 to 2006 were uncontested in the general election, only 9.8 percent of female incumbents were given such a "free pass" (Palmer and Simon 2006, 149; see also Milyo and Schosberg 2000). Palmer and Simon (2006) examine the Republican primary races in 1994 against all forty-three first-time Democrats who supported President Bill Clinton's deficit reduction bill. They find that contested primaries occurred in only 32 percent of districts with male Democratic representatives, but in 59 percent of those held by females (127–28).

Utilizing data made available from the Brookings Institution Primaries Project, we assessed the data for all 2014 congressional elections, and find that women legislators continue to the present to face more impediments on their way to reelection. As shown in figure 2.6, female House incumbents are more likely than males to face challenges in both their primary and general elections. Almost half of female incumbents face primary challengers (48.6 percent) as opposed to only 44.8 percent of male incumbents. The numbers become more striking when we move to the general elec-

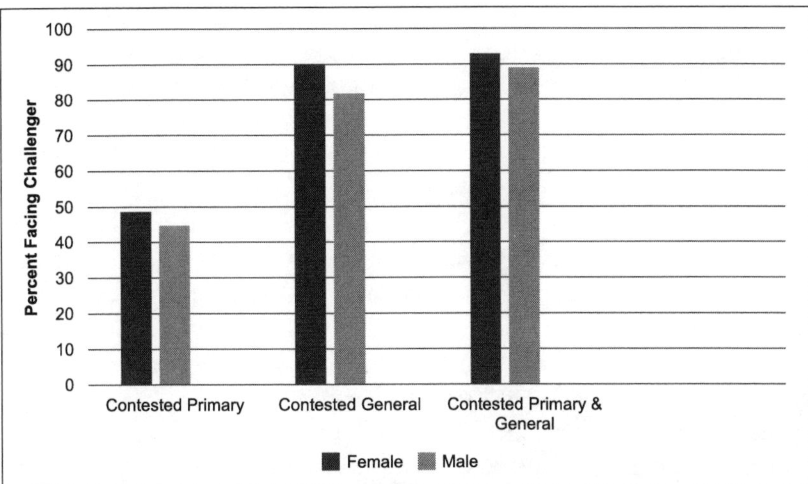

Figure 2.6. Primary and general election challengers faced by male and female incumbents during 2014 House elections

tion: while 18.3 percent of male incumbents lacked a general election challenger, only 10 percent of females could say the same. Overall, 11 percent of males faced no opposition to their reelection at any stage, while only 7.1 percent of females could say the same.

A closer examination of these primary data from 2014 reveals that even seniority and leadership positions do not necessarily protect one from a challenge, even from one's own partisans. During the 2014 elections, House Minority Leader Nancy Pelosi (D-CA) was challenged by two fellow Democrats in the primary, as well as Republican and third party candidates; she won reelection in 2012 with 85.1 percent of the vote and triumphed again in 2014 with 83.3 percent of the vote. Donna Edwards (D-MD) also faced a primary challenge, even though she won the 2012 general election with 77 percent of the vote; she ultimately won reelection in 2014 with 70 percent of the vote. Vicky Hartzler (R-MO) won her newly drawn district in 2012 with 60.3 percent of the vote. She still faced a primary challenger in 2014, however, as well as a strong general election challenger. She won the general election in 2014 even more decisively, with 68.1 percent of the vote. Notably, she again faced a Republican primary challenger in 2016, but again emerged victorious. Marsha Blackburn (R-TN) has represented the 7th District since 2003, currently serving as the Vice Chair of the Energy and Commerce Committee and a Republican

Party whip. She has never won reelection with less than 66 percent of the vote; she won reelection in 2012 with 71 percent of the vote. Nevertheless, she still faced a primary challenge in 2014. Finally, Eddie Bernice Johnson (D-TX) has served continuously in the U.S. Congress since 1993. She is the Ranking Member of the Committee on Science, Space and Technology and served as Chairwoman of the Congressional Black Caucus during the 107th Congress. And, since 1998, she has garnered at least 70 percent of the vote in all nine subsequent reelections. But, like many of her female colleagues, she also routinely faced primary challenges, as well as those in the general election.

Not only are female officeholders more likely to face primary and general election challengers, but the challengers they face are, on average, stronger than those faced by male incumbents. Their challengers are more likely to be politically experienced (in the sense that they held an elective office prior to running) and are on average better funded than the challengers facing male incumbents (Berch 2004; Milyo and Schosberg 2000; Niven 1998b; Palmer and Simon 2005). These findings hold true even for female incumbents who are electorally safe by conventional standards (Palmer and Simon 2005). In fact, Milyo and Schosberg (2000) suggest that female incumbents are generally of higher quality than male incumbents, but still must contend with "the irrational tendency [of] challengers to overestimate their likely success against female incumbents" (44).

Outside group spending reinforces this gendered imbalance: the Center for Responsive Politics reports that in the 2016 elections outside groups spent twice as much to defeat female Senate incumbents as they did to defeat male incumbents (Balcerzak 2017). On average, outside group spending against Senate Democrats totaled $6.7 million if the incumbent was female, but only $3.3 million if the incumbent was male. For Republican incumbents, spending totaled $4.3 against females, and $2.2 against males. Groups similarly targeted female nonincumbents, spending $10.6 million on average against their candidacies, but only $6.9 million against male nonincumbents. Similar patterns were also seen with respect to House races.

As a result, females must assume that they will face attacks in the next election and prepare accordingly. Even a challenge from a weak candidate still requires that the incumbent spend valuable time and resources that could be spent otherwise. Female candidates may also suffer from what Stout and Kline (2011) dub the "Richards Effect": preelection polls are much more likely to underestimate support for female candidates than males, particularly in states with more traditional cultural attitudes.

Although up to 70 percent of female candidates perform better on Election Day than polls predict, these polling discrepancies further exacerbate the tendency among elites and voters to view female candidates as weaker—and reinforce female candidates' personal perceptions of vulnerability and the need to overcome obstacles linked directly to their gender. The Richards Effect can also work to negatively influence efforts to attract donors or other prominent supporters.

We argue these electoral forces exacerbate female officeholders' perception of their gendered vulnerability. Our interviews confirm that sitting representatives and senators both anticipate and fear these challenges, even if their past electoral performance was strong. As one staffer noted, "Women are viewed as more vulnerable [come election time]. Men are systematically not as threatened by women so they are more likely to run against them." This same staffer suggested that the two representatives she worked for were very similar to one another as to their districts, and relative "safe-ness" of their seats, but "she got two primary opponents and he got zero." And, one of those primary opponents declared on just the 100th day she was in office. (A two-year House term lasts 730 days; the 100th day is considered very early for a challenger to declare for office). Similarly, another staffer explained that a senior female senator "was always approaching [elections as if] she was vulnerable. Absolutely, she won by 69 percent, but she always . . . had to prove she was the best." This staffer further commented: "I do think that at least for the two women I worked for there was a different perception of vulnerability. . . . I mean [Senator X] was a force to be reckoned with without a doubt here, but she didn't let that make her comfortable. We were always like, you are winning by 61, 69, whatever, why are we killing ourselves with this. . . . Because you know you can never be comfortable, which was her perspective and her mindset." The result is that female legislators are socialized to expect challenges, even within their own parties, and thus they must act accordingly while in office to try to mitigate and/or prepare for these electoral attacks.

Media Coverage

Elizabeth Warren ran for a U.S. Senate seat from Massachusetts in 2012; she ultimately won, defeating incumbent Scott Brown. Along the way, however, she faced a number of media stories about whether she needed to "soften her image." For example, a *New York Times* piece suggested that "[t]here have also been worries that Ms. Warren comes across as a scold when she speaks directly into the camera." The *Boston Globe*'s Joan Vennochi

(2012), while calling for substance over style, also stated, "Agreed: Democratic challenger Elizabeth Warren wasted millions on ads that turned her into every man's worst nightmare: a smarter-than-thou older woman sporting granny glasses and sensible hair." These are just a couple of examples of how media portrayals of female candidates reinforce the electoral difficulties discussed above. There exists a rich scholarly literature outlining differences in media coverage between male and female candidates. Female candidates receive less media coverage than male candidates, on average, and this finding holds true for both incumbents and challengers (Kahn 1994; Kahn and Goldenberg 1991; Kropf and Boiney 2001; Niven and Zilber 2001a; but see Devitt 1999; Smith 1997). Kahn's (1994) examination of newspaper coverage of U.S. Senate candidates finds that female candidates receive less coverage than men regardless of whether the race is competitive or whether the female candidate is the incumbent. News reports about female candidates are more likely to focus on questions of candidate viability than reports about male candidates, and these reports generally evaluate female incumbents as less viable than their male counterparts (Kahn 1994; Kahn and Goldenberg 1991). Furthermore, the media may help further gendered stereotypes about female candidates. Kahn (1994) reports that "female" issues are discussed 40 percent of the time in newspaper articles about female candidates, but only 30 percent of the time with male candidates. Similarly, an analysis of media coverage of campaign ads reveals that while female candidates overwhelmingly emphasize "male" traits (78 percent to 22 percent) in their ads, the media discusses such traits in connection with female candidates much less frequently (Kahn 1993).

Some recent literature suggests that some gender differences in media attention are lessening with time (see, e.g., Bystrom 2010; Lawrence and Rose 2009; Hayes and Lawless 2015). However, other studies continue to find these differences. For instance, Fowler and Lawless (2009) find that male gubernatorial candidates were more likely than females to receive media coverage that portrayed their actions, even though females were slightly more likely to receive coverage of their issue positions. Coverage of female candidates tends to deemphasize their policy positions while focusing on more gendered information such as what the candidate is wearing or her marital and family status (Bystrom et al. 2004; Palmer and Simon 2006; see also Devitt 1999; Kahn 1994, 1996; Kahn and Goldenberg 1991; Smith 1997). Women are also less frequent guests on Sunday morning political television shows; Baitlinger (2015) argues that guest decisions are most likely a function of there being fewer potential female guests, particularly if shows emphasize those with seniority or leadership positions. The result, however, is a dearth of women appearing on these shows, further exacerbating the gendered media landscape. Relatedly, an analysis of the front page of newspapers the day after Hillary Clinton became the first major party nominee for president found that only 24 percent of covers included a picture of Hillary; in almost half, the only picture was of Bill Clinton (Christensen 2016).

Further, even if inequities in the *amount* of coverage have lessened (Bystrom 2010; Lawrence and Rose 2009), the *content* continues to differ. Headlines, designed to catch viewers, may also reinforce gendered tropes: a *Nation* article about Michelle Bachmann's 2012 presidential ambitions was entitled, "Michele Bachmann, Wife in Chief?" while *CBS News* delved into Hillary Clinton's aspirations with the tagline, "Hillary Clinton: Grandmother-in-Chief?" A *New York Times* piece asked about a 2014 female gubernatorial candidate, "Can Wendy Davis Have It All? A Texas-Size Tale of Ambition, Motherhood and Political Mythmaking." The Davis piece led to a rebuke by the *New York Times*'s public editor, acknowledging that "this relentless second-guessing [of female politicians] hits hard and cuts deep," while the subheadline "comes close to suggesting that Ms. Davis is spinning a big lie" (Sullivan 2014). These portrayals many times carry over into the articles themselves: for example, a *Washington Post* piece about then-freshman Representative Kyrsten Sinema (the first openly bisexual member of Congress) stated she became "lecturing, hectoring, defensive, accusatory, pouty and curiously repetitive" when asked about her sexual orientation (Roig-Franzia 2013).

More broadly, most studies find that women receive more trait or character coverage than men, but less issue coverage (but see Hayes and Lawless 2015). An analysis of media coverage during the 2000 Republican presidential primary revealed that coverage of Elizabeth Dole focused more on personal traits, and less on her issue positions, than the coverage given to her opponents, George W. Bush, John McCain, and Steve Forbes (Aday and Devitt 2001). Fowler and Lawless (2009) find more broadly that 64 percent of the media's coverage of topics such as marital and family status and appearance appeared in articles about female gubernatorial candidates, while Falk (2008) similarly finds that coverage of female presidential candidates concentrates more heavily on "character" coverage. And Dunaway et al. (2013) find that when the media cover female gubernatorial candidates they focus disproportionately on personal traits, but focus on issue positions when covering male candidates.

The media also provides increased coverage of female politicians' sartorial choices: one example of this is Hillary Clinton, who, during her campaign for the 2008 Democratic presidential nomination, was the subject of numerous articles about her colorful pantsuits (see, e.g., Givhan 2007; Skenazy 2008). An article about Nancy Pelosi the day after she became the presumptive (and first female) Speaker of the House in November 2006 was devoted solely to her fashion choices, and the "neutral-colored, softly tailored power suit" she wore for her press conference (Givhan 2006). Many articles about female candidates also drop in a short note about their clothes, information not usually included about male candidates. While a comment about one's "red suit and black heels" may seem insignificant, at least one study finds that such commentary negatively impacts evaluations of female candidates: an experimental study found that simply adding information about a female candidate's clothes to a news story, whether negative or positive, decreased respondents' likelihood of voting for the female candidate (Lake et al. 2013).

Female politicians are, not surprisingly, aware of the inequalities in media coverage. Niven and Zilber's (2001b) survey of U.S. House members' press secretaries reveals that press secretaries for female members are much more likely to believe the media treats their member "unfairly" than press secretaries serving male members. Female members' press secretaries are also less likely to believe that the media equally covers their issues and events and more likely to believe that the existent coverage indicates a "lack of respect" for their member.

The media may also add to the pressures facing female candidates in other ways: Lawrence and Rose (2011) argue Hillary Clinton faced more media "exit talk" and pressure to end her 2008 presidential campaign than comparable male candidates in past races. Importantly, a number of studies find that these disparities in media coverage are not a function of differences in how female and male candidates present themselves in speeches, campaign advertisements, or campaign websites; rather, they seem to reflect enduring, stereotypical differences in how the media itself views male, as opposed to female, candidates (Dolan 2005; Kahn 1993; Niven and Zilber 2001a). As Meeks (2013) concludes, after assessing the gendered coverage of Hillary Clinton and Sarah Palin during the 2008 presidential election, "Citizens are embedded in a society that fosters gender stereotypes, the news they consume reinforces those stereotypes, journalists grow up in this environment, carry it with them in their coverage, and start to foster the process all over again, thereby reinforcing gender barriers for women [to elected office]" (533).

Impact on Female Candidates

Sitting politicians customarily attend presidential inaugurations regardless of party ties. At Donald Trump's inauguration in January 2017, a Getty photograph captured some of these attendees commemorating the event by taking a photograph of themselves (see figure 2.7). Getty Images captioned the picture, "A woman takes a selfie with Sen. John McCain (R-AZ) and Sen. Bernie Sanders (D-VT) (R) on the West Front of the U.S. Capitol on January 20, 2017 in Washington, DC." The only problem with this photo seemingly showing senators taking photos with members of the public? Everyone whose face is in the picture was a sitting U.S. senator, not just the men; the "woman" in the photo is Senator Amy Klobuchar (D-MN). Klobuchar's office noted the discrepancy in how the caption writer treated her and the male senators in the photo. She said, "Since only senators were seated in that section (with many layers of security) it did seem a bit odd that they didn't try to pin down who the random 'woman' was sitting next to Senators McCain and Sanders. . . . Next time I will wear a big name tag or better yet a Vikings jersey with my name on the back" (Herreria 2017).

As figure 2.7 and its original caption illuminate, female legislators confront indignities related to their gender even in situations where their presence should not be noteworthy. We argue that the heightened electoral pressures outlined above, combined with persistent gender socialization and gender-related indignities, result in female candidates' perception that they are vulnerable simply because they are women, what we call gendered vulnerability. Even if they win at the same rates as their male colleagues, and even if voters are becoming increasingly accepting of female politicians, the perception—and we would argue the fact—remains that female candidates must work harder than male candidates to win elections, even when, as highlighted by the story of Senator Barbara Mikulski, they are highly popular incumbents.

Women contend with persistent societal stereotypes as to what traits women should possess and what issues women are better equipped to deal with competently; and also with party elites, other office-seeking individuals, and a media that reinforce these same stereotypes in a variety of ways. As Thomas (1997) argues, "No matter how women try to fit into the present system, they are still apart from the norm. Only when the norm itself is redefined will the situation be ameliorated" (49). While important advances in recent decades have moderated these concerns—particularly when it comes to the media—women still face significant barriers to obtaining and retaining elected office. Fowler and Lawless (2009) rather

Figure 2.7. Original caption: "A woman takes a selfie with Sen. John McCain (R-AZ) and Sen. Bernie Sanders (D-VT) (R) on the West Front of the U.S. Capitol on January 20, 2017 in Washington, DC. In today's inauguration ceremony Donald J. Trump becomes the 45th president of the United States." (Photo by Joe Raedle/Getty Images).

bleakly conclude that "regardless of the amount and type of media coverage a woman receives, or the characteristics of her challenger, contest, state or newspaper, her sex remains a serious liability" (527). For better or worse, the evidence suggests that a pervasive gendered vulnerability faces women legislators, and their own perceptions reinforce this conclusion.

Even more poignantly, our argument is not dependent upon women facing an objectively more difficult road to reelection (even though we find the evidence that they do to be persuasive). Rather, the question is whether female candidates *perceive* that they do. And the answer appears to be a resounding "yes." Surveys of potential candidates, our interviews with members and congressional staff, and multiple first- and second-person accounts of female legislators all conclude that women believe, due simply to their gender, that it is harder for them to get elected and succeed in politics than a similarly situated man.

The question we ask in this book is how this gendered vulnerability influences women once they attain elected office. Do these electoral concerns, along with the broader social forces women confront on a daily basis, lead women to pursue different legislative activities or otherwise act differently than their male colleagues? We contend that the answer is yes. The pressures facing female legislators create the conditions for gendered vulnerability. This unique form of vulnerability, in turn, forces women to proactively combat the challenges they will likely face come reelection—even if conventional signs suggest that, in the absence of gender, they should easily win reelection. Thus, as members legislate in anticipation of their next race for reelection (Mayhew 1974), the existence of gendered vulnerability leads women to approach the legislative process and other aspects of their representational duties differently than men. Specifically, we argue that women will provide increased attention to constituent services and constituents' policy preferences and needs.

How Do Men and Women Legislate Differently?

Before exploring those differences, however, we first summarize what the literature already knows about how men and women legislate differently or otherwise distinctly approach the legislative process. Prior work on the subject focuses primarily on the question of whether gender diversity within legislative bodies leads to discernible differences in legislative outputs.[10]

The notion of "descriptive representation" posits that institutions gain legitimacy when their members reflect the demographic makeup of the citizenry (Mansbridge 1999; Phillips 1995; Pitkin 1967). One effect of such diversity may be that citizens view the legislature as more legitimate. Under this theory, legislative bodies gain more support when members of the public see people who look like them serving in the legislature, and consequently lose support when certain segments of society, such as women or minorities, believe they (and their views) are not fairly represented in the institution. Descriptive representation also serves to combat the legacies of past discrimination by sending the message that "certain features of one's identity do not mark one as less able to govern" (Mansbridge 1999, 651; Sapiro 1981b). However, there is little evidence that descriptive representation—at least as the idea applies to gender—actually boosts public confidence or trust in government (Lawless 2004b; Rosenthal 1995).

However, diversity may provide other, more tangible benefits. For example, both Lawless (2004b) and Rosenthal (1995) suggest that females may prefer women representatives because they believe women representatives are more likely to support their political interests, thus providing an increased level of the amount of "substantive representation." Substantive representation refers to the extent to which societal groups' interests and policy preferences are reflected in a legislature's policy debates and outputs. Diversity is necessary because otherwise the views of groups who are not physically represented in the legislative body will not be reflected in the policies created by the institution (Krislov 1974). Advocates of a descriptive-substantive representation link maintain that more women legislators are necessary for reasons beyond female citizens being more accepting of the legislature's actions. Rather, an increase in the number of women legislators will in turn increase the attention the body pays to issues of concern to women. In Pitkin's (1967) phrasing, female legislators may inherently see part of their job as "acting for" women, "in a manner responsive" to their concerns (209). Critics (including those desiring increased diversity) note, however, that it is problematic to assume that all members of a particular group, such as women, share the same interests and goals (Dovi 2002; Phillips 1995; Williams 1998).

The first studies on the descriptive-substantive representation link answered this question in the negative (Diamond 1977; Schlozman and Mansbridge 1979; Mezey 1978; Carroll 1984; though see Sapiro 1981b). From this, scholars inferred that an overly strong focus on women's issues may harm female politicians electorally. As Carroll (1984) explains, "too much emphasis on women's issues in a campaign might lead to speculation that the candidate is narrow in her interests and would not adequately represent all the people" (319); similarly, female legislators may fear being stereotyped come reelection (321).

More recently, however, a large body of work has found that female legislators concentrate their substantive legislative efforts on issues that are of interest to women in the electorate, more than male legislators do. Studies find, for example, that female legislators are more likely to introduce or support legislation on topics of interest to women (Reingold 2000; Swers 2005) and vote differently on roll-call votes (Gehlen 1977; Leader 1977; Swers 1998; Welch 1985; but see Reingold 2000). These substantive differences have been found across several different stages in the legislative process, including bill introduction, committee and subcommittee work, and roll-call voting (see, e.g., Bratton and Haynie 1999; Reingold 2000; Swers 1998, 2002, 2005; Thomas 1991, 1994; Thomas and Welch 1991; Vega and Firestone 1995). Swers (2002) and others highlight the normative implication that greater numbers of women in government will result in better representation of women and their interests. And interviews with female legislators reveal that they feel a personal sense of responsibility to use their positions to act on behalf of women and see themselves as acting as representatives for women in general (Burrell 1994; Carroll 2003; Reingold 2000; Swers 2002).

Finally, diversity can lead to changes in how the organization itself operates. For example, women legislators may simply approach the process of legislating differently, which can influence the policies produced by the lawmaking body or simply alter the way in which decisions are made. In particular, female legislators may adopt different legislative or leadership styles than male legislators, leading to fundamental changes in the process of legislating. For example, scholars in numerous fields find evidence that women are more likely to lead democratically, rather than autocratically, and to use supportive rather than competitive language (see, e.g., Blair and Stanley 1991; Coates 1993; Duerst-Lahti and Johnson 1990; Eagly and Johnson 1990; Kelly, Saint-Germain, and Horn 1991). Lyn Kathlene's work brings this idea to the legislative arena. For instance, women in leadership positions, such as committee chairs, are more likely to use these positions to encourage and moderate debate and discussion, rather than to use their leadership powers to control witness testimony or the committee's discussions (Kathlene 1990, 1991, 1994). Specifically, female chairs and legislators more generally speak less, take fewer turns, and make fewer interruptions than men (Kathlene 1994). Other studies find female legislators utilize more collegial and consensual styles of decision making (Flammang 1985; Reingold 1992) and focus more on process-oriented, rather than power-oriented, goals (Jewell and Whicker 1994; but see Dodson and Carroll 1991; Kelly, Saint-Germain, and Horn 1991; Thomas and Welch 1991). Female legislators are also found to behave distinctly in other ways. For example, women are more likely than men to favor direct contact with constituents and contact through newsletters (Sussman and West 1995). Reingold (1996, 2000) argues, however, that such gender differences are most likely to arise in institutions that lack strong institutional norms of behavior.

These studies highlight a number of ways in which women legislators act differently than male legislators, and how these differences influence legislative politics and outputs as a whole. Since many of these studies focus on whether female officeholders provide descriptive and substantive representation to female constituents, they necessarily focus on whether women offer distinctive leadership styles or are better at representing "women's" interests. They do not necessarily address, however, whether broader patterns of gender-related behavior differences exist. We thus introduce the concept of "gendered vulnerability" and discuss its implications for differences in legislative activity between men and women.

Gendered Vulnerability and Legislative Behavior

Due to broad socialization pressures and the obstacles they face in the electoral process, we argue that all women legislators—regardless of how safe their electoral position might appear to be by objective standards—must contend with gendered vulnerability. For better or worse, females confront a society that sends the signal that, as women, they must continually prove their skills and worthiness in a way men do not. This is particularly true when women enter an arena that is traditionally considered "male" or "masculine," such as the political arena. The current electoral landscape reinforces these perceptions, suggesting to women candidates that they are particularly vulnerable to attacks and challenges. This vulnerability is not because women hold seats that are unsafe by conventional standards. Rather, this vulnerability is grounded in female legislators' gender, and the ways in which their gender causes other political actors to treat them differently. Gendered vulnerability thus captures the notion that women are both socialized to perceive that their efforts will be discounted relative to their male counterparts—and are socialized to themselves discount their abilities compared to men—and are aware that they are more likely to be challenged in their quest for reelection.

Moreover, gendered vulnerability is not mitigated by incumbency status. As highlighted in chapter 1, Senator Barbara Mikulski faced considerably more challenges along her path to reelection, even though she also consistently won her primary and general elections by considerable margins. In 2004, eleven candidates vied against her, even though she won by more than 70 percent of the vote in her last two elections. The implication is that Senator Mikulski was viewed as "vulnerable," but not in the traditional sense of having won election by a relatively close margin; rather, her vulnerability appears to be a function of her gender and "the irrational tendency [of] challengers to overestimate their likely success against female incumbents" (Milyo and Schosberg 2000, 44).

We suggest—along with the long line of literature we reference above—that this condition is not unique to Senator Mikulski, but common to most, if not all, female politicians. And, even if, as Hayes and Lawless (2015) suggest, the media is beginning to use a "non-gendered lens" to assess congressional candidates, they also acknowledge that potential female candidates *believe* they will face gendered media coverage and potential gender backlash from voters (see also Lawless and Fox 2010, 2012); these perceptions are mirrored in both the CAWP 2008 Recruitment Study of state legislators as well as numerous national polls discussed earlier in the chapter. Regardless of their objective level of electoral vulnerability—that is, whether they reside in a "safe" district or whether they won office with a substantial proportion of the two-party vote—women politicians continue to perceive that their position is inherently vulnerable. We argue that this perception is one women hold specifically as a consequence of their gender, and so its effects are widely felt by the females currently serving in the United States Congress, as well as in other elected bodies. And, as discussed above, this perception of vulnerability and not belonging may also be reinforced by the subtle (and not-so-subtle) actions of male members of Congress.

We posit that this belief that women are electorally vulnerable—a belief held by both female legislators and others in the electoral arena—significantly influences women's behavior in office. The result is that female legislators will, more so than males, consciously focus their efforts on those activities and policies that most benefit their constituents and offer the most electoral benefits. Mayhew (1974) introduced the triad of credit-claiming activities (which send the message to constituents that the legislator is responsible as an individual for getting the government to do something desirable), position-taking activities (expressing judgments on issues of interest), and advertising (simply raising one's name recognition among voters) (see also Fenno 1978a). Since female legislators must be concerned with overcoming their gendered vulnerability and proving their worth to the voters (as well as to colleagues, party elites, and potential challengers), they will simply do more advertising, position-taking, and credit-claiming activities, and be more attuned than their male colleagues to representing their constituents' interests. And, since gendered vulnerability applies to all women elected officials, its effects will be broadly felt and result in clear gender-based patterns of behavior. This strategy has clear payoffs: the overwhelming conclusion is that voters reward members of Congress who engage in these activities, particularly on Election Day (Cain, Ferejohn, and Fiorina 1987; Box-Steffensmeier, Arnold and Zorn 1997; Eulau and Karps 1977; Parker and Goodman 2009; Rocca and Gordon 2010; Serra and Moon 1994). And, as shown in figure 2.5, this strategy has benefited women incumbents, shielding them from defeat—even if they still face challenges along the way—and providing them with high reelection margins.

This gendered behavior is independent of any effects we might see for either traditional notions of electoral vulnerability, seniority, or other forces that usually explain broad trends in legislative behavior. Specifically, we argue that female legislators—simply by virtue of the fact that they are female—focus more time and attention on legislative activities that reflect their constituents' needs and interests, and that provide a higher reelection payoff. Our argument thus moves beyond the descriptive-substantive representation linkage debate to contend that we will see gender differences in legislative behavior across the multitude of issues that legislators address. As we show in the next four empirical chapters, women simply do more in terms of bill sponsorship and cosponsorship, distributive benefit procurement, and constituent-based work, and they are more likely than their male colleagues to hew more closely to their districts' interests, whether in terms of committee work, roll-call voting, or the policies they pursue. Importantly, we find these effects go beyond women simply representing women, and instead show that women represent everyone.

Some recent studies have argued that differences in legislative activity and output may be the result of which women seek and/or win elected office. Like our own theory, this one begins with the premise that while female candidates face a more difficult path to elected office than male candidates, they are also just as likely to win (see, e.g., Darcy and Schramm 1977; Smith and Fox 2001), and voter sexism has generally not been found to be an explanation for the lack of women in elected office (see, e.g., Rosenwasser et al. 1987). This school of thought reconciles these two apparently divergent patterns by arguing that those women who ultimately choose to seek elected office, and those who actually win election despite the outsized challenges facing women in that arena, must be the hardest-working and most qualified (Anzia and Berry 2011; Fulton 2010; Milyo and Schosberg 2000). Once in office, these women continue to utilize these same traits and skills and become highly effective legislators. Given that female candidates must in many ways be superior to male candidates in order to attain the same electoral outcome (i.e., winning office), this theory acts as a "selection model" and suggests female legislators are in fact likely to be more effective legislators than their male counterparts in many aspects of legislative life—in terms of accruing chamber power, securing distributive benefits, or seeing their legislative priorities enacted.

Our theory does not necessarily conflict with the selection-based theory. Rather, it moves beyond simply labeling women as "better legislators" or "better politicians" by offering a more cohesive and substantive-oriented explanation for potential gender differences. Most previous studies measure legislative effectiveness by assessing levels of "entrepreneurship" or legislative activity (Anzia and Berry 2011; Fulton 2010; Wawro 2000; Schiller 1995; Mayhew 2000). We argue there is an effect on legislative behavior beyond what the selection-based theory proposes: women will be more likely than men to emphasize activities that cater to their constituents' needs, to pursue policies that reflect their constituents' interests, and to prioritize those activities with the highest constituent and electorally oriented benefits. That is, we provide a comprehensive framework for understanding what being "better" looks like.

The normative implication of our theory is that women more faithfully seek to represent all of their constituents. While scholars have previously examined whether women better represent women, our focus on broad patterns of legislative behavior reveals that women better represent everyone. Women in the U.S. Congress orient themselves toward their constituents. And this orientation appears not to be solely focused on single groups (such as women) or copartisans, but rather on the distinctive needs of the district. A potential side benefit of gendered vulnerability is thus the improved representation of those living in districts represented by women; we discuss these important normative implications more in chapter 7. We turn now in chapters 3 through 6 to an in-depth examination of what women's reaction to their gendered vulnerability looks like in practice.

THREE

A Constituent Way of Life?

Gender and Constituency Services

Senators Kay Bailey Hutchison and Debbie Stabenow differ in a number of ways. One is a Republican, while the other is a Democrat. One represents a large, red state, while the other represents a midsize blue state. One has a consistently conservative voting record while the other is considered quite liberal. However, one thing they have in common is that these two female senators tied during the 110th Congress for the highest number of district-based staff at twenty-six each. This was not idiosyncratic to the 110th Congress, but rather a continuing pattern: during both the 108th and 109th Congresses they tied for second.

Unlike most congressional staff who work on Capitol Hill, district staff are tasked with directly helping constituents. They help constituents with federal grant proposals, issues with Social Security or other benefits checks, Medicare and Medicaid eligibility, and any other issue that may arise in relation to the federal government. Generally, members of Congress who want to focus on constituency issues hire more staff to work in the district, and members who want to focus more on legislation hire more DC staff. This is a zero-sum choice—each member of Congress has a fixed budget for hiring all staff, so every dollar they spend on a district staffer is one they cannot spend on someone to help in DC. The number of staffers a member of Congress employs in his or her district is not a perfect measure of how much constituent work a member does, but it suggests how important constituency concerns are to the member of Congress. And while Hutchison and Stabenow are only two senators, we argue that their heightened attention to constituency services is part of a broader pattern. Because women are vulnerable in ways that men are not, female members overall devote more time and resources to constituent services than men do.

In chapter 2 we laid out our theory of gendered vulnerability—that female political candidates and elected officials face more doubts about their political acumen and a tougher road to winning election and reelection. This translates into significant gender-based differences once in office. Most notably, women are more likely than men to pursue activities that directly target the needs of their constituents and provide high reelection payoffs. Returning to Mayhew's triad of activities, women utilize advertising, position-taking, and credit-claiming strategies more heavily and more often than men. In this chapter, we begin our empirical analysis of the implications of gendered vulnerability with an assessment of the services members of Congress provide to constituents.

Many times, our understanding of Congress focuses on the legislative process. However, providing services to voters outside of the legislative process is just as much a part of members' job as legislating is. As constituents' official representative in the federal government, members take it upon themselves to inform voters of what the government is doing and (more importantly from the member's point of view) what the member is doing. Members also intercede on their constituents' behalf whenever constituents have a problem with the government, helping to untangle the bureaucratic snags that people inevitably run into. These services are so much a part of the representative's job, in fact, that the government pays for members of Congress to provide them. Each member is given a budget that she can use to furnish an office in Washington, to rent and operate offices in her state or district, to hire staff for each office, and for other things that allow them to interact with their constituents. This budget is referred to in official circles as the member's allowance, and the amount varies from member to member.

In this chapter, we argue that, as a result of their gendered vulnerability, women devote more time and attention while in office to providing services to constituents. In a classically Mahewian bargain, when members directly aid individuals and groups of constituents the member can then obviously claim credit for providing the assistance. Female legislators thus utilize constituency services to clearly illuminate how they are working for their districts. And, the impetus is twofold: there are clear electoral benefits to engaging in high levels of constituency services, and gender socialization studies suggest women are more likely than men to engage in behaviors that help others. We look for and find evidence for that proposition by examining how members of Congress use their allowances to aid their constituents.

Nonlegislative Constituency Service

Go to any Congress member's website and one of the most prominent links will be to a page where a site visitor can submit a request for the member to help them with some problem. Sometimes there are more specific links for people dealing with specific problems—veterans' issues, consumer protection, immigration, student loans, or whatever that specific member gets the most requests for. This link's prominent placement on members' websites tells us that members see such constituent outreach as a high priority. Members are making themselves and their staffs available to constituents—they *want* constituents to ask them for help.

Of course, members do not provide these services out of the goodness of their hearts. True, it is part of their job as the peoples' representative in the government to help constituents deal with that government. But there's another factor a work as well—members also believe that casework and other services help them win reelection. (We discuss whether it actually helps below—short answer, it probably does.) The thinking among members is, "After I help this person she'll probably vote for me, and voters in her family will probably vote for me, *and* some of them will tell their friends and then the friends will like me better—and maybe they'll vote for me as well." In other words, every time a constituent contacts a member's office to ask for help with something it creates a win-win situation: the member can perform a public service for their constituents, and their constituents (hopefully) will be grateful come election time. The belief that casework generates votes helps keep casework near the center of every congressional office.

When a member of Congress helps a constituent solve a problem he or she is having with the federal government, the common name for this type of service is "casework." The type of problem could be anything—perhaps someone's government benefits check did not come on time, or a family is waiting for paperwork to clear a federal agency so they can conclude an international adoption, or a company that provides food services to a military installation did not get paid, or an enlisted soldier with an ailing mother had her request for leave denied. Casework can involve virtually any area of life a powerful member of government might have some influence over. One congressional staffer we interviewed explained in detail the types of services her member's office provides:

> We help modify mortgages, help with VA benefits. We'll go to the hospital weekly to check on people. . . . It is about customer service. We also do really big events. We host a jobs fair every March—14,000 people came this year. We ensure companies really have jobs and people can be hired at the fair. We did a huge media blitz—local churches, radio, TV, and [we] used people who have been hired. . . . Same with the annual health fair in August—about 3,000 people came. We do screenings and got people to the hospital to save them. [These services] show [the member] is concerned.

Another staffer explains that her office does not wait for constituents to approach them. Rather, the representative and his staff members actively seek out people who might have a problem they could help with:

> You go to a restaurant or a senior center or something like that and as people show up you just have a conversation. And you bring a district representative so if you have a VA concern, or disability, or Social Security, or whatever, bring your concern and we will get the process started to getting the problem fixed.

Virtually any time a constituent has a problem with a federal agency—or even, as the second quote indicates, some other problems that the government might be able to deal with more tangentially—a member's office is willing and even eager to help. Members make it their business to fix these problems for their constituents.

We show in this chapter that female Congress members devote more effort to serving constituents than male members.[1] The literature has focused on three such measures of this effort. One is the number of staff a member employs who work in the member's state or district. Every member employs a number of staffers both in Washington and in their home districts or states. However, Washington staff focus primarily on different aspects of legislative work—legislation itself, public affairs, meeting with constituents, and to some extent casework. On the other hand, staff who work in the state or district are much more focused on helping constituents with the problems they bring to the member's office. One DC staffer we interviewed explained his office's constituency service operation: "Back in the district we had about eight or nine staff spread over two [full] offices and one satellite office. . . . The district was . . . really spread out. . . . We placed a big part of our strategy in constituent service."

The second measure of constituency service is the amount of time the member spends in her state or district, as opposed to in Washington, D.C. Most members travel back and forth between Washington and their district several times a year (or several times a month) and the cost of the travel comes out of the members' allowance. Members do not need to be in the district to help with casework, and most do not personally do a lot of casework. Nonetheless, time in the district is constituency-focused in a way that time in Washington is not. As Representative Northup commented about being "home" in the district, "you have to be on the street from 8 o'clock in the morning till late in the evening every day you are in town. And it just bristles me when I have people talk about 'Congress's on vacation' because vacation was coming back here and doing a lot of work." Similarly, a staffer explains that when her member was in district, "He was going to ribbon cuttings, and high school sporting events, and anything just trying to be seen. And we would put up his schedule before we went home on the website, and send [it] to media and invite people to come up and see him." Fenno's (1978a, 1978b) classic accounts of House members interacting with their constituents shed light on how members interact with their voters, and how they use these meetings and other gatherings to help themselves win reelection. Each member uses a different strategy tailored to his or her personality and constituents' preferences, but the common theme among all members is that when she in the district, she is probably working on constituent relations. So another way to measure how much time and attention a member spends on constituent-related services is to observe how much time he or she spends in the district.

The third measure is the amount of mail members send to constituents. Even in the twenty-first century members of Congress still keep in contact with their constituents through the mail because, as a staffer explained to us, "that was one of the easy ways to communicate with constituents. [News]papers were contracting so much and it was just harder, and you weren't getting covered as much. . . . To actually get a message across and make sure people know what you are doing, you really had to [send mail]." Members send mail to constituents via "the frank," which allows them to replace a paid-for postage stamp with their signature. The franking privilege, as it is known, was unlimited for many years—members could send literally as much mail as they felt like, as long as it fell within certain parameters, and for free. However, that changed in 1991, and in the modern era the cost of sending mail comes out of members' mail allowance; members' mail allowance is determined by a formula based on the cost of a first class stamp and the number of nonbusiness addresses in a district. There are a few restrictions on what kinds of mail members can frank, and they are not allowed to send anything explicitly connected to their reelection campaign. Nonetheless, members use the frank to tell their constituents about what they are doing in office—what bills they are sponsoring, what spending projects they have secured for the district, and what issues are coming up for consideration that voters care about. Moreover, typically members send the largest amount of mail in the months leading up to an election. In other words, it is well accepted by everyone—Congress members, staffers, journalists, academics, and others—that the frank is a reelection tool in everything but name.

Importantly for our purposes, members do not all employ the same number of staffers in the district, frank the same amount of mail, or travel between DC and their districts with the same frequency. Rather, there is wide variation in each of these measures. That variation is explained by a number of factors, and we argue that a member's gender is an important one. Gendered vulnerability theory holds that female legislators need to advertise their actions on behalf of their constituents and claim credit for various accomplishments more than men do; as such, they should devote more resources than men to keeping in contact with constituents.

Previous Work on Constituency Service

Empirically, the measures we utilize in this chapter are the number of staff a member places in the district, congressional travel to the member's district, and the use of the franking privilege. And we predict that female members do all of these things more than men. But before we discuss the role gender plays in these activities, there are two questions we need to address: Are these valuable tools for members of Congress, in that they actually help members win reelection? And do members who are electorally vulnerable (in the traditional sense) use these tools more than safe members do?

These are questions that congressional scholars have been asking for decades. Looking at the first question—whether constituent services help members win reelection—the answer seems to be "yes," but it took a while for scholars to get there. This issue was the subject of intense debate among academics throughout most of the 1980s. One group of scholars focused on the district level, looking for evidence that attentive members (those who performed more casework, hired more staff in the district, and so forth) received higher vote shares than their less-attentive counterparts. They found no evidence for this and concluded somewhat counterintuitively that casework does not really help members get reelected, despite the fact members spend so much time on it (Johannes and McAdams 1981; McAdams and Johannes 1981, 1988; Ragsdale and Cook 1987; Bond, Covington, and Fleisher 1985). A second group looked at individual-level data, searching for evidence that voters who had benefited from casework evaluate their member of Congress more favorably than voters who had never gotten help from their member. Contrary to the first set of studies, these studies typically found that constituent service made voters more favorable to their member (Fiorina 1977, 1981; Cain, Ferejohn, and Fiorina 1987; Rivers and Fiorina 1989; Yiannakis 1981). This debate involves a Gordian knot of methodological claims and counterclaims, and was never fully resolved by those who originally participated in it even though it went on for about a decade.[2]

However, two sets of later studies shed new light on the question, and both indicate that constituent services do help members win reelection. First, scholars reexamined the individual-level connection between members' constituent service and voter evaluations, addressing the methodological shortcomings Johannes and McAdams (1981, 1988) identified in Fiorina and coauthors' original work.[3] Studies of the House (Romero 2006; Parker and Goodman 2009) and the Senate (Parker and Goodman 2013) collectively examine the empirical connection between several constituency related activities on one hand, and survey respondents' evaluations of their Congress members on the other hand. All three studies find that, even while controlling for other factors, members who provide more constituent services receive better evaluations from their constituents.

A second set of studies attempts to isolate the causal effect of district service by employing experimental and quasi-experimental research designs. Cover and Brumburg (1982) worked directly with a House member who, every month, sent informative child-rearing literature to all the new mothers who gave birth in a hospital in his district. For one month, the member agreed to let the scholars randomly select half of the women to not receive the pamphlet, and to let the scholars contact the district's new mothers to perform follow-up interviews. Serra and Cover (1992) obtained from a member of Congress a list of constituents who had received help from the member via a casework request, and also constructed a control group of constituents who had not received help; they likewise contacted members of both groups to perform interviews. Serra and Pinny (2004) replicated the second research design using state legislators. In all three studies, researchers found that constituents who had been helped or contacted by the member were more likely than the constituents in the control group to recognize the member's name and to give the member more favorable evaluations. Cover and Brumburg (1982) additionally examined how long the effect lasts, finding that the differences between treatment group and control group caused by receiving a single piece of mail would eventually disappear, but not for two years. This implies that the mail Congress members send to voters within two years of an election might still influence them on Election Day.

In the end, the evidence appears pretty convincing that constituent service does indeed help members of Congress win reelection—it results in constituents who are more likely to know who their members are, who evaluate their members more favorably, and who are more likely to vote for the member come election time. So it makes sense that members focus so heavily on casework—it is a nonpartisan, nonideological way to reach out to voters. Casework is especially useful for winning over moderate or undecided voters who might not otherwise pay attention to politics. But if a constituent who is otherwise disengaged from politics has a problem that the member or her office can solve, that constituent might become a voter, and a proincumbent voter to boot. In general, the best evidence suggests that casework has the effect Congress members intend for it to have—it helps them win reelection.

On the other hand, the answer to the second question—whether vulnerable members use constituent services more than safe members—depends on which type of constituent service is examined. For franking, the evidence is unambiguous: vulnerable members use it more than safe members. This is true in both the House (Cover 1980; Goodman and Parker 2010; Hall, Nesbit, and Thorson 2012; Edwards, Stephenson, and Yeoh 2012) and the Senate (Mikesell 1987), even though senators rely on franking much less than House members do. However, there is not any evidence at all that electorally vulnerable members travel to the district more than safe members do (Fenno 1978a; Parker and Parker 1985; Goodman and Parker 2010). Nor is there much evidence that vulnerable members hire more district staff than safe members (Fenno 1978a; Schiff and Smith 1983; Bennett and DiLorenzo 1982; Epstein and Frankovic 1982). Taken together, all of this research appears to indicate that, out of the three distinct types of constituent services that scholars have investigated, franking is the only one that members of Congress most reliably turn to when they are in electoral trouble or feel insecure about their reelection chances.

Gendered Vulnerability and Constituency Service

What role does gender play in determining members' levels of constituency service? Scholars have long argued that women are more concerned than men with providing constituent services. Early research on female politicians focused on so-called female traits—the idea that women are by nature more people-oriented, consensual, and caring than men. For legislative officeholders of all types (members of Congress, state legislators, and city council members were all examined), these traits imply that women are more attuned and attentive to their constituents' needs than men are, and more willing to devote their office resources to helping alleviate these needs. Scholars also argued that constituents consciously or unconsciously recognize these traits when they are represented by women, and as a result view their female representatives in government as being more willing to help them solve their own problems. In interviews, female legislators have said that they believed themselves to be more approachable than men—that they are more willing to listen to constituents, and more likely to help constituents with their problems, than men are (Mezey 1978; Bers 1978; Flammang 1985; Merritt 1980). For example, Diamond (1977) writes, "The female legislator is perceived as being ever available by her constituents. This . . . enable[s] the legislator to solidify relationships with constituents, thereby enhancing reelection prospects. . . . There was a definite consensus among the women . . . that women legislators received considerably more calls than their male colleagues" (86).

Later studies surveyed larger numbers of state legislators using more systematic methodology, asking them how much time they spent on various activities including constituency service. In these surveys, female legislators consistently reported hearing from constituents more often, spending more time keeping in touch with constituents, and spending more time helping constituents with their problems than male representatives do (Thomas 1992; Richardson and Freeman 1995; Carey, Niemi, and Powell 1998; Epstein, Niemi, and Powell 2005; but see Hogan 2008 and Reingold 2000).

These prior works all comport with our primary hypothesis: women legislators engage in each of these constituent-oriented activities more than their male colleagues. However, one methodological shortcoming these previous studies share is that none directly examines officeholders' actual levels of constituency service. Rather, they all discuss members' self-reported levels of interaction with constituents. This distinction is important precisely *because* female officeholders view themselves as being much more available to constituents than their male counterparts. It is thus possible that when members are asked about how much time they spend on constituency service, women and men both answer the question while accessing their beliefs about their relationships with constituents rather than directly recalling how much time they spend on those relationships.[4] Thus, one of our goals in this chapter is to directly assess this gendered effect for the first time by investigating the actual behavior of members rather than their self-reported assessments. Before turning to the quantitative analysis, however, we first discuss the insights gained from our interviews with congressional staff.

Interviews with Congressional Staff

Our interviews provide considerable support for the notion that female officeholders provide more and better constituent services than men. Indeed, this gender difference in constituency services was one of the most prominent themes emerging from the interviews, particularly those we conducted with staff members who had at different times worked for both female and male members. We were struck by the number of staff members who—without prompting—explicitly compared the level of constituent service provided by their female bosses to that provided by their male bosses. In each of these cases, the staffer indicated that his or her female boss devoted more effort to constituent services than the male boss did. For instance, this theme emerges from our interviewees' comments on how often members visit their states and districts. One Senate staffer explained that when she worked for a female senator, spending time in the state was one of the member's highest priorities:

> There was a lot of emphasis placed on what we can do to improve [the state]. . . . We had the economic development administration. . . . I was brought [to the state] a couple of times to look at economic development opportunities. . . . With [the female senator] that was pretty much everything we did the whole time I was there . . . although she did not have very tough races. We were up in the district a lot more meeting with people. Maybe I went to [the state] twice during my entire five or six years in [the male senator's] office.

A similar comparison was made by a House staffer who had previously worked for two male members, but at the time of the interview worked for a woman: "All three [members I have worked for] have DC residences. But only [the female member] spent most of her time in the district."

The same theme emerges when the staffers discussed congressional offices' franking activity. One staffer noted that the female senator he worked for put more pressure on staff members to get mail out than his previous boss, a male House member.

> Mail was always an issue in [female Senator's] office. . . . Are you answering the mail? We would be called out if we weren't, but that was never the case in [male House member]'s office. Not that he didn't care to know what was happening, but there wasn't as much pressure to sit down and get it done.

Another staffer indicated that this pressure went beyond just getting a certain number of pieces of mail out. The female House member she worked for was also more controlling of the *content* of the letters their offices sent out than her previous boss, a male senator:

> The House member I worked for was a woman, and she got very into the mail. . . . She would go through [the letters] with a fine-toothed comb, practically writing the letters, whereas other members—you know [male senator] just looked at the number. He wanted to know what our mail number was [but] he did not necessarily read the letters, did not necessarily want to know what was in them.

Staffers we interviewed also indicated that female members placed a higher priority on meeting constituents while they were in Washington. Some staffers for female members indicated in a static way that these meetings were important: "Mornings are devoted to meeting with all constituents and groups that are in town." Or "constituents always came first, even before interest groups." But on this topic as well, other interviewees provided direct comparisons between their male and female bosses, and found the women to be more attentive:

> [Female House member's] office's policy was to meet with constituents whenever there wasn't a hearing or something that was already on the schedule. Which was different from when I worked for [male House member]—all of those requests went straight to the legislative staff unless it was a somebody. . . . He wanted to have free time in case things came up or to meet with other members whereas [female House member] was much more "What's going on with the constituents? I want to know everything that's happening."

And another, telling a similar story:

> One of the things [female senator] always did and I believe continues to do is she dedicates a chunk of her time every day from Tuesday, Wednesday, and Thursday to constituents' meetings. . . . It was her belief that a constituent was flying all the way from [the home] state to see her, then she wanted to see them. . . . [Male senator] did not always do the small constituent groups in DC all the time.

Other interviewees more succinctly acknowledged the difference in how male and female members of Congress approach constituency services. One said, "[Female senator] was always aware of what was happening in the district, whereas [male House member] knew that there would have been things he probably could have done, he just didn't want to." A second shared a similar sentiment about her male and female bosses: "With casework, [the female member's] operation is more robust than [that of male members I have worked for]. Her biggest priorities are helping with immigration, Social Security, and supporting grant requests." And finally, one of our interviewees summed up our position as well as or better than we could: "Maybe women tend to focus more on the constituent services side of things, just making sure that the folks back home are taken care of." We turn now to a systematic examination of the notion that female legislators emphasize constituency-based work more than their male counterparts. We first examine franked mail usage, and then turn to members' trips home and district staff allocations.

Franking

In this section, we present the results of the first-ever study of gender differences in officeholders' constituency activities that uses data on the activities themselves, rather than self-reports gathered from surveys. For our analysis of franking we focus primarily on House members, because House members send more mail than senators, and rely on it as a communication tool to a much greater extent.[5] We examine House members' franking activity over five Congresses, from the 103rd (1993–94) through the 107th (2001–02).[6] We count members' mass mailings, and exclude letters written to individual constituents in response to queries about the status of legislation, requests for casework, voters expressing their opinions on political issues, or other constituent-generated responses. For each member, we observe the amount of money they spend on sending franked mail to their constituents, how many pieces of mail they send, and how many pieces of mail they send per 1,000 constituents.

Looking first at the bivariate relationship between gender and the amount of mail that a member sends, all three measures of mail volume tell the same story: over the time period we examine, female House members sent significantly more mail than men did. Female members spent an (inflation-adjusted) average of $103,000 per Congress on franked mail, nearly 12 percent more than the $91,520 spent by male members of Congress ($p<.003$) (see figure 3.1). Similarly, female members sent an average of 581,695 pieces of franked mail, 17 percent more than the 496,385 sent by men ($p<.003$). Finally, even though House districts are nominally equivalent to one another in population, in practice there can be some significant differences owing to the allocation of House districts between the states, and population change within census periods. Thus, we also look at the population-adjusted number of pieces of mail sent by each member of the House. On average female members sent 999 pieces of mail per 1,000 residents every Congress, 19 percent more than the 840 pieces per 1,000 residents sent by male members ($p<.001$). All three of our measures point to the same conclusion: women send more mail to their constituents than men do.

We replicated these bivariate analyses with multivariate models using the same dependent variables—dollars spent franking, pieces of franked mail, and population-adjusted pieces of franked mail. We estimate spending and population adjusted mail with ordinary least squares, and the raw number of pieces of franked mail with a negative binomial count model. In each model, the key independent variable is a dummy variable indicating which members of Congress are female. We included several control variables that also potentially influence the number of pieces of franked mail members send—how far their district is from Washington, DC; each member's seniority in years; a dummy variable indicating that the member is a freshman; the member's vote in his or her most recent election (to account for traditional notions of electoral vulnerability); and a set of dummy variables indicating which Congress each data point is taken from. Results are presented in table 3.1, and in all three cases the original finding holds: *Female* is positive and significant. The coefficients in the negative binomial model is not directly interpretable, but the OLS models indicate that even after accounting for the control variables, gender differences are comparable to the bivariate differences reported above: on average, women spend approximately $11,760 more per Congress than men, and send 145 more pieces of mail per 1,000 constituents than men do.

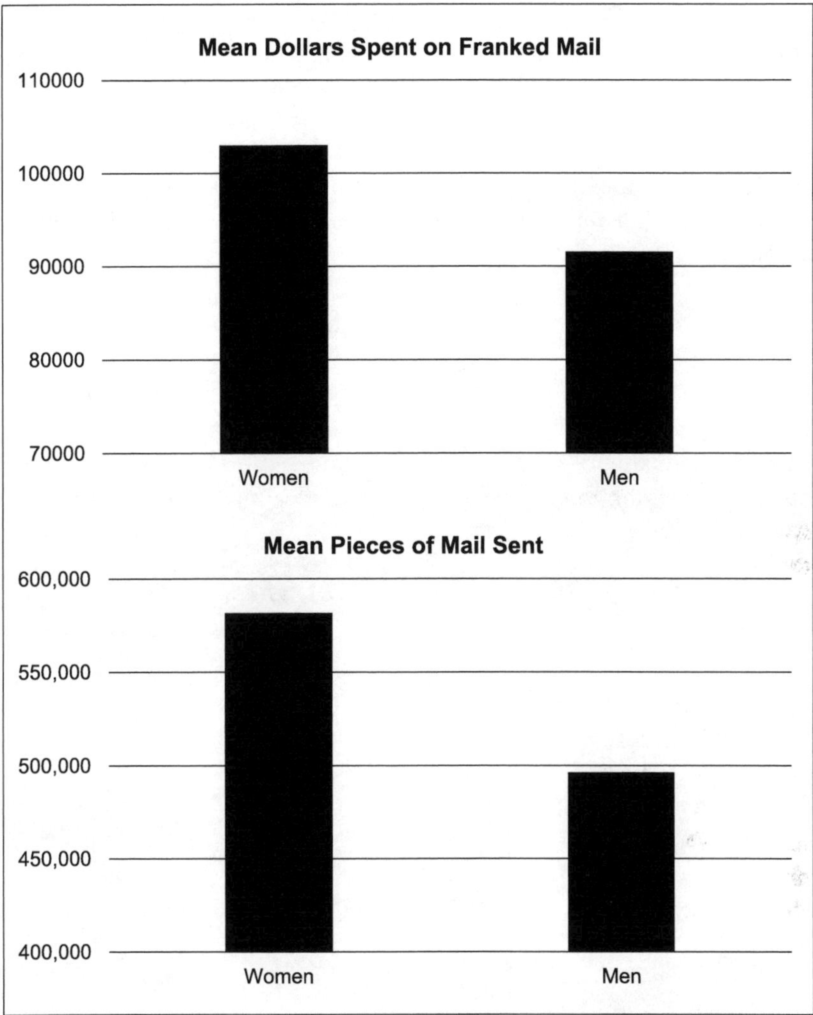

Figure 3.1. Gender differences in franking—House members, 103rd–107th Congresses

In the Senate, the franking privilege is not nearly so important a tool for reelection (or any other goal). Over half of the observations in our Senate dataset spanning the 103rd through the 108th Congress consist of senators who sent zero pieces of franked mail. Even if we isolate the senators who did send mail, on average they only sent fifty-two pieces of mail per 1,000 constituents, whereas House members sent over 850. Nonetheless, we analyze the data. Forty-six percent of male Senators and 48 percent of female senators sent at least some franked mail; of those who did, women sent fewer pieces overall than men (61,584 and 111,470 pieces, respectively, p<.123) and fewer pieces per 1,000 residents than men (2.3 and 5.6 pieces, respectively, p<.020). When we analyze both dependent variables using multivariate Tobit analysis (using a similar specification as above), the dummy variable indicating female senators is not significant in either model, suggesting we cannot attribute variations in franked mail usage in the Senate to gender.

Travel to the District

Ideally, we would measure congressional travel by taking note of how many times a member of Congress visits his or her district over the course of a year, or the total number of days a member spends in her district. Unfortunately, obtaining this information is a logistical nightmare.[7] Instead we

TABLE 3.1. Determinants of Franking—House Members, 103rd–107th Congresses

	Dollars spent franking (1,000s)	Pieces of franked mail	Pieces of franked mail, per 1,000 residents
Female	11.76**	.155**	145.5***
	(3.93)	(.056)	(51.9)
Distance from DC	.003*	.101	–.001
	(.001)	(.210)	(.019)
Seniority	.552	.012*	11.68*
	(.371)	(.006)	(5.09)
Freshman	34.3***	.398***	408***
	(7.24)	(.081)	(87.12)
Lagged vote	–.334***	–.005***	–4.07***
	(.052)	(.0009)	(.756)
Constant	74.59***	13.18***	833***
	(4.68)	(.081)	(67.95)
N	1948	1605	1603
R-squared	.113	—	.0464
Log likelihood		–21805	
Wald chi²		79.47	
p > chi²		.000	
Overdispersion		2.90	
		(.164)	

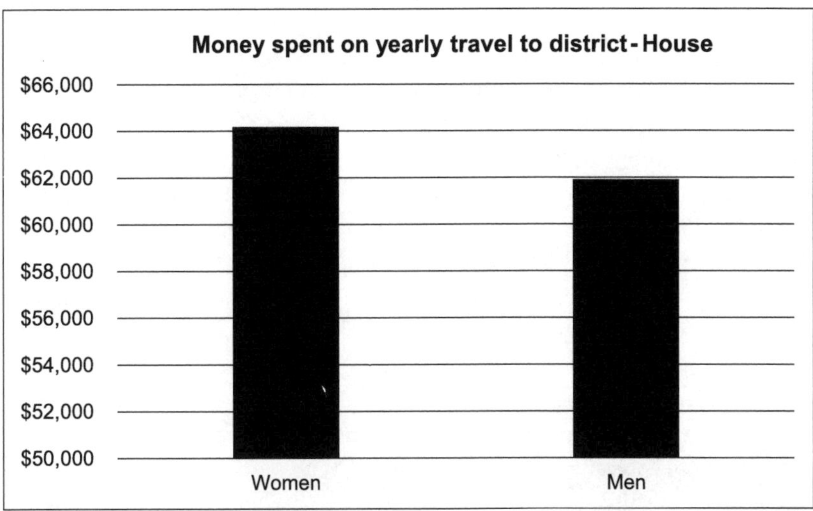

Figure 3.2. Gender differences in spending on travel to the district, House members, 103rd–107th Congresses

examine information about the amount of money House members spend traveling to and from the district in each Congress from the 103rd to the 107th Congresses. Looking first at the direct relationship between that variable and a member's gender, it appears that women do spend slightly more than men: on average in our dataset women spend $64,173 on travel, while men spend $61,901. However, the difference is not statistically significant ($p<.141$).

This lack of statistical significance is confirmed when we estimate travel spending using a multivariate OLS model. The most important covariates when it comes to determining how much a member travels to his or her district are both geographical. First, a member of Congress whose district is farther away from Washington, DC, will take fewer trips home per year, on average, than a member of Congress whose district is closer (Fenno 1978b). However, when the dependent variable is not the travel itself, but the money spent on traveling, this is offset by the fact that each trip will be more expensive—compare, for example, traveling from Washington, DC, to Oregon on one hand, and to central Virginia on the other. Either way, it is necessary to control for the distance between the district and Washington. Second is the size of the member's district. Members will spend more time and money traveling between locations within the district when the district is geographically large and the population density is low (say, Wyoming's at-large district) than when it is geographically small and has high density (for example, midtown Manhattan). We include these two variables as control variables, along with the member's tenure, the population of the district, the member's vote share in his or her most recent election, and by-Congress dummy variables. Results are presented in table 3.2, and indicate that once these other factors are controlled for, gender is not significantly related to the amount of money a member spends traveling.

These empirical findings contradict the story told by our interviewees. Many of them spoke about how female members, particularly senators, appeared to be more worried about traveling back home whenever they could. For example, one interviewee commented, "You know the stories you see about the senators or the members of congress who lose touch and move to Washington? It is not the women. . . . I mean, [Alaska Senator Lisa] Murkowski goes home every weekend, and that is the other side of the world. [California Senator Barbara] Boxer and [California Senator Dianne] Feinstein—even though they lived far away they have always gone back home."

What might explain such a discrepancy? One obvious answer is that we only have data on House member travel. Perhaps if senator travel data were available for us to examine, we would find a significant overall relationship between gender and travel spending in that chamber. Another possibility is that the way we measure member travel limits our ability to capture the

TABLE 3.2. Determinants of District Travel—House of Representatives, 103rd–107th Congresses

	Dollars spent traveling
Female	.886
	(1.80)
Distance from DC	.010***
	(.001)
District Square Miles (logged)	7.99***
	(.407)
Seniority	–1.68***
	(.152)
District Population (thousands)	–.031**
	(.011)
District Ideology	.345***
	(.055)
Constant	16.94
	(8.81)
N	2173
R^2	.3825

relationship: perhaps we would see a difference if we were able to accurately capture how many trips home each member took, rather than simply the amount of money they spent. Finally, it is possible that, as in early studies of how gender influences legislative behavior, the perception still holds that woman devote more attention to this component of legislative duties.

District Staff

The final constituent-related measure we examine concerns how members allocate their staff. Each member is given a certain amount of money to hire underlings, both to staff their official Washington, DC, office and to staff however many district offices they decide to establish. In most congressional offices, district-based staff focus primarily on casework, as opposed to legislative activities. Since measuring the amount of casework each member does is difficult, accounting for the number of district staff each member employs serves as a reasonable proxy. Taking advantage of the Congressional Staff Directory, we collected data on the number of staff members each Congress member, from both chambers, employed in their districts between the 103rd and the 110th Congresses.

Looking at the Senate first, women do employ more staff in their home states than men (14.9 versus 13.8, $p<.01$) (see figure 3.3). However, this is one case where the bivariate relationship may be misleading. Many female senators represent large states (Barbara Boxer and Dianne Feinstein from California, for example). Senators from big states receive more casework requests—and therefore need to hire more staff—than senators from smaller states.[8] A more appropriate measure might be the population-adjusted number of staffers—how many district staffers does each member employ per one million state residents? Calculating this number flips the results: male senators employ 6.5 staffers per one million residents on average, and female senators only 4.16 ($p<.001$). But this too is misleading. Senators pay staff out of a personnel allowance, and senators from large states receive a larger allowance than those from smaller states. But unfortunately for large-state senators the allowance does not come close to keeping up with population differences between the states. For instance, California has more than sixty times the population of Wyoming, but senators from the largest states receive only about 1.5 times the personnel allowance of senators from the smallest states. Thus, senators from large states do not have the funding to hire as many staffers as they would need to, to reflect the number of constituents that they have.

As a result, the only accurate way to isolate gender's effect on home-

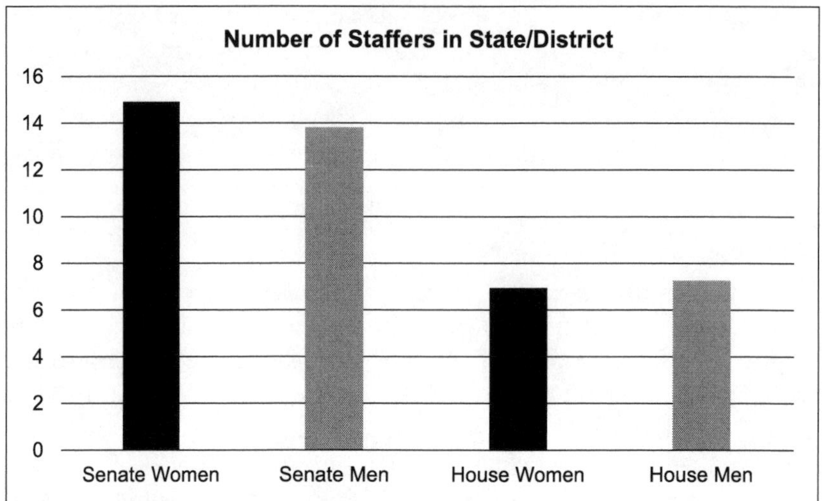

Figure 3.3. Gender differences in district staff, 103rd–110th Congresses

state staffing patterns is with multiple regression. We estimate the number of staff as a function of gender, population, and office allowance, along with other control variables. Our control variables include the senator's vote share in the most recent election; a dummy indicating whether the senator's seat is up in the upcoming election; seniority and seniority squared; the state's land area (more land potentially means more offices to staff); and the size of the senator's staff in Washington, DC. (Senators hire in-state staff and Washington staff out of the same pool of money, meaning there might be some zero-sum trade-offs between the two). We also include an interaction between the state's population and the allowance. We estimate two models—one where the dependent variable is the raw number of senators' in-state staff, and one where the dependent variable is the population-adjusted district staff. In the second model we omit the population independent variable, as population is already accounted for in the dependent variable. We also include dummy variables indicating which Congress the data are taken from (not reported). Both models take data from the 103rd through 110th Congress, and are estimated using OLS.

Results are presented in table 3.3, and in both cases the coefficient on Female—the dummy variable indicating that the senator is a woman—is positive and significant. The in-state staff model indicates that women employ 1.5 more in-state staff than men do on average. However, the more nuanced population-adjusted staff model indicates that women employ 0.79 in-state staff per million residents than men do on average.

Here are a few practical examples to illustrate what these population-adjusted results mean in real terms. The states that have the median population size (Louisiana and Kentucky) each have about 4.5 million residents. The model predicts that in the median state, a female senator would hire approximately 3.5 more in-state staffers than a male senator. In a smaller state , say one with approximately 1.5 million residents, a female senator would hire about one more in-state staffer than a male senator would, on average. In a very large state with about twenty million residents, like Florida or New York, a female senator would hire almost sixteen more in-state staffers. In the end, both models clearly indicate that female senators hire more staff to work among their constituents—presumably to handle more casework—than males do. More concretely, we see these differences when we examine the actual staff utilized by senators serving in the 110th Congress. In Texas, Kay Bailey Hutchinson had twenty-six staffers in the

TABLE 3.3. Number of Staff Members in the State—Senators, 103rd-110th Congresses

	In-state staff	Population adjusted staff
Female	1.52**	.787***
	(.542)	(.187)
Lagged vote	–2.19	–1.89
	(1.73)	(1.17)
Seat up	.094	.011
	(.321)	(.209)
Seniority	.099*	.052
	(.048)	(.031)
Seniority 2	–.004**	–.002*
	(.001)	(.001)
Population (logged)	17.13***	—
	(2.62)	
Allowance	.111***	.062***
	(.192)	(.0002)
Population*allowance	–.000006***	–.000003***
	(.000001)	(.0000001)
Land area (logged)	.293**	.074
	(.108)	(.099)
DC Staff	–.066	–.048
	(.044)	(.028)
Constant	–266.5***	–29.2***
	(44.6)	(2.02)
N	793	793
R^2	.159	.792

state while John Cornyn had only sixteen. In Minnesota, Amy Klobuchar's state offices had twenty-two staffers, while Norm Coleman employed only fifteen. And, in Arkansas, Blanche Lincoln had eighteen staffers in the state, while Mark Pryor used only twelve.

Among House members in the 103rd through 110th Congresses, the bivariate relationship indicates that female House members actually employ slightly fewer district staffers than men (6.94 versus 7.26, $p<.001$). House members similarly hire their staffers out of an allowance that varies, but in the House the allowance varies by how far the district is from Washington, DC.[9] Thus we estimate House members' district staffing decisions with a similar set of independent variables as we used in estimating Senate staffing decisions above, with a few differences. Most important, we do not have a direct measure of House members' representational allowance, so we use the distance between the district and Washington as a proxy. Additionally, we exclude the variable indicating whether a member's seat is up (meaningless in this context) and include a variable that indicates the district's logged geographic size.

We use the same dependent variables as in the Senate analysis above—the raw number, and population-adjusted number, of district staff. Results are presented in table 3.4, and in both cases the coefficient on Female is negative but not significant. Thus, once we control for other factors, the slight difference between the number of district staffers hired by male and female members becomes indistinguishable from zero—neither gender appears to hire any more staff in their districts than the other in the House of Representatives.

Conclusion

Women spend more time and effort on their constituents than men, that much is clear. We find the same results from our interviews with Congress members and congressional staffers and from our quantitative analysis. However, the ways in which women in the House and Senate differ from their male counterparts is not consistent across the two chambers. Rather, that extra effort appears to be limited to one particular aspect of constituency service, and which aspect of service applies is different in each chamber of Congress.

In the House, female members spend about 20 percent more money sending mail to their constituents than the men do, even after controlling for other member and district traits that influence the volume of mail members send. Since mail is paid for out of a fixed allowance, this extra money represents a substantive decision to focus resources on constituent communication, rather than using them on other priorities. Female House members spend more of their office allowance telling voters what they are doing in office, what positions they are taking stands on, what bills they are introducing, and what government spending projects they have procured for the district. This extra communication is especially notable when combined with the findings from other chapters, that female House members get more pork and sponsor more legislation than male members. These additional findings, which we elaborate upon later in the book, imply that female House members have more to tell their voters about, which could be the source of some of the difference we uncover in this chapter. Even in the Internet age, House members still rely on mail to communicate with voters, and female members use this tool more than male members.

In the Senate, quantitative analysis reveals that female senators hire more staff to work in the state than male senators do. Overall, female senators hire about 1.5 more in-state staff than men do, but this number varies with the size of the state a senator represents. The average senator in our

TABLE 3.4. Number of Staff Members in District—House Members, 103rd–110th Congresses

	District Staff	Staff per 100,000 constituents
Female	–.142	–.016
	(.079)	(.013)
Lagged vote	.001	–.00001
	(.002)	(.0003)
Seniority	.048***	.008***
	(.010)	(.002)
Seniority 2	–.001***	–.0002***
	(.0003)	(.0003)
Population	.207***	—
	(.053)	
Land area (logged)	–.002	–.003
	(.002)	(.011)
Distance from DC	.228***	–.040***
(1,000s of miles)	(.032)	(.005)
DC Staff	–.217***	–.037***
	(.02)	(.004)
Constant	7.20***	1.40***
	(.459)	(.052)
N	3466	3466
R^2	.059	.1201

dataset employs about fourteen staff members in the state, so these models indicate that female Senators employ between 11 percent and 25 percent more staff in the state than males do. Regardless of the precise difference, the extra in-state staffers would be a big help in processing requests for help that come in from constituents, or—as one of our interviewees indicated earlier in the chapter—a big help in seeking out constituents for the member's office to help. Female senators, or more accurately their offices, have more capacity to deal with casework than male senators do. This allows them to help more people and to do so more quickly than male senators can.

Our quantitative analysis did not reveal that female members spend any more money on travel than male members do. However, in our interviews several staffers indicated that they believe female members spend more time in, or at least devote more attention to, their districts. This notion was a common theme in the interviews, so even though we do not find a clear gender difference in this area, the *idea* that there is a gender difference appears to be a common belief. What explains this discrepancy? One possibility is that female members so thoroughly outstrip the men in attending to constituency needs and preferences in so many different ways that the impression of the difference exists even in those areas where the women are not actually doing more than the men. Or perhaps there is a gender difference in members' travel to the district that our analysis failed to identify. Either way, it is pretty clear that a significant portion of staffers experience their female bosses as spending more time in the district than their male bosses.

In the end, whether it is via franked mail usage in the House of Representatives, through additional caseworkers in the Senate, or a staffer-identified discrepancy in district travel, the differences all point in the same direction: female members pay more attention to their constituents than the men do. One of our staffer interviewees who worked for a female House member at the time of our interview sums up the difference between male and female members this way:

> The ego is the same. [Members] all do have an ego or they wouldn't be here. But I think there is a difference in going back and serving, that's what you are here for, right? You are not here to grace everybody's presence. You are going back [to the district], you are working for them there. You know, we did a lot of stuff in the district, a lot of stuff in the state, and I can't remember working that hard when I was working for [male House member]. I can't remember a male

House member that I have worked for being that obsessed with that part of it.

This notion of working harder and simply doing more was a consistent theme in our interviews, and underlies the theory we present in this book: women legislators, to overcome their gendered vulnerability, do more for their constituents, whether in terms of constituent services, various legislative activities, or simply attending to constituent needs and interests. This chapter finds evidence of women doing more in terms of direct constituency services. We turn in chapter 4 to another tool legislators can use to aid their constituents: procuring distributive benefits that go directly to the district and visibly aid constituents.

FOUR

Bringing Home the Bacon Is a Woman's Job

Gender and Pork Barrel Spending

The newsletter is an important tool for Congress members looking to keep their constituents informed of what they're up to in Washington, DC. From time to time, a member (or more likely their staff) will compile some information, format it to look vaguely like a newspaper, and mail it to constituents—although these days, it is just as important to post it on the member's website and send out an e-mail blast to the member's list with a link to the newsletter. The contents of the newsletter reveal a lot about what members want their voters to know about—what they think voters will appreciate come reelection time. And consistently, for member after member, what you see in the newsletter are announcements about pork barrel spending—the money that the federal government spends in her district on projects that will mostly benefit her constituents.

For example, former Representative Lynn Woolsey was a veteran Democratic House member in a safe seat just north of San Francisco. She used newsletters sparingly, just once each election cycle. Just before the 2004 election, Woolsey's newsletter highlighted transportation projects: "With Congress set to pass a major transportation bill . . . I have been working aggressively and successfully to ensure that California's Sixth District gets its fair share." The newsletter then listed the federally funded projects benefitting her district; the most eye-catching of these was a $60 million grant for seismic retrofitting of the Golden Gate Bridge. Her 2008 letter gave over a quarter of its space to spending projects, in sections called "Bringing Home Transportation Dollars for the North Bay" and "Congresswoman Lynn Woolsey Working for You." Woolsey's 2010 newsletter added a URL that took interested voters to a twenty-five-page document with detailed information on ninety-one distinct spending projects, and also trumpeted federal funding coming to the district's medical community from the recently passed American Recovery and Reinvestment Act (Woolsey 2004, 2008, 2010).

While Woolsey used newsletters sparingly, Kyrsten Sinema (D-AZ) puts out several a month, and one of them is devoted exclusively to telling voters about what funding is coming her district's way. In these newsletters, Sinema uses a different credit-claiming strategy than Woolsey did—she highlights all federal spending being delivered to local residents whether Sinema is responsible for them or not. A naïve reader might assume that Sinema played a role in procuring all of these grants. For example, the "January Grants newsletter" from January 2017 mentions federal research grants going to Arizona State University faculty; a grant going to a local daycare center; and one that was awarded to a hospital on a local Indian reservation. The newsletter also has information about upcoming grant opportunities, and links to the granting organizations' web pages.

As a whole, voters do not like pork barrel spending. Most people think of it as a waste of government funds. Nonetheless, members of Congress see it as an essential tool that helps keep them in office. Representative Woolsey's and Sinema's newsletters were hardly unique—nearly every member of Congress actively seeks out spending for their district, and brags about that money to their voters. But Representatives Woolsey and Sinema are women, and female members of Congress need pork barrel spending more than the men do. The reason is gendered vulnerability. Gendered vulnerability causes women to concentrate on activities that have the most electoral value. Just as gendered vulnerability causes female legislators to spend more time and effort on constituent services, as we showed in the last chapter, here we show that female legislators likewise procure more federal spending for their districts.

In this chapter we first ask whether pork barrel spending helps members win reelection. Since so many people think pork barrel spending is a waste of time and money, it is something of an open question why so many members are so devoted to it. The answer is, because it works. From there, we move on to discuss the role gender plays, which leads us to the hypothesis that female members deliver more federal projects and dollars to their constituents. We test these hypotheses with two different types of pork barrel spending: congressional earmarks, and the money coming out of the American Recovery and Reinvestment Act. For both kinds of spending, we find that female members deliver more money for their voters than male members do for theirs. We also hypothesize that the dollars female members secure will more closely reflect their constituents' needs, which we look at with the ARRA data.

An Overview of Pork Barrel Spending

Pork barrel spending is the term used to describe money that the federal government spends on projects that chiefly or solely benefit local groups. Members of Congress love pork barrel spending because this money is almost always spent on something visible to voters—something that members can point to (sometimes physically) and claim credit for. Congress members have been using pork barrel spending for as long as there has been a Congress—less than six months after the First Congress convened in 1789, members authorized spending to build a lighthouse on Chesapeake Bay in Virginia (Frisch and Kelly 2011). Individual Congress members work hard to direct as much spending as possible to their individual districts. They also try to make it seem as if they are personally responsible for the projects, even if those claims stretch the truth.

Academics and other observers of Congress have long argued about the purported goods and ills of pork barrel spending. Indeed, the phrase "pork barrel spending" originated over 100 years ago as a derogatory description of wasteful government spending projects—the kind of thing that might help a few people but is unnecessary from the point of view of most Americans. A variety of lobbying organizations have sprung up around the issue, focusing on eliminating waste from the federal budget. Every year, groups like Citizens Against Government Waste and the National Taxpayers Union publicize the projects they see as being emblematic of unnecessary spending—Citizens Against Government Waste even calls its publication "The Pig Book." One of the most notorious projects in recent years was a proposal to spend $400 million on a bridge linking a sparsely populated Alaskan island (Gravina Island, population fifty) to a larger island with an airport. This "Bridge to Nowhere," even though ultimately not built, served as a potent symbol of pork barrel spending run amok.

On the other hand, to some extent pork is in the eye of the beholder. Defenders of government spending point out that each project is designed to help a specific group of people solve a pressing problem in their community—the Bridge to Nowhere was designed to replace a ferry service that carries enough traffic to run every fifteen minutes and charges $5 per person and $6 per car. Other spending projects might help local law enforcement agencies or emergency responders upgrade their communications technology or other equipment—Presidio, Texas, Whitemarsh Township, Pennsylvania, and Molalla, Oregon all received this type of funding in 2008. Spending projects that some may label as pork might also improve the quality of life for soldiers and their families living on military bases by building or improving barracks, hospitals, or schools. A former House Appropriations Committee staffer summarizes this point of view: "A [pork barrel project] is something that flows into 434 congressional districts and not yours. When it comes into your district it is a federal investment in jobs and education" (Cohn 2006). Rahm Emanuel—a member of the House of Representatives before he was White House chief of staff and later mayor of Chicago—similarly defended pork barrel spending: "[M]ost members believe it is their prerogative and their duty to channel federal resources to important public purposes. . . . I make no apologies for these earmarks, which serve important public purposes—and might even save a life. I'm happy to defend them in the well of the House or against attacks from campaign opponents" (Emanuel 2008). And, as one of the staffers we interviewed noted, "At the end of the day, there's a press release saying, 'I have secured money for Highway 101 that will make your commute better.' That is better than 'I passed the bill slapping . . . some unnamed bank on the wrist.' At the end of the day, all politics is local."

Our aim is not to take a side on this multifaceted issue, but simply to highlight that pork is an important tool Congress members use to aid their constituents and (of course) help themselves win reelection. By taking public credit for pork barrel projects, members of Congress publicly tie themselves to the benefits that the pork barrel spending bring to the district. For instance, in a local news item, Representative Mike Thompson (D-CA) said of a joint military-business earmark, "I am pleased that I was able to secure funding that both protects our brave men and women in uniform and keep[s] American families safe while simultaneously supporting a business important to our local economy" (Payne 2008). Congresswoman Lucille Roybal-Allard (D-CA) used a press release to announce the passage of a spending bill that "makes key investments to improve the quality of life for residents in my district. . . . Critical federal dollars included in the measure will be used to ease gridlock, improve safety, provide greater transportation options for residents and keep more youth off the streets and in school, while providing needed jobs in our communities." The release also lists several spending projects that appeared in the bill "due to the efforts of Congresswoman Roybal-Allard" (Roybal-Allard 2010). In one month alone leading up to the 2010 elections, Senator Susan Collins of Maine issued eight press releases to announce spending projects in Maine. Beyond these few examples, Bickers et al. (2007) found that in the 109th Congress (2005–06), the median House member claimed credit for three spending programs per month just in their online press releases. Clearly, members of Congress want their voters to know about these projects.

The question then becomes, do spending projects actually help members of Congress win reelection? Classic academic accounts of member motivation (Mayhew 1974; Arnold 1990) suggest that regardless of whether they do or not, members certainly think they do. Pork barrel spending is a particularly attractive credit-claiming opportunity in Mayhew's (1974) terms, since the funded project is often visible and local in nature, and claims of individual credit are plausible. Ferejohn (1974) argues that pork barrel spending demonstrates to voters that the member is an effective legislator and "can do things for [voters] in Washington." Moreover, they may also advertise electoral security and inhibit political opposition. Thus, distributive spending may not only directly help in attracting voters but it may also discourage potential challengers from running against the incumbent. Bickers and Stein (1996) take this argument a step further, claiming that district spending can be targeted to the preferences of groups within the district, and that incumbents use this spending to purchase these groups' good will. This dissuades local groups from supporting a challenger in upcoming elections and ultimately results in weaker challenges.

More directly, the empirical evidence that pork barrel spending helps members of Congress win reelection is considerable. At the individual level, pork barrel spending ties voters to members in a variety of ways. Voters are better able to recognize their member's name and identify a reason to like him or her if the member procured high levels of funding (Stein and Bickers 1994; Alvarez and Schousen 1993). They also give House members more positive evaluations if the member seeks and publicizes grants for his or her district (Cain, Ferejohn, and Fiorina 1987). Most important, however, voters are more likely to vote to reelect a House member if they can recall something the member has done for the district (Johannes and McAdams 1981; McAdams and Johannes 1988; Pew Research Center 2010), and when the member has actually procured higher levels of pork barrel spending (Stein and Bickers 1994; Alvarez and Schousen 1993; Sellers 1997; Sidman and Mak 2006).[1]

Other studies examine pork barrel spending's effect at the district level.

Although the earliest studies of this type found very little effect (Anagnoson 1980, 1982; Chernick 1979; Rundquist 1978; Feldman and Jondrow 1984), more recent studies show a clear link between a member's ability to procure district-based spending and electoral payoffs. For instance, the Federal Assistance Awards Data System contains records of federal outlays in every federal domestic spending program, and identifies which congressional district each award goes to. Using this data, numerous studies find that members—particularly Democratic members—receive a higher vote share if their districts receive more federal spending (Levitt and Snyder 1997; Alvarez and Saving 1997; Sellers 1997; Lazarus and Reilly 2010). Bickers and Stein (1996) find that members in districts with higher outlays are also less likely to face a strong electoral challenger when seeking reelection. Looking at a different type of spending, both Rocca and Gordon (2013) and Lazarus, Glas, and Barbieri (2012) find that earmarks directly help members of Congress raise more money for reelection.

Put together, the empirical evidence all points in the same direction—pork barrel spending helps members of Congress win reelection. This means that members who seek out programs and projects for their voters so that money flows to their constituents will have their efforts rewarded in the form of higher vote totals come election time. And so they do. Members of Congress work hard to get money for their district, working with bureaucrats to fund projects (Ferejohn 1974; Arnold 1979) and lobbying members of the Appropriations Committee in their chamber to fund earmark requests (when earmarks are put into bills; Savage 1991). Members of Congress also encourage their constituents to apply for federal spending programs or alert them to the presence of little known programs. Bickers and Stein (1996) describe one way in which members of Congress encourage their constituents to apply for federal aid, and hope to benefit themselves in the process: "A legislator speaking before a civic group in their district could set up a table where small business owners in the audience could receive help in filling out an application for assistance from the SBA [Small Business Association]. Usually within a week the applicants would receive a decision on the application, a time frame short enough for the applicant to link the legislator's help to the receipt of the new award" (1312–13).

Gendered Vulnerability and Federal Spending

Gendered vulnerability leads female legislators to perceive themselves as vulnerable, and thus pursue legislative activities that shore up support from voters and mitigate potential challenges. We thus argue that female members will engage in these activities more than male members, and also do so in a way that more closely hews to their constituents' needs. As we discussed above, directing federal spending projects to the district is one activity that helps members win reelection. As such, vulnerable members should pursue spending projects more aggressively than safe members. Since female members are inherently vulnerable in a way that men are not, they should likewise pursue and secure more projects and federal spending than men do, on average. Further, female members should be more cognizant of their district's interests, and attempt to secure funds accordingly. In particular, for spending that is specifically designed to alleviate economic distress (i.e., the American Recovery and Reinvestment Act) we expect to find a closer correspondence between a district's level of economic distress and the amount of money going to the district for female members than for male members.

Anzia and Berry (2011) have already tested the proposition that female Congress members bring home more pork barrel spending than male members. They examine the Federal Assistance Awards Data System dataset, mentioned above, which includes all discretionary domestic spending projects that are funded by bureaucratic agencies. It is by far the most comprehensive set of information on federal spending, and is the standard dataset for scholarly examination of federal bureaucratic award procurement. Using this data in the period 1984 to 2004, Anzia and Berry find that districts represented by females received more spending than those represented by males: specifically, female members have "a spending advantage of 9 percent [which] amounts to approximately an extra $88 per capita per year for districts represented by women. Given that the average district has 563,732 residents, the aggregate spending increase for the district is roughly $49 million [measured in 2004 dollars] when it sends a woman to Capitol Hill" (Anzia and Berry 2011, 18). In other words, a House district that elects a woman receives nearly $50 million in extra federal spending per year, just for having elected a woman. Their results provide evidence for our hypothesis—women procure more spending for their districts than men on a consistent basis, and this effect reaches into nearly every corner of the domestic political spending universe. Below we examine other, more directed types of federal spending.

If devoting more time and effort to pork barrel spending can help members secure more of it, then *all* vulnerable members—not just members who are subject to gendered vulnerability—should get more pork. A handful of prior studies have tested this hypothesis, but they provide mixed results.

Some find no relationship between vulnerability and the level of spending procured (Balla et al. 2002; Lee 2003; Frisch 1998) and others find evidence of a weak relationship (Bickers and Stein 1996; Stein and Bickers 1994). The most recent study finds that if vulnerable members are in the majority party they get more pork barrel spending, but vulnerable members in the minority do not (Lazarus 2009). Thus there is only lukewarm support for the proposition that traditional electoral vulnerability induces members of Congress to procure extra spending for their district. Nonetheless, gendered vulnerability is qualitatively different than prior conceptions of vulnerability, which rely on the member's vote share in the prior election. Gendered vulnerability is a constant among all female members of Congress, and we argue and find in the empirical examination presented below that, similar to Anzia and Berry (2011), women do indeed procure more spending for their districts. This indicates that pork barrel spending is an important tool that female members use to combat their unique brand of vulnerability and highlight their work for their constituents.

We investigate the quantity of federal spending in our examination of ARRA and earmarks in the 110th Congress. Our primary hypothesis is that female members obtain more spending than male members. We additionally argue that while increased funds are good, female legislators' attention to constituent needs—a direct result of their gendered vulnerability—also leads them to procure funds in a manner that better reflects these needs. We therefore move beyond just a simple calculation of quantity to one that also reflects the substantive, constituent-based orientation of female legislators' actions in our examination of funding coming out of the ARRA; it is similar to the analysis we present in chapter 6 with respect to members' policy responsiveness. Finally, as in our other empirical chapters, we assess the actions of members of both the House and the Senate.

Earmarks

The first type of distributive spending we examine is earmarks. Earmarks are items in spending bills that designate money for specific spending projects and are placed in bills at the request of members of Congress. Ultimately, the authority to fund earmarks lies with the subcommittee chairs in each chamber's Appropriations Committee. Nearly all Congress members send funding requests to these chairs on behalf of organizations in their district that have themselves requested funding from the member. Those requests that are ultimately funded are placed in the bill. Neither the subcommittee nor the full Appropriations Committee votes directly on the earmarks before the bill is reported out of committee, and from there the earmarks travel through the legislative process as part of the larger spending bill. Later in the budgeting process, most individual earmarks are overshadowed by larger and more visible spending priorities, so the vast majority of earmarks never receive a vote at any stage of the legislative process, or a public hearing on the merits of the project.

Members are attracted to earmarking because the earmarking process prominently features the individual member as one of only two actors (along with the Appropriations subcommittee chair) who directly influence final funding decisions. This high degree of individual responsibility sets earmarking apart from bureaucratic awards, and holds several political advantages for members of Congress. First, it maximizes the degree to which an individual congressperson can claim credit for the spending. Members of Congress (or their staffs) personally arbitrate among the requests they receive to decide which to forward on to Appropriations subcommittee chairs, and heavily publicize their successfully funded earmarks. Second, earmarks provide individual members with the opportunity to concentrate funding on the projects that are likely to confer the greatest political benefits. Finally, the overwhelming majority of projects are local in nature—they are requested by a constituent, and, if funded, the money stays in the district. Collectively, these features mean that credit for procuring the earmark is unmistakably attributed to the procuring member of Congress. Such easily identifiable and narrow boundaries create opportunities for exchange: beneficiaries can offer electoral support to members of Congress, either before or after the member selects earmarks to forward on to the subcommittee chair.

For example, Senator Amy Klobuchar (D-MN) is a strong supporter of the STARBASE program, which provides STEM (science, technology, engineering and mathematics) education to the children of active-duty military, particularly minority children. Between 2001 and 2017, Klobuchar successfully funded nine earmarks for STARBASE—which operates an educational facility on a National Guard base in Minnesota, along with locations in thirty-nine other states—totaling $94 million. Nominally, STARBASE's funding runs through the Department of Defense's budget, but that funding must be renewed each year, and is often threatened in the political back-and-forth that goes on over the annual budget. Klobuchar's earmarks helped smooth out funding for the program, ensuring its survival during lean budget years. Patty Murray (D-WA) similarly used the earmark process in 2016 to enable the Army Corps of Engineers to replace

Native American fishing villages that were flooded by the construction of the Dalles Dam on the Columbia River in the 1930s. Sometimes earmarks are not quite so local—NASA's New Horizons mission, which sent a probe to Pluto for the first time, was funded in large part by a 2003 earmark requested by Senator Barbara Mikulski (Chang 2015).

The gendered vulnerability theory predicts that female members of Congress will procure more earmarks than male members. We test this hypothesis with data from the earmarks funded in the fiscal year 2008 Appropriations bills. The FY 2008 Appropriations bills included over 7,000 earmarks requested by one or more specific members of Congress, collectively totaling $13.7 billion. Since both senators and representatives may request earmarks, we are able to directly test whether the predictions of the gendered vulnerability theory work similarly in the House and the Senate. In the House, the majority of earmarks (>80%) were requested individually by a single member. The remainder were jointly requested by more than one member; for these we divided credit for these earmarks among all requesting members.[2] In the Senate, approximately two-thirds of the earmarks were requested by an individual senator, and nearly all of the remainder were jointly requested by both members of a state's delegation. We examine the solo-requested and dual-requested Senate earmarks separately from one another in order to determine whether the presence of a female senator in a delegation results in that delegation procuring more benefits for its state. Finally, we examine two dependent variables for each set of earmarks: the total number of earmarks each member placed into the spending bills, and the aggregate dollar value of these earmarks. We therefore utilize six distinct dependent variables—Senate solo dollars; Senate solo earmarks; Senate dual dollars; Senate dual earmarks; House dollars; and House earmarks. We test to see if women score higher than men, on average, for each of these measures.

The differences between women and men for all six dependent variables are presented in figures 4.1–4.3. Figure 4.1 presents the data for House earmarks. On both measures, women have a modest, though not statistically significant, advantage. In the 2008 bills, female members placed an average of 20.1 earmarks collectively worth $20.2 million into the spending bills, while male members placed an average of 18.7 earmarks collectively worth $18.6 million ($p<.200$, $p<.308$, respectively). In the Senate, gender differences were considerably more significant both substantively and statistically. Figure 4.2 presents the data for earmarks that senators requested individually. Here, female members placed an average of 51.6 earmarks into the spending bills, collectively worth $10 million, while male members

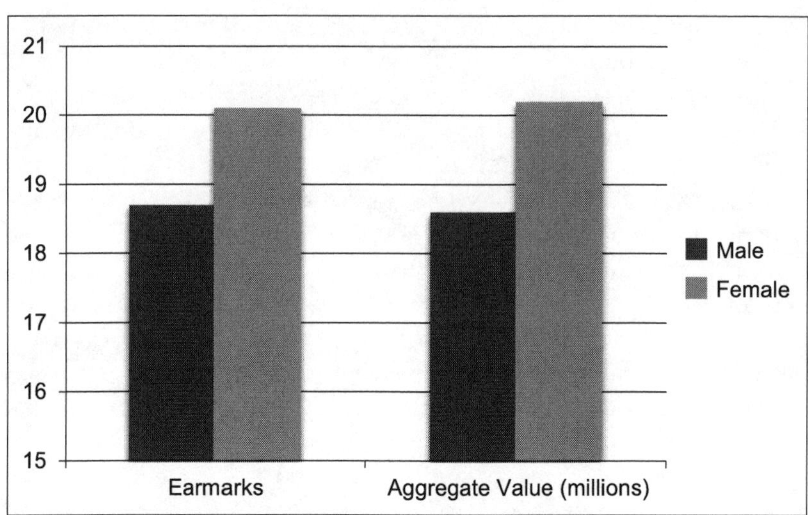

Figure 4.1. 2008 House earmarks and gender

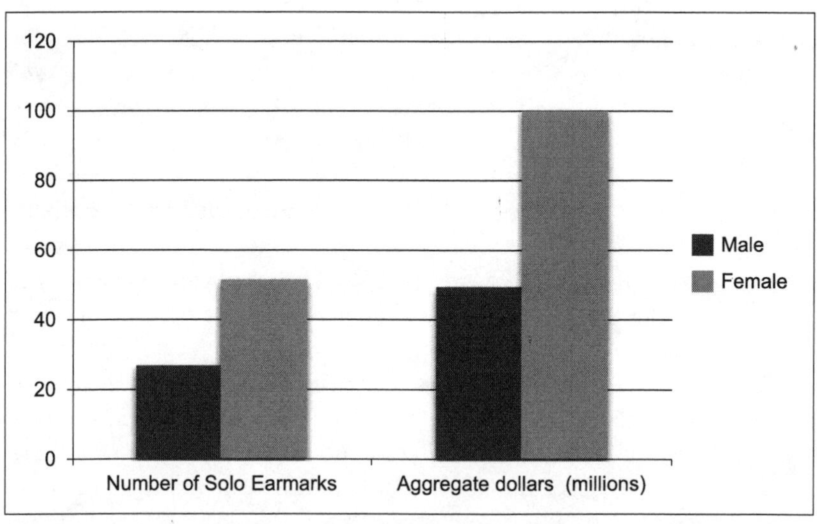

Figure 4.2. Solo-requested 2008 Senate earmarks and gender

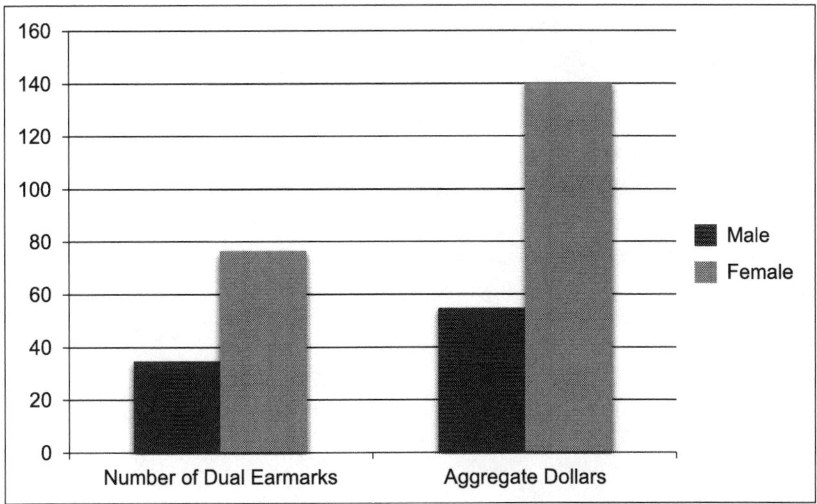

Figure 4.3. Dual-requested 2008 Senate earmarks and gender

placed an average of 26.8 earmarks into the bills, collectively worth $4.9 million (p<.011, p<.029, respectively). Figure 4.3 presents the data for earmarks that senators requested jointly with their same-state partner (note the change in unit of analysis from the individual member to the state delegation). Delegations with at least one female senator placed an average of 52.7 dual-requested earmarks into the bills, collectively worth $14 million; state delegations with no female members collectively placed an average of only 34.8 earmarks into spending bills, collectively worth $7.6 million (p< .042, p<.009, respectively).

We tested the robustness of these relationships by estimating each dependent variable in a multivariate model. We estimated dollar values by taking the natural log and employing OLS, and we estimated the total number of earmarks using negative binomial regression. In the House models and those looking at solo-requested Senate earmarks, the unit of analysis is the individual member and the primary independent variable is the dummy variable *Female*. The models of aggregate dollar values exclude members who received no earmarks.

In the House models, independent variables include the member's share of the vote in his or her *prior* election (to account for traditional notions of electoral vulnerability); a dummy variable indicating whether the member is a *Democrat*; the member's *DW-NOMINATE* score (included as separate variables for Democrats and Republicans); the district's *presidential vote* as an indicator of voter ideology; the member's *seniority*, or the number of years each member has been in the House; and dummy variables indicating whether the member is a *committee chair*, a *party leader*, a member of the *Appropriations Committee*, or a subcommittee chair on the Appropriations Committee, known as a *cardinal*. Finally, we include economic distress indictors to account for a district's need for government funding: the district's *unemployment* rate, its *poverty rate*, and its median *income*.

Results are presented in table 4.1. *Female* is positive and significant in both estimations, contrary to the fact that the difference between men and

TABLE 4.1. Distribution of 2008 Earmarks among House Members

	Aggregate dollar value	Total # of Earmarks
Female	.408*	.104*
	(.171)	(.048)
Prior vote	.293	–.624
	(1.35)	(.394)
Democrat	–1.49	–.389*
	(.944)	(.187)
NOMINATE (Democrats)	1.38*	.173
	(.686)	(.193)
NOMINATE (Republicans)	–5.44**	–1.55***
	(1.94)	(.330)
District Presidential Vote	–.014	–.006
	(.011)	(.003)
Seniority	.026*	.008*
	(.011)	(.003)
Committee Chair	–.386	–.008
	(.321)	(.113)
Party Leader	–.723	.835***
	(2.29)	(.248)
Appropriations Member	1.27***	.832***
	(.170)	(.072)
Cardinal	–.105	.250*
	(.294)	(.104)
Unemployment	1.45*	.275*
	(.678)	(.135)
Income	.833	.206
	(.894)	(.224)
Poverty rate	–.037	–.008
	(.025)	(.004)
Constant	17.1***	.187***
	(1.31)	(.272)
N	428	435
Adjusted R^2	.176	—
Log likelihood	—	–1481
Overdispersion	—	–2.07
		(.166)

Note: Robust standard errors in parentheses; $^*p < .05$; $^{**}p < .01$; $^{***}p < .001$

women was not significant when we examined them in the bivariate relationship. The confounding variable is most likely *seniority*: it is significantly related to both measures of earmarking, and in the 110th Congress females were significantly less senior than males (a mean of 11.5 years of seniority for males, but only 8.7 for females). In other words, we find that less senior women achieved the same level of success—or even a little higher—in earmarking that more senior men achieved. The substantive predictions of the models highlight this difference. The model estimating the number of earmarks predicts that the average female House member inserted 20.4 earmarks into the 2008 spending bills, while the average male House member inserted 18.4. This difference is similar to the bivariate difference reported in figure 4.1. However, the model estimating the logged dollar values of these earmarks indicates a more substantial difference: once seniority and other confounds are controlled for, the aggregate value of female-requested earmarks was nearly 50 percent higher than the aggregate value of male-requested earmarks (with the exact dollar figures being fluid because the dependent variable is nonlinear).[3]

Table 4.2 presents results for solo earmarking in the Senate. Independent variables are similar to those used to estimate House earmarking activity, with the following differences: we include a dummy variable to indicate senators who would be running for election in the current election cycle (*seat up*), and a variable indicating the logged state population (*state size*). We exclude *cardinal*, as nearly every majority member of the Appropriations Committee in the Senate heads an Appropriations subcommittee. Mirroring the results of the House models, *Female* is significant in both estimations. For both models, the predicted values of the dependent variables for men and women have differences that are substantively similar to those shown in figure 4.2. The model estimating senators' number of earmarks predicts that female senators placed ninety-three earmarks into spending bills, while male senators placed sixty; the model estimating the dollar value of these earmarks predicts that female senators' earmarks were, on average, collectively worth 147 percent more than male senators' earmarks (with the exact dollar figures again being fluid because the dependent variable is nonlinear).

Table 4.3 presents results for joint earmarking in the Senate. Here, the unit of analysis is the state delegation, rather than the individual senator, and so a slightly different set of independent variables is used. The primary independent variable, once again named *Female*, indicates states with at least one female senator. Control variables indicate if the state's Senate delegation is unified *Republican* or is unified *Democrat*; the baseline comparison group is split delegations. We include the state's *poverty rate* to indicate economic need; the Senate delegation's mean *seniority*; the *ideological distance* between the two senators by taking the absolute value of the difference between their DW-NOMINATE scores; the mean of the senators' solo earmarking activities; and the logged population of the state. Results indicate that the difference between states with a female senator and states

TABLE 4.2. Distribution of Solo-Requested 2008 Earmarks among Senators

	Aggregate Dollar Value	Total Earmarks
Female	.903^	.861*
	(.516)	(.413)
Prior vote	.015	.014
	(.014)	(.012)
Seat up	.158	.230
	(.313)	(.234)
Democrat	1.92*	.717
	(.854)	(.794)
NOMINATE (Democrats)	.749	1.09
	(1.30)	(1.31)
NOMINATE (Republicans)	4.18**	.820
	(1.46)	(1.24)
State Presidential Vote	.007	.021
	(.022)	(.015)
Seniority	.020	.017
	(.019)	(.016)
Committee Chair	.589	–.044
	(.508)	(.374)
Party Leader	1.27	1.07
	(.975)	(.657)
Appropriations Member	1.59***	.914***
	(.322)	(.200)
Unemployment	–.156	–.427
	(.258)	(.300)
Income	.731***	.544***
	(.212)	(.167)
Poverty rate	–.099	–.034
	(.051)	(.039)
State size (logged)	.537***	.306**
	(.151)	(.109)
	9.86***	–.067
Constant	(2.91/)	(2.18)
N	92	100
Adjusted R^2	.471	—
Log likelihood	—	–418.6
Overdispersion	—	.041
		(.175)

Note: Robust standard errors in parentheses; *$p < .05$; **$p < .01$; ***$p < .001$

without a female senator is significant with regard to the total dollar value of these earmarks; the substantive prediction of the model is that delegations with a female senator receive earmarks worth 79 percent more money than delegations with no female senators. On the other hand, the variable *Female* is not significantly related to the number of earmarks procured. This result could be driven by the fact that unified Republican delegations received significantly fewer earmarks than others, and there are few female Republicans in the Senate; in fact, out of five Republican women in the Senate, two (Susan Collins and Olympia Snowe) represent the same state. Alternatively, the result could be driven by the model's relatively low n.[4]

In sum, our examination of earmarks, which allows us to directly test whether female members of both the House and Senate secure more funding for their districts than their male counterparts, reveals that women consistently procure more earmarks than men. In the House, female legislators procure both more earmarks as well as earmarks worth more money than males. In the Senate, individual female senators similarly secure both more earmarks and higher dollar totals than male senators. And, when we look at earmarks jointly requested by Senate state delegations, we find that

TABLE 4.3. Distribution of Jointly Requested 2008 Earmarks among Senators

	Aggregate Dollar Value	Total Earmarks
Female senator	.585*	.174
	(.248)	(.175)
Republican delegation	–.479	–.571**
	(.386)	(.199)
Democratic delegation	–.180	.246
	(.324)	(.177)
Poverty rate	–.062	–.007
	(.041)	(.029)
Mean seniority	–.040*	–.018
	(.016)	(.010)
Ideological distance	.234	–.168
	(.408)	(.245)
Mean solo earmarks	.577***	.007
/mean solo dollars	(.181)	(.005)
Logged population	–.289	–.200*
	(.151)	(.092)
Constant	23.4***	6.89***
	(2.12)	(1.35)
N	44	50
Adusted R^2	.409	—
Log likelihood	—	–1.35
Overdispersion	—	(.209)

Note: Robust standard errors in parentheses; *$p < .05$; **$p < .01$; ***$p < .001$

women again hold the advantage: states with a female member of the delegation secure more expensive earmarks than all-male delegations. Earmarks provide a clear mechanism of credit claiming, and female legislators in both the House and the Senate work hard to maximize this advantage.

American Recovery and Reinvestment Act

The other type of spending we examine is the money coming out of the American Recovery and Reinvestment Act of 2009 (ARRA). More commonly known as the Obama Stimulus package, it was proposed by president-elect Barack Obama prior to assuming office in January 2009 in the wake of the economic crisis that began in the fall of 2008. This bill was one of his top legislative priorities: it was the first bill introduced in the House during the 111th Congress (HR 1) and moved relatively quickly through the legislative process, taking only a month to move from introduction to enrollment as public law. The money appropriated by the stimulus package began flowing to recipients almost immediately thereafter. Estimates differ on how much money the stimulus package authorized the government to spend, but the Congressional Budget Office estimated that the package was worth a total of $787 billion, with approximately 75 percent in the form of government spending and 25 percent in the form of tax cuts. The spending was allocated among dozens of programs and administrations. The text of the bill provided each bureaucratic division receiving funds with instructions regarding how the money was to be distributed. Each division would accept applications for funding and be responsible for adjudicating among the applications according to the guidelines in the bill. In this respect, the stimulus package is similar to bureaucratic government spending generally. Thus, examining the money distributed by the ARRA provides a window into how the bureaucracy distributes federal funds, Congress members' ability to influence that distribution, and whether districts represented by female members receive a disproportionate share of federal funds. We also utilize this data to further investigate the notion that female representatives are more likely to procure federal funds in a way that more closely reflects their districts' needs.

We investigate whether districts represented by female House members received more federal spending under the ARRA using data on the allocation of stimulus funds during the first two quarters during which the money was distributed to recipients. During this time period, the federal government awarded almost 65,000 contracts and grants collectively worth

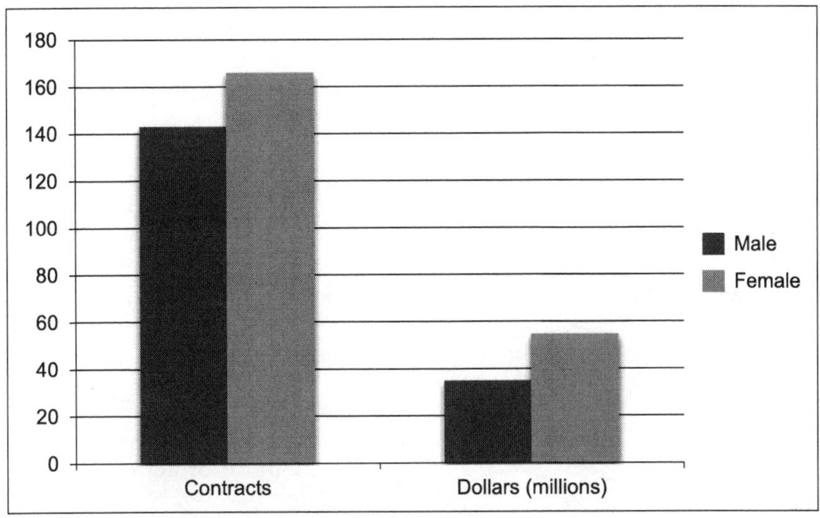

Figure 4.4. 2009–2010 Stimulus funds and House member gender

over $165 billion. We examine two dependent variables related to stimulus spending. The first is the aggregate dollar value of all grants and contracts awarded to each congressional district; the second is the total number of grants and contracts awarded to the districts.

Looking at the bivariate relationship between gender and ARRA funding reveals that House districts represented by female House members did better under ARRA than those represented by male members. These differences are shown in figure 4.4. Districts represented by female members received a mean of 166 contracts throughout the first two quarters of funds distribution, 17 percent more than the mean of 143 contracts received by the districts represented by men. The percentage difference is even greater when looking at the dollar value of these projects—the projects going to women's districts were collectively funded to the tune of $54.6 million; the projects going to men's districts, only $34.8 million. Women's House districts thus received 56 percent more funding than men's House districts.

We further investigate this disparity by estimating multivariate models of both dependent variables. We estimate the aggregate dollar value of contracts going to a district by taking the natural log of the variable and employing OLS; we estimate the number of contracts won by each district using negative binomial regression. In each case, the primary independent variable is the dummy variable *Female*, coded 1 for districts represented by female members and 0 for districts represented by male members. We employ a wide variety of control variables to account for the many factors, both economic and political, that might also influence the flow of economic stimulus dollars to each congressional district. All of the data come from the 111th Congress, the time when the stimulus money was distributed. One group of variables accounts for factors internal to the House that influence members' ability to channel money to their district. *Republican* is a dummy variable coded 1 if a member is a *Republican* and 0 if a member is a Democrat. *Tenure* is the logged number of years each member has served in the House of Representatives. Dummy variables also indicate members who hold powerful chamber positions: separate variables identify *committee chairs*, committee *ranking minority members*, members of the *Appropriations Committee*, and the top three ranking *party leaders* in either party. *Lagged vote* is the member's share of the two-party vote in his or her most recent election.

Since the stimulus package was primarily an initiative of the Obama administration, we include a second group of variables to indicate factors that influence presidential politics. For instance, if spending is being targeted for presidential reelection purposes, we should see a disproportionate amount directed to House districts located in *battleground states*.[5] We include the natural log of *state population*. We also include two variables that provide a rough indication of the working relationship between each state government and the Obama administration. Separate dummy variables indicate whether the district lies in a state with *unified Democratic control* or *unified Republican control* of the elected branches of the state government. The baseline comparison group is states with divided government.

The third group of control variables indicates the extent to which a district can make a substantive claim to stimulus funds. These include the district's *population* (because districts do vary somewhat in population especially near the end of a decennial redistricting cycle) and the geographical size of the district measured as *logged square miles*. Additionally, we employ variables that directly indicate economic need, to capture the stimulus's goal of jump-starting economic growth and employment. We employ three variables in this vein: the House district's *poverty rate*; its *unemployment* rate; and its median *per capita income*. Finally, a dummy variable indicates whether a congressional district is located in a *state capital*, and we include an interaction between *state capital* and state population.

Results are presented in table 4.4, Models 1 and 3. In the model of aggregate dollar value (Model 1), *Female* is positive and significant. This result indicates that even after controlling for a wide variety of other fac-

TABLE 4.4. Distribution of 2009–2010 Economic Stimulus Funds among House Districts

	Aggregate dollar value		Total number of awards	
	Model 1	Model 2	Model 3	Model 4
Female	.263*	–955**	.115	–.696*
	(.135)	(.330)	(.109)	(.305)
Poverty rate	.087***	.074***	.053***	.043***
	(.016)	(.016)	(.013)	(.013)
Female*Poverty rate	—	.091***	—	.059**
		(.023)		(.023)
Unemployment	.018	.004	–.006	–.010
	(.054)	(.054)	(.037)	(.038)
Per capita income	1.73***	1.76***	1.15***	1.13***
(logged)	(.327)	(.315)	(.283)	(.279)
Population	.248	.227	2.19*	.197
	(.155)	(.154)	(.108)	(.108)
Square miles (logged)	.061	.076*	.083***	.092***
	(.036)	(.035)	(.026)	(.025)
State Capital	1.82***	1.81***	.811***	.827***
	(.226)	(.223)	(.174)	(.174)
State Capital* state	.563***	.552***	.217*	.203*
population	(.152)	(.151)	(.089)	(.089)
Republican	–.282*	–.278*	–.333***	–.339***
	(.112)	(.110)	(.081)	(.081)
Tenure	.013*	.011*	.011*	.010*
	(.006)	(.006)	(.005)	(.004)
Committee Chair	–.346	–.272	–.193	–.154
	(.232)	(.238)	(.182)	(.181)
Committee Ranking	.438	.406	.060	.044
Minority Member	(.288)	(.284)	(.120)	(.119)
Appropriations	.068	.072	.133	.149
Committee	(.148)	(.145)	(.110)	(.111)
Party Leader	.248*	.277*	.187	.235
	(.123)	(.137)	(.188)	(.206)
Lagged Vote	–.001	–.0002	.004	.005
	(.004)	(.004)	(.003)	(.003)
Battleground State	–.089	–.095	.006	–.006
	(.134)	(.132)	(.110)	(.111)
State Population	–.004	–.004	–.006**	–.007**
	(.003)	(.003)	(.003)	(.003)
Unified Dem control	.340*	.358*	.178	.187
of state gov't	(.156)	(.154)	(.121)	(.119)
Unified GOP control	–.121	–.143	–.200*	–.202*
of state gov't	(.134)	(.132)	(.092)	(.092)
Constant	–2.76	–2.85	–9.94**	–9.52**
	(3.67)	(3.53)	(3.20)	(3.16)
N	435	435	435	435
Adjusted R^2	.516	.530	—	—
Log likelihood	—	—	–2458	–2452
Overdispersion	—	—	–.865	–.887
			(.077)	(.075)

Note: Robust standard errors in parentheses; $^{*}p < .05$; $^{**}p < .01$; $^{***}p < .001$

tors that might influence the distribution of stimulus dollars, districts represented by female House members received more stimulus spending than those represented by male House members. Because the dependent variable is logged, the coefficients are not directly interpretable even though they are OLS coefficients. However, taking the inverse log indicates that the predicted difference between the median male representative and median female representative is approximately $23.8 million of stimulus funding. This finding is similar to the bivariate difference shown in figure 4.4. Looking at the model of the number of contracts procured (Model 3), *Female* is not significant. Nonetheless, the results of the dollar value model provide strong evidence that having a female member of Congress substantially boosted the amount of funding a district received from ARRA.

We next test for the possibility of a Senate gender effect by focusing on stimulus money going directly to state governments. This money was identified in the dataset of ARRA awards as going to the congressional district that houses the state capital. As indicated by the very large and highly significant coefficients on *State Capital* and the interaction term *State Capital*State Population* in table 4.4, an outsized share of the money distributed under ARRA went directly to the states. We hypothesize that having a female senator would result in a larger share of money going to the state government, and test this by examining the per capita dollars and per capita number of contracts going to each state. However, we find no support for this hypothesis. States represented by a female senator received an average of $500 per capita; states with no female senator received $510 per capita, a difference that was not close to being statistically significant. Similarly, states with a female senator received 1.85 contracts per thousand residents; states with no female senator received 1.93 contracts per thousand residents. Multivariate tests similarly indicated that there was no significant difference between states with and without a female senator on either measure. Thus, there is no evidence of a Senate gender effect in the distribution of ARRA funds, though we cannot discern definitively whether that is because of a lack of gender effects in the Senate vis-à-vis stimulus fund distribution or because our measure of senator-secured funding was not an accurate proxy for such funding.

Finally, we use the stimulus data to investigate whether female members show a more constituent-oriented focus when it comes to securing federal dollars. We specifically hypothesize that in addition to female House members obtaining *more* dollars for their constituents, it should also be the case that female members are more *responsive* to their districts' needs in procuring dollars. This claim substantively means different things in different contexts; the context surrounding ARRA was economic stimulation. We accounted for this originally in our econometric models by including three indicators of economic need. Of these, *unemployment* was not significantly related to the distribution of either dollars or contracts, and *income* was positive and significant, indicating that wealthy districts received more money, all else equal.[6] *Poverty rate* was also positive and significant in both models, indicating that a district's poverty rate was the metric that decision makers most relied upon to deliver stimulus funds to economically distressed districts. In other words, districts with more need, as evidenced by a high poverty rate, received more stimulus funds. We propose that because female members of Congress are more responsive to constituent needs than male members, districts with high poverty rates will benefit even more when they are represented by females as opposed to males.

We test this proposition by reestimating Models 1 and 3 (see table 4.4), and including the interaction variable *Female*Poverty Rate*. The hypothesis is that districts with higher poverty rates will benefit more when they are represented by female members as opposed to male members; thus the coefficient on the interaction term should be positive and significant. The results are presented as Models 2 and 4 in table 4.4, and in both models the coefficient is indeed positive and significant. The substantive predictions of the models are presented in figures 4.5 and 4.6. These display the relationships between poverty rate and, respectively, the dollar value of stimulus projects and the total number of projects awarded, and do so independently for districts represented by male and female members.

In both figures, the curve for female members is significantly steeper. For low values of poverty, the gender difference is negligible. However, as the poverty rate rises from a low of 5 percent to a high of 30 percent, in male-represented districts the predicted number of projects increases by 227 percent and the dollar value of these projects increases by 507 percent; comparatively, in female districts the predicted number of projects increases by 777 percent and the dollar value of these projects increases by an overwhelming 3,797 percent. Thus the "returns" to poverty-stricken districts in terms of stimulus spending were significantly and substantively greater in districts represented by female members, suggesting women not only secure more benefits for their districts overall but also do so in a manner that reflects their constituents' needs.

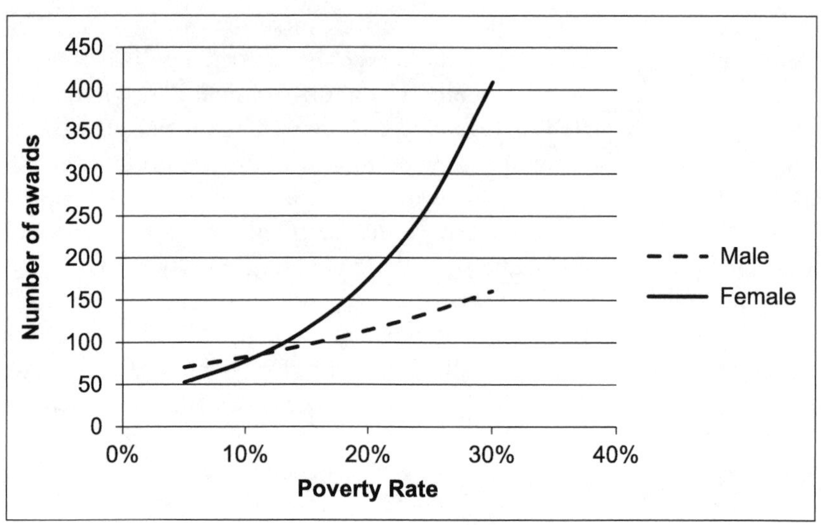

Figure 4.5. Number of Stimulus awards, by House member gender and district poverty rate

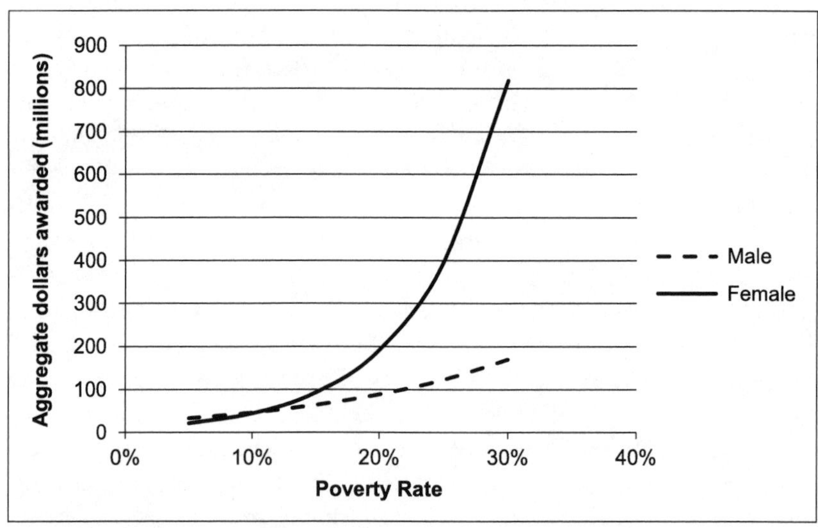

Figure 4.6. Aggregate dollar value of stimulus awards, by House member gender and district poverty rate

Conclusion

In this chapter we investigate two different types of distributive spending. The first is the earmarks included in the FY2008 appropriations bills, which members of Congress are more directly responsible for than any other form of spending. The second is stimulus spending distributed under the 2009 American Recovery and Reinvestment Act; this spending originated from federal agencies as a result of very contextualized political and economic conditions. In both cases, we find that voters represented by women have more money spent in their districts and states than voters represented by men. These findings comport with those of Anzia and Berry (2011), who investigate the continuing bureaucratic outlays that federal agencies make on a day-to-day basis. In all three cases, the evidence points to female members of Congress procuring more spending for their districts than male members. Thus, in a variety of theoretically distinct settings, we find evidence that female members are more focused than male members on procuring constituent-oriented benefits. The evidence is somewhat stronger for House members than senators, but we see at least some signs of a gender gap in both chambers. In the House, female pork barrel spending outstrips male spending in all three cases. In the Senate, we find evidence of gender differences only with earmarks. However, the differences in earmark procurement were extremely large: female senators out-earmarked their male counterparts by almost, and in some cases more than, 2–1. All told, the evidence is strong that female Congress members procure more outlays than their male counterparts.

In addition to the quantitative difference in spending for their constituents of male and female members, we also find evidence of an important qualitative difference in the patterns by which male and female House members procure money. In the federal funds distributed out of the ARRA, as the poverty level in a district increases, female members procured more stimulus projects and a greater amount of stimulus funds than males did. In other words, female members' procurement of funds comported more closely with their districts' levels of need than male members' procurements did. This is one indication that female members are also more substantively responsive to their districts' needs; we show further evidence of this substantively oriented responsiveness in chapter 6.

Securing targeted spending that directly benefits one's district offers a clear credit-claiming opportunity for members of Congress, and there is substantial evidence that such spending substantially helps members win reelection. However, while most members of Congress seek the rewards that come along with procuring pork barrel spending—as figures 4.1–4.6 show, the average requests for all types of distributive benefits are fairly high—we clearly show that women seek them *more* than men. We further show that women are more attuned to the needs of their constituents with respect to stimulus funds: not only did women procure more stimulus funds overall, they also did so more effectively than men when representing those districts with the highest levels of need. In order to produce the differences uncovered in this chapter, female members must devote more of their time, energy, and resources to procuring federal benefits for their voters.

Gendered vulnerability provides a clear and parsimonious explanation for these findings. By directing spending to their districts, and ensuring the interests of their constituents are met, women legislators seek to overcome the difficulties caused by their gendered vulnerability. Returning to Representative Woolsey, her efforts to secure federal dollars for her district both show her constituents tangible evidence of her successful work on their behalf while also working to undercut potential challengers. And she needed to do so: even though she won reelection in 2002 with 67 percent of the vote, she faced a primary challenger in 2004; she eventually won the general election in 2004 with 73 percent of the vote, only to face a strong primary challenger (a three-time city councilman) again in 2006. Thus, regardless of objective assessments of their electoral safety, women must guard against potential challengers, and we show that they do so in part through the procurement of federal funding.

We turn now in chapter 5 to an assessment of how gendered vulnerability influences legislative activities.

FIVE

Legislating, Position Taking, and Gendered Vulnerability

Congresswoman Carolyn Maloney (D-NY) won reelection in 2004 handily, outspending her opponent almost 40–1 and collecting 81 percent of the vote. Thanks to her efforts and her favorably liberal district (in the 2004 presidential race, John Kerry won 75 percent of the vote), Rep. Maloney was among the safest members in the House. For many members, a safe seat provides some leeway to focus one's legislative goals, as well as the latitude to pursue a more focused legislative agenda that may even depart somewhat from the district's views. But that's not the path Representative Maloney took. Rather, Representative Maloney introduced sixty-five bills in the 109th Congress, more than five times the average for members of the House, and the third highest total among all 435 members of the House of Representatives during the 109th Congress.

Not only did Representative Maloney introduce a large number of bills, but she also introduced bills that were targeted directly at the concerns of her constituents. For instance, Maloney's New York City district is mere blocks away from the former site of the World Trade Center. Only three years removed from the tragedies of 9/11, Maloney introduced ten bills that were directly or indirectly related to the events of that day—two proposed improvements to federally funded health care for 9/11 responders, three proposed extensions to the benefits going to the families of victims, four related to disaster preparedness more generally, and one called for bolstering security screening for airport operators. Four other bills were designed to attract the support of Maloney's large Jewish constituency—two pertaining to Nazi war crimes, one pertaining to Holocaust education, and the fourth proposing a Congressional Gold Medal (one of the two highest civilian awards the United States government award) for human rights activist Rabbi Arthur Schneir, who led a congregation in Maloney's district. Maloney also introduced bills that proposed federal funding for urban parks and new radio equipment for the New York City Fire Department.

The downside to the high volume of Representative Maloney's legislative activity was that not a single one of these bills received any formal consideration by the House of Representatives. None were debated on the floor, none were reported out of committee, and none even received a committee hearing. Rather, all sixty-five were introduced by Maloney and then subsequently ignored by the entire chamber.[1]

Even though only about 5 percent of bills introduced in a given Congress eventually become law, about a quarter of them at least are considered by the relevant committee (Krutz 2005). Representative Maloney thus not only introduced an unusually high number of bills but she also experienced an unusually high rate of legislative futility.

We argue that this pattern of legislative behavior is not unusual for women in Congress, and that once again the culprit is gendered vulnerability. Our theory of gendered vulnerability is premised on the idea that female legislators perceive that they must constantly work to show both their constituents and colleagues that they deserve to be in Congress, and to be returned to Congress. In this chapter, we explore how women's unique position in the legislature influences their approach to one of the basic activities of legislators, bill sponsorship. Sponsoring and cosponsoring bills provides a clear signal to voters that a member is working to address their needs and interests by seeking policy changes. Introduce more bills, and you send more signals to constituents. We show that women are more active than men in this aspect of the legislative arena, in the sense that they introduce more bills and resolutions. This helps them forestall any doubts about their willingness to work hard for their constituents.

The constituent-oriented focus of gendered vulnerability influences more than just the raw number of bills or resolutions women sponsor or cosponsor. In addition, gendered vulnerability induces female members to sponsor *qualitatively different types* of bills than male members. Specifically, we posit that women introduce a disproportionately high number of "messaging" bills—bills that members introduce primarily, if not solely, to send a message to their constituents. Looking at the thousands of bills members introduce each year it is hard to specifically identify which are messaging bills and which are not, but collectively they have certain characteristics. First, because messaging bills are designed to showcase legislators' efforts to work on issues of interest to their constituents, they are unlikely to advance very far within the chamber. They tend to be introduced and then forgotten about. Additionally, because they are designed to be vehicles for their authors to take public positions, they offer the same potential benefit to other legislators as well. As such, messaging bills should receive more cosponsors than other bills, all else being equal.

We argue that these trends should be detectable when looking at all the bills that men and women introduce: if women truly introduce more messaging bills than men, then the bills they introduce should get more cosponsors, and be less likely to advance in the legislative process, than men's bills. Thus, while Representative Maloney's lack of success is particularly notable, we show that the broader trend is shared among women: simply put, women do not see as many of their bills become law as men do despite the fact that their bills attract more cosponsors than male-sponsored bills. A further dimension to this argument, which we explore in chapter 6, is that gendered vulnerability induces women legislators to hew more closely to their constituents' needs. As a result, women focus the content of their legislative work on issues most salient to their districts more than men do.

We turn now to a more in-depth examination of the link between gendered vulnerability and legislative activity. We then empirically test our hypotheses related to the volume of legislative activity members undertake and whether women's increased volume is in part a function of prioritizing the position-taking aspects of the legislative process in order to combat their gendered vulnerability.

Legislative Activity and Gendered Vulnerability

There is no clean distinction between electoral activity and legislative activity. Members of Congress use the legislative process to help themselves win reelection, and are not usually shy about it. Members think strategically about how their roll-call votes will play with voters in the district (e.g., Kingdon 1989), deliver speeches on the chamber floor calculated to win the support of hometown groups (Hill and Hurley 2002), and, perhaps most prominently, procure federal spending for their district with an eye toward pleasing people and winning votes (e.g., Ferejohn 1974; Arnold

1979). Yet another way that members of Congress use the legislative process to their electoral advantage is by introducing bills that highlight positions their voters favor (Lazarus 2013).

There are no limits on what bills members can sponsor; so long as Congress is in session, any member may introduce any bill and the chamber will, at least nominally, consider it. As a result, members of Congress sponsor thousands of bills, resolutions, and amendments every year. However, very little of this legislation is enacted—as we noted above, in recent Congresses only 5 percent of bills that were introduced became law, and only 22 percent received even the most cursory level of formal legislative consideration, a hearing in front of a standing committee. Since most bills have virtually no chance of becoming law there must be another reason members go to the trouble of researching, writing, and introducing bills to the chamber—or, more likely, having their staff do the research and writing while the member does the introducing. That reason is electoral position-taking.

With every piece of legislation he or she sponsors, a member specifically endorses a position on a political issue. There is tremendous variety in the issues contained in the text of legislation: the issue at hand may be serious or frivolous, it may be national or local in scope, and it might draw the member of Congress a lot of attention or (more likely) very little. Nonetheless, every time a member of Congress puts his or her name on a piece of legislation, it represents an official, public endorsement of the principles and arguments embodied within it. Introducing bills provides a prototypical example of Mayhewian (Mayhew 1974) position-taking. Indeed, Mayhew even notes that "the electoral requirement is not that [a member of Congress] make pleasing things happen, but that he make pleasing judgmental statements. The position itself is the electoral commodity" (1974, 62). From the perspective of a member of Congress trying to secure reelection, it does not matter whether the bill passes. As long as the bill publicly stakes out a popular position on an issue that is important to the member's voters, the bill has done at least one of its jobs.

Even though legislative activity can help members win reelection, there are downsides. Most important, whenever a member takes a position on an issue, whether in a public speech, in a town hall meeting, or by introducing a bill, she might antagonize voters or interests opposed to the position. This opposition "can harm a [member's] reputation, influence and ultimately the chance to be reelected" (Schiller 1995, 198), so members must be cautious before staking out any type of position. Second, there is also a time cost—at some point, a member of Congress (or more likely staff) must study the issues, craft policy positions, and draft the legislation (Schiller 1995; Hall 1996; Wawro 2000). Even cosponsorship—which formally requires a member only to sign his or her name to a sheet of paper—forces the prudent member to read the bill closely enough to ensure nothing in it will embarrass him or her.

The presence of at least a small amount of cost means that making a public statement on an issue is not automatic. Rather, like most things there is a (at least an informal, mental) cost-benefit analysis that members must perform—before writing the bill or resolution, members ask themselves, is this worth the time and trouble? And some members will find that going through the trouble is worth it more often than others do—presumably the members who need to reach voters the most. Thus there is a fairly widely accepted expectation that electorally vulnerable members take more public positions—in this context, sponsor or cosponsor more bills and resolutions—than safe members, all else equal.

Prior analyses have not been kind to this hypothesis, however. It has been tested fairly extensively in the context of cosponsorship—several prior studies ask whether electorally vulnerable members cosponsor more bills. In the House, where most of these studies look, there is virtually no evidence that they do (Campbell 1982; Kessler and Krehbiel 1996; Wilson and Young 1993; Koger 2003), although among senators, the electorally vulnerable do appear to cosponsor more (Harward and Moffett 2010). Thus, the cosponsorship literature has not shed much light on the issue of electorally motivated legislating. On the contrary, it has cast doubt on whether members of Congress use legislation toward this end at all. Lazarus (2010) suggests, though, that these findings may be a function of resources: when members face a difficult reelection, they have to devote their time, energy, money, and staff toward winning reelection and may simply not have enough resources to both campaign vigorously and participate in the legislative process. As a result those who lack the resources withdraw from the legislative arena while concentrating on keeping their seat. Noting that senators enjoy significantly more resources than House members, Lazarus (2010) finds that while electorally vulnerable senators legislate more than safe senators, electorally vulnerable House members legislate *less* than safe House members.

The Implications of Gendered Vulnerability for Legislating

Previous investigations of the link between vulnerability and legislative activities focus on traditional notions of electoral vulnerability, utilizing members' vote share in their last election. We argue, however, that examining legislative activity offers a prime example of how gendered vulnerability is distinct from traditional notions of electoral vulnerability. Gendered vulnerability reflects women's *perception* that they are inherently vulnerable to attack—female members may, in reality, reside in a safe seat, and even have won election handily in prior years, but they perceive that they must take additional steps to reassure their constituents that they are the best person suited for the job of representing them. Gendered vulnerability thus leads women legislators to focus on activities that target their constituents, and provide high reelection payoffs, even if these activities are not traditional *campaign* activities.

One particularly effective way to achieve this goal is to utilize the legislative process. Several of our interviewees explained, a la Mayhew, that members use the legislative process to posture to voters. According to one staffer, members "need to look active. That is always true. I think you are always looking for an option to sign onto bills or to sign on initiatives that look good vote-wise. . . . It wasn't necessarily doing so for purposes like passing stuff . . . it was more for amassing points. I mean, reelection is of supreme importance here." Members thus sponsor and cosponsor bills to show they are active and working for their constituents. Another interviewee noted that being "a 'good' member means being active in a number of ways . . . and members want to show what they are doing. 'I stand on this issue and this is what I'm doing.'" Stated more baldly, "If we have to choose to either drop [introduce] 100 amendments or pass one bill . . . I'll choose the amendments every time. We want to do anything we can do to be active and show [our constituents that we are] engaged in the process." And our interviewees contend that there is a clear link between position-taking through legislating and voters' behavior on Election Day: "[Constituents] vote [for a member] because they like the person and believe the member likes the same stuff, as evidenced by sponsorship and cosponsorship activity."

In addition to bills, members also use other legislative tools to send policy signals to voters. One interviewee noted that "everything you do legislatively creates a certain persona or message that you're trying to get across." As a result, in the empirical analysis below we look at not only bills but also resolutions and cosponsorships. In Congress, a resolution is a piece of legislation that expresses an opinion: the resolution may endorse a position on a political issue, recognize the accomplishment of a citizen or group, or condemn unpopular behavior. For example, a member of Congress might introduce a resolution recognizing the achievements of the local high school basketball championship team, approving or disapproving of the president's policy toward a foreign nation, or declaring the third Thursday in February national turnip day. If and when one or both chambers votes on a resolution, the position in the resolution becomes the official position of the chamber, or of Congress. Unlike bills, which have a position-taking component and a policy component, resolutions are pure position-taking devices. But, as a result, introducing resolutions allows members to send signals to voters without the distraction of the legislation potentially making substantive policy.

Representative Maloney—the member we discussed at the opening of the chapter—introduced a number of resolutions closely tied to her voters' interests. One called on Congress to recognize the 60th anniversary of the United Nations, which is located in her district. Another called for recognizing the 65th anniversary of the American Ballet Theatre, also located in her district. Maloney also introduced five resolutions related to the domestic politics of Greece and its historic rival, Turkey—largely because Maloney's district includes the heavily Greek neighborhood of Astoria, home to the largest Greek population in the world outside of Greece (Schumach 1977).[2]

A third legislative device, cosponsorship, allows members of Congress to signal their support for a bill or resolution introduced by another member. Among all of the different ways members participate in the legislative process, cosponsoring bills takes the least effort—in principle all the member has to do is sign his or her name to a document that someone else has written. But once again, that signature is a public indication of support for what is in the document, and that potentially gives it electoral value. One staffer we interviewed argues that cosponsoring legislation makes it "easy to appease interest groups. . . . It is a very low-cost, high-return thing to do, especially for rank-and-file members."

Studies confirm that voters reward members who actively participate in the legislative process by writing and introducing bills: Box-Steffensmeier et al. (2003) and Parker and Goodman (2009) both find that survey respondents' ability to identify a reason for liking a House incumbent correlates positively with the number of bills he or she introduces. Box-Steffensmeier et al. (2003) also find that survey respondents are more likely to vote for incumbents who have introduced more bills. Romero (2006) finds that House members who sponsor more bills receive higher vote shares than their less legislatively active counterparts. Rocca and Gordon (2010) find that, among House members, bill sponsorship correlates positively with political action committee campaign donations. Finally, Schiller (2000) finds that senators who sponsor more bills receive more local media coverage.

We thus contend that, unlike members who are electorally vulnerable in the traditional sense who focus on campaign activities (perhaps to the detriment of other priorities; e.g., Lazarus 2010), women take an active role in the legislative process in terms of bill introductions and cosponsorships. They want to look active to their constituents and show that they deserve to be returned to Congress. We thus formally hypothesize, first, that *women introduce more bills and resolutions than men*, and second, that *women cosponsor more bills than men*.

In this vein, one of our interviewees provided an example of how the goal of messaging can take over the content of a bill. She told us about a bill she had written about endangered species protection. When she showed it to her boss he directed her to change the language to make it more understandable to voters, even though the changes would mean that the bill would not be compatible with the United States Code. The staffer described how her boss reacted when she showed him the initial draft: "He said, 'That is not what I asked for. I want to say protect this animal . . .' And I was like 'But that doesn't really work with the way the [United States] Code is written. I mean we have to point to statute and regulation and rewrite things.' And he said, 'Well, if I show this to someone at home they're not going to know what it says.'" In this case at least, messaging was not just a secondary goal for the bill, it was the primary reason the member wanted the bill introduced.

We therefore further expect, due to their gendered vulnerability, women's legislative activities to lean more heavily on the position-taking function of legislating, leading them to introduce more "messaging" bills than those with the clear purpose of being enacted into law. As one of our interviewees noted, the member might " candidly say to constituents, 'This is too uphill a battle; [but] I will introduce it to keep the issue alive.'" We investigate this notion in two ways. First, we examine the percentage of each member's bills that reach certain benchmark stages of the legislative process, up to and including final passage in the chamber. When we calculate the percentage of an individual legislator's bills that, say, clear committee or pass the chamber, women's denominators (the total number of bills they introduce) are going to be inflated because of the disproportionate number of messaging bills they introduce. This artificially drives down the percentage of bills that advance through the legislative process. Thus, even if women and men manage to advance the same overall *number* of bills through the chamber (which we think is likely the case), the larger number of bills women introduce means their success *rate* is artificially low. We formally hypothesize that *compared to men, a smaller percentage of the bills that women introduce receive serious consideration in the chamber, and a smaller percentage of their bills likewise pass.*

Second, messaging bills are written specifically to communicate popular positions to voters, so they should attract more cosponsors than bills that are crafted for the purpose of becoming law. Since female members sponsor more messaging bills than males do, on average bills sponsored by female members should secure more cosponsors than bills introduced by their male counterparts. We thus hypothesize that *bills sponsored by women, due to their position-taking orientation, will garner more cosponsors than those sponsored by men.* The dual implication of these two analyses is that women, induced by their gendered vulnerability, prioritize the position-taking aspects of legislative activity. We turn now to an empirical examination of how women and men contribute to the pile of legislation that Congress considers every year.

Volume of Legislative Activity

We begin our empirical investigation of legislative activity by exploring potential gender differences in the *volume* of legislation members produce. What has prior literature said about women's propensity to introduce bills and resolutions as compared to men? Although the literature on how women approach the legislative process is robust (see Reingold 2000 for a review), little of it directly asks whether women participate more or less than men do. Rather, the dominant share of the literature asks whether women focus on different policy issues than men and specifically the question of whether women are more likely than men to introduce bills that address "women's issues" (e.g., Barnello and Bratton 2007; Bratton 2002, 2005; Swers 2002; Saint Germain 1989). On the question of volume, when surveyed, female legislators indicate that they spend less time on legislative matters than males (Thomas and Welch 1991; Thomas 1994), but when scholars have looked directly at the volume of Congress members' legislative activity they find that women actually introduce more bills (Volden, Wiseman, and Wittmer 2013; Swers 2002; Tamerius 1995) and cosponsor more legislation (Swers 2002; Tamerius 1995) than men. We interpret these prior findings as preliminary support for our hypotheses.

We expand on these previous studies by offering a more comprehensive and systematic examination of three different types of legislative activity: bill introductions, resolution introductions, and cosponsorships. We collected data on each of these measures for each member of both chambers of Congress in the 103rd through the 110th Congresses. In each of these eight Congresses, we observed the total number of HR-designated or S-designated bills each member sponsored in his or her respective chamber. We also observed the total number of resolutions each member sponsored, and the total number of bills and resolutions each member cosponsored. Descriptive statistics for all six of our measures of legislative activity, aggregated over all eight Congresses, are presented in table 5.1. These numbers suggest, for instance, that Representative Maloney was well above the House mean and median when she introduced sixty-five bills in the 109th Congress.

Figures 5.1, 5.2, and 5.3 present simple gender differences in the mean number of bills, resolutions, and cosponsorships, respectively, across all the Congresses for which we collected data. Figure 5.1 shows that in both the House and the Senate, women sponsor more bills than men. In the House, the difference is just under two bills per Congress, while in the Senate the difference is almost eight bills per Congress. The percentage difference is also larger in the Senate: females sponsor 14.5 percent more bills than males in the House, and 26.4 percent more bills than men in the Senate. In both cases, bivariate difference-in-means tests indicate that the differences are statistically significant ($p<.000$ in both chambers).

Figure 5.2 displays the number of resolutions sponsored by members of each chamber. The results indicate that, like bills, women sponsor more resolutions than men. In the House, women sponsor just under one more resolution per Congress, while in the Senate they sponsor 1.3 more resolutions per Congress. Here the percentage difference in each chamber is nearly identical: 27.7 percent in the House and 27.1 percent in the Senate; once again, both differences are statistically significant ($p<.000$ in the House, $p<.012$ in the Senate). Finally, figure 5.3 displays the aggregate

TABLE 5.1. House and Senate Legislative Activity

	Mean	Median	SD	Minimum	Maximum
Bills					
Senate	30.8	26	20.1	0	140
House	12.6	10	10.5	0	119
Resolutions					
Senate	5.0	4	5.1	0	43
House	2.3	1	3.0	0	35
Aggregate cosponsored					
Senate	208.7	190	93.3	0	614
House	271.3	240	145.6	1	1,051

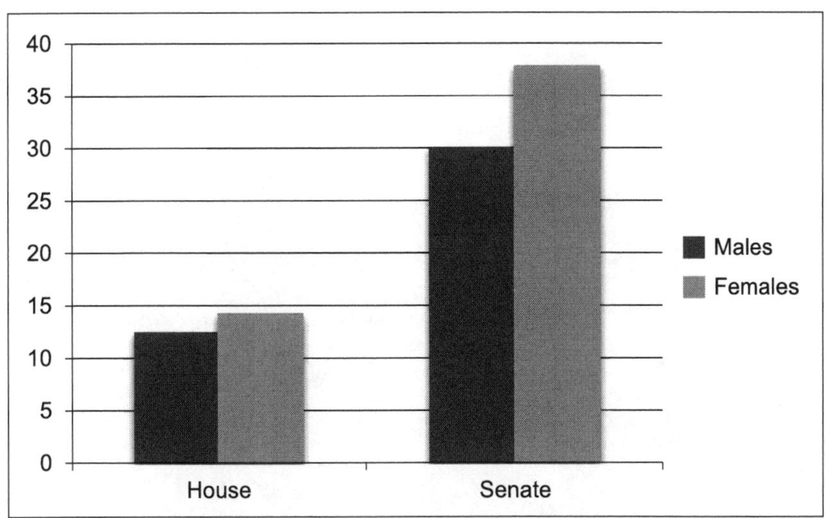

Figure 5.1. Average number of bills sponsored

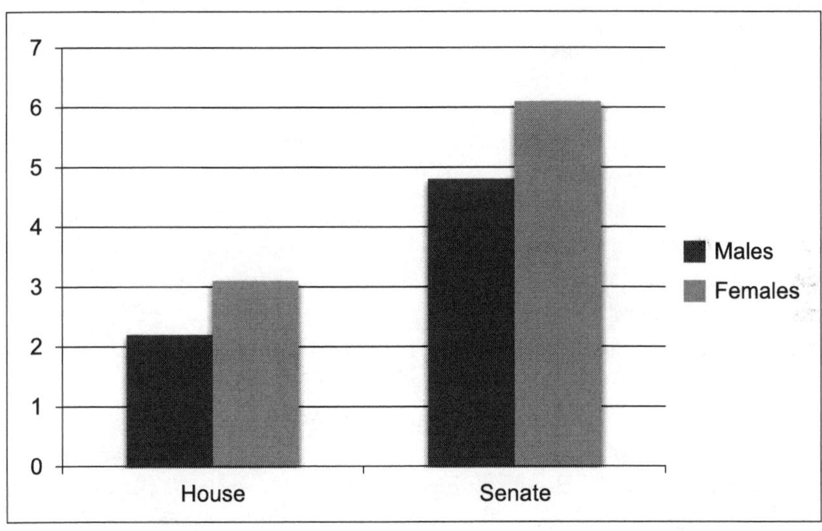

Figure 5.2. Average number of resolutions sponsored

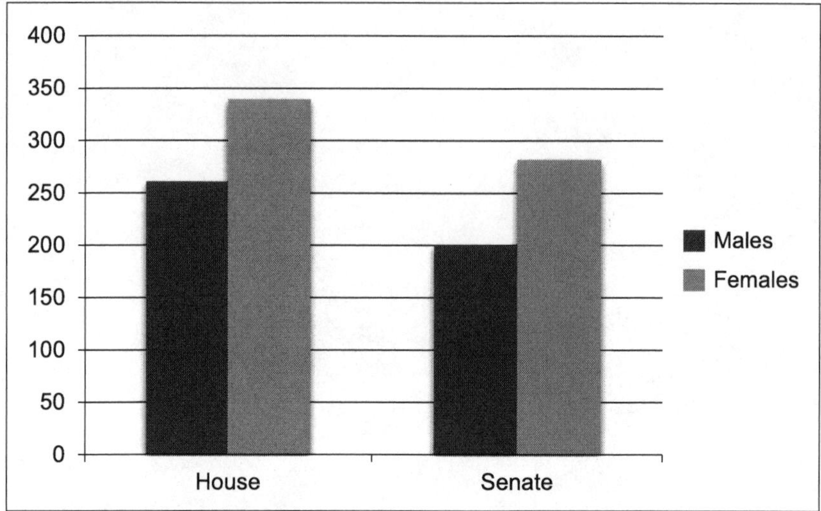

Figure 5.3. Average number of cosponsorships

number of bills and resolutions that members of each chamber cosponsored. Again, the pattern is the same: women cosponsor more items than men. In both chambers, females cosponsor approximately eighty more items per Congress than males, though lower absolute numbers in the Senate mean the percentage difference in that chamber is larger than in the House. In the Senate, women cosponsor 41.3 percent more items than men, while in the House women cosponsor 23.1 percent more items. Once again in both chambers the differences between males and females are statistically significant ($p<.000$ in both chambers).

To further investigate whether gender independently influences the volume of legislative activity that members produce, we also estimate multivariate models for each of our six dependent variables (the number of bills, resolutions, and cosponsorships in each of the two chambers). All of the dependent variables are count variables with significant overdispersion; as a result we employ negative binomial regression in all six estimations. For all of the models, the primary independent variable is a dummy variable indicating whether the member is *Female*.

We include numerous control variables drawn from the previous literature to account for other factors that may potentially influence members' levels of legislative activity; the operationalization of each of these variables, as well as our dependent variables, is summarized in table 5.2. As discussed

TABLE 5.2. Variable Descriptions for Chapter Analyses

Variable Name	Variable Measurement
Dependent Variables	
Bills Introduced	Total number of HR-designated or S-designated bills each member sponsored in each Congress in his or her respective chamber
Resolutions Introduced	Total number of resolutions, joint resolutions, and concurrent resolutions each member sponsored in each Congress in his or her respective chamber. We exclude, however, resolutions that are procedural in nature, such as those calling for an adjournment or appointing a member to a committee, since these have no significant position-taking value
Bills and Resolutions Cosponsored	Total number of bills and resolutions each member cosponsored in each Congress in his or her respective chamber
Committee Action	Percentage of each member's sponsored bills that received any official action from the standing committee to which it was referred (or relevant subcommittee within the committee), including having a hearing held in conjunction with the bill or considering the bill in a markup session.
Reported by Committee	Percentage of each member's sponsored bills that were reported out of committee to the floor
Scheduled for Floor Action	Percentage of each member's sponsored bills that were scheduled for any type of action on the floor of the bill's home chamber
Passed Chamber	Percentage of each member's sponsored bills that passed the chamber (i.e., received at least a majority vote from the full chamber)
Became Public Law	Percentage of each member's sponsored bills that were enrolled as public law
Average Cosponsorships on Sponsored Bills	We counted the number of cosponsors that signed on to each of the member's sponsored bills in a particular Congress, and then took the average.
Independent Variables	
Female	Female members are coded 1, and males 0
Lagged Vote	Member's share of the two-party vote in his or her most recent election
Seniority	Logged number of consecutive years the member has served in his or her (current) chamber
Ideological Extremity	Absolute value of each member's Poole and Rosenthal (1995) DW-NOMINATE score
District Partisanship	Percentage of the district that voted for the presidential candidate of the member's party in the most recent presidential election
Majority Party	Majority party members are coded 1, and minority party members 0
Party Leader	Members serving as a party leader, whip, or conference/caucus chair for each party, as well as the Speaker of the House, are coded 1, and all others 0
Appropriations Committee Member	Appropriations Committee members are coded 1, and 0 otherwise
House Rules Committee Member (House model only)	House Rules Committee members are coded 1, and 0 otherwise

TABLE 5.2.—*Continued*

Variable Name	Variable Measurement
Committee Chair	Members serving as the chair of any committee in their respective chamber are coded 1, and 0 otherwise
Committee RMM	Members serving as the ranking minority member of any committee in their respective chamber are coded 1, and 0 otherwise
Reelection (Senate model only)	Senators who face reelection at the end of a particular Congress are coded 1, and 0 otherwise
State Size (Senate model only)	Log of the size of the state's congressional delegation

above, most congressional literature assumes that members facing electoral peril will engage in more Mayhewian position-taking behavior than their more electorally secure colleagues. To test for this conventional notion of electoral vulnerability, *lagged vote* reflects the member's share of the two-party vote in his or her most recent election. Given the time and resource constraints facing members who wish to draft bills, those who have more legislative experience, and resulting lower start-up costs to learning about issues and understanding current law and areas for potential change, are more likely to draft legislation than more junior members (Schiller 1995). *Seniority* thus indicates the (logged) number of consecutive years the member has served in his or her (current) chamber. *Ideological extremity* indicates how far to the left or right a member of Congress is, and is operationalized as the absolute value of each member's Poole and Rosenthal (1995) DW-NOMINATE score. We include a variable to indicate how strongly partisan each district is; *district partisanship* is indicated by the district's vote for the presidential candidate of the member's party in the most recent presidential election. A dummy variable indicates whether each member is in the *majority party* (coded 1) or not (0); majority party members are generally found to be more legislatively active (see, e.g., Garand and Burke 2006; Wawro 2000). A series of dummy variables indicate whether a member holds an institutional position that might influence her legislative activity levels (Cox and Terry 2008; Schiller 1995; Sinclair 1989). Respectively, they indicate whether a member is a *Party Leader*, a member of the *Appropriations Committee*, a member of the House *Rules Committee* (included, of course, only in the estimations of House legislative activity), a *Committee Chair*, or a committee *Ranking Minority Member*. Two further variables are included in the Senate models only: a dummy variable indicating that the member is facing an imminent reelection, and a variable indicating the (logged) *state size* (Schiller 1995). Finally, we include a series of fixed-effects dummy variables indicating the Congress each observation is taken from; these are not reported in any of this section's results.

Results of these analyses are presented in table 5.3 for the House and table 5.4 for the Senate. In all six estimations, the coefficient on the dummy variable *Female* is positive and significant. These results indicate that even after controlling for other factors that influence legislative activity, gender remains a significant factor in explaining how many bills and resolutions members sponsor and cosponsor. We used CLARIFY (Tomz, Wittenberg, and King 2003) to generate predicted gender differences for each dependent variable based on the models in tables 5.3 and 5.4. Results are not substantively different from those presented above in figures 5.1–5.3. Thus, we find that, in six independent tests of legislative activity, female

TABLE 5.3. Multivariate Analysis of the Volume of Legislative Activity, House of Representatives

	Bills introduced	Resolutions introduced	Bills and resolutions cosponsored
Female	.238***	.288***	.179***
	(.037)	(.053)	(.020)
Seniority (logged)	.345***	.216***	.040
	(.021)	(.032)	(.012)
Lagged vote	–.078	–.256	.029
	(.110)	(.151)	(.066)
Ideological extremity	.243*	.241	.117*
	(.095)	(.135)	(.053)
District partisanship	–.103	1.08***	.561***
	(.001)	(.002)	(.093)
Majority	.223***	.077	–.209***
	(.028)	(.041)	(.016)
Party leader	–.660***	.435**	–.532***
	(.143)	(.158)	(.131)
Appropriations Committee	–.483***	–.363***	–.183***
	(.040)	(.062)	(.023)
Rules Committee	–.235**	.305*	.078
	(.082)	(.124)	(.063)
Committee chair	.236***	.315**	–.202***
	(.056)	(.110)	(.048)
Committee RMM	–.131*	.140	–.102*
	(.066)	(.114)	(.044)
Constant	1.88***	.130	565***
	(.089)	(.138)	(.054)
N	3470	3470	3470
Log likelihood	-11677	-6801	-21092
Overdispersion	–.966***	–.355***	–1.70***
	(.034)	(.046)	(.028)

members of Congress are more active in the legislative process than males are. In both the House and the Senate, and regardless of whether we look at the bivariate relationships or control for other influences on activity, women introduce more bills, introduce more resolutions, and cosponsor more actively than men. These results provide strong initial evidence that female members of Congress more heavily use the legislative process to produce public positions than males.

We also contend that this emphasis on using the legislative process as a position-taking activity leads to qualitative differences in the *types* of bills women introduce as compared to men: women are more likely to introduce

TABLE 5.4. Multivariate Analysis of the Volume of Legislative Activity, Senate

	Bills introduced	Resolutions introduced	Bills and resolutions cosponsored
Female	.190**	.179^	.208***
	(.064)	(.094)	(.040)
Seniority (logged)	.127***	.131***	–.005
	(.029)	(.043)	(.018)
Lagged Vote	–.100	–1.42***	–.095
	(.270)	(.401)	(.165)
Reelect in 2	.110**	.128*	.067**
	(.042)	(.063)	(.026)
DW Nominate	–.467***	–.645***	–.396***
	(.107)	(.159)	(.067)
District/State partisanship	–.610	1.09**	.012
	(.267)	(.411)	(.168)
Democrat	–.182^	–.565***	–.076
	(.095)	(.141)	(.058)
Majority	.141**	.173*	–.002
	(.050)	(.073)	(.031)
Party Leader	.215^	1.32***	.025
	(.128)	(.180)	(.081)
State size (logged)	.118***	.228***	.034**
	(.019)	(.030)	(.012)
Appropriations Committee	–.143**	–.142*	–.074**
	(.045)	(.068)	(.036)
Committee Chair	.310***	.278**	–.046
	(.063)	(.096)	(.048)
Committee RMM	.025	.038	–.036
	(.065)	(.099)	(.040)
Constant	3.21***	1.71***	5.58***
	(.206)	(.305)	(.125)
N	800	800	800
Log likelihood	–3276	–2016	–4308
Overdisperson	–1.34***	–.831***	–1.94***
	(.056)	(.080)	(.005)

"messaging" bills. If women introduce a disproportionality high number of messaging bills, two important by-products should be observable. First, while undoubtedly all members wish to see all of their efforts successfully enacted, our interviews reveal that many members recognize the benefits of simply introducing messaging bills that address constituent concerns. Given the zero-sum nature of legislative resources, increased front-end activity in terms of sponsorship likely means less success at the end of the enactment process. We argue that women's gendered vulnerability induces them to introduce a disproportionate percentage of messaging bills, and that these bills are less likely to become law—even if the number of substantive bills they introduce (and see enacted) is equivalent to that of men. Second, introducing more messaging bills should result in a member also gaining more cosponsors for these bills. By definition, messaging bills are written to be attractive to various constituencies, and so they should disproportionately garner more cosponsors than other bills as other members seek to capitalize on the position-taking benefits of these bills. We thus expect that bills introduced by women, given their constituent orientation, will garner more cosponsors than men. We turn in the following sections to testing these two hypotheses.

Legislative Success

In this section, we examine whether a disproportionate emphasis on messaging bills influences how successful members are in getting their bills through the chamber. Variations in members' motivations influence what happens to their bills within the legislative process. When a member sponsors a bill whose primary goal is policy change, he or she will likely devote considerable time and effort to helping the bill pass the chamber and become law. But no such effort is made on behalf of messaging bills; the bill has already achieved its purpose simply upon being introduced because there is little if any additional electoral gain to be had from legislative success (Frantzich 1979; Mayhew 1974). All else being equal, then, the higher the level of policy-making intent behind a bill, the more effort the bill's sponsor will expend to move the bill through the legislative process. If we make the safe assumption that this effort translates into some amount of legislative success (Hall 1996; Wawro 2000), it follows that bills motivated primarily by a member's policy concerns are more likely to successfully navigate the legislative process than those motivated primarily by a member's electoral concerns.

Since even the bills' sponsors do not put much effort into moving messaging bills through the chamber, the decision makers who pick which bills advance through the legislative process to receive attention in committee or, later, the floor, will similarly avoid working on messaging bills. Position-taking bills are likely sorted from policy-making bills at the very beginning of the legislative process, when committee chairs (often in consultation with party leaders) decide which bills to take up for action. Under the regular legislative process, bills that fail to make it past this initial "winnowing" stage of consideration (Krutz 2005) cannot advance through the rest of the legislative process.[3] As a result, the consequences of women's disproportionate number of messaging bills can reach all the way through to the end of the process. Thus it is not a coincidence that none of Representative Maloney's 109th Congress bills received any formal consideration in the House of Representatives. Her example represents an extreme case, but it illustrates the possible or even likely result of focusing one's legislative effort so heavily on messaging bills. We posit that female Congress members' disproportionate focus on messaging bills results in female members having fewer of their bills (percentage-wise) advance through the legislative process, and ultimately fewer of their bills passing the chamber to become law.[4]

Our interviews bear out the perspective that enacting legislation provides relatively little payoff (Mayhew 1974). One staffer said, "I agree very much with the notion that voters care less about whether a bill is signed into law than did [the member] do something important on particular issues? When they go into the voting booth, they're not going to say 'introduced but not signed.' They'll be glad [the member] introduced [a bill] and advocated for the position." A second staffer, from a different office, tells a virtually identical story:

> Cosponsorship, sponsorship, getting cosponsors, are all stuff that takes relatively little effort, but [there's] a ton of political payback. You can tell your constituent that you are going to fix the problem and you got thirty-five others to agree. The electorate then says she's influential, and getting people to stand up. [But] getting legislation passed is a lot more work, and as far as the electorate is concerned, meh. . . . Passage is icing to the electorate, and they really do not care.

A staffer from a third office adds that members can even use the nonpassage of a messaging bill as a method to attack political opponents: "There is always an angle, there is always a political opportunity, so if you can't get a bill through Congress, then you have the opportunity to turn this around and say, well, this didn't pass, or this wasn't successful because of my opponents x, y, and z, or my opponents' party." Thus it seems reasonable to expect that a group of members—such as women—who introduce more messaging bills should see a smaller percentage of their bills ultimately become law. Most previous examinations of the differences between men and women's legislative success rates have primarily focused on state legislators. At that level of government, the findings are consistent: there is no appreciable difference between men and women in the percentage of their bills that ultimately pass the chamber or become law (Thomas and Welch 1991; Saint Germain 1989; Bratton and Haynie 1999; Bratton 2005; Thomas 1994; Ellickson and Whistler 2000). Two studies examine members of Congress, and produce mixed results. Jeydel and Taylor (2003) examine House members' bills and amendments, finding no gender difference among minority party members but that majority-party women have lower success rates than their male counterparts. On the other hand, Volden, Wiseman, and Wittmer (2013) find no gender difference among majority party members, but that minority party women are more successful than their male counterparts.

Volden, Wiseman, and Wittmer (2013) employ a more complex methodological approach to the study of legislative success than most prior studies. Traditionally, scholars count all the bills that a member introduces and how many of these pass the chamber, and use these two numbers to calculate a "hit rate," or the percentage of a member's introduced bills that pass. Indeed, this is the approach we take below. Alternatively, Volden, Wiseman and Wittmer weight bills by their perceived importance, with "commemorative/symbolic" bills receiving the least weight. (In their accounting, a commemorative bill is worth either one-fifth or one-tenth of a more substantive bill, depending on the substantive bill in question.) From a legislative perspective, this is a reasonable methodological response to the fact that not all bills are created equal, and lesser bills will likely be ignored by the chamber more often than more important bills. If you want to test which members are the most effective legislators, as they do, it makes sense to put the most methodological weight behind the same bills that members put the most legislative weight behind.

However, our purpose here is different. We are not trying to figure out whether women are more or less effective legislators; we are trying to determine what kinds of bills they introduce. From an electoral perspective, each bill is worth the same amount—voters likely do not know or care that one bill is only symbolically important while another has tremendous policy consequences. Moreover, in the context of our theory, the whole point is that bills differ from one another in their degree of legislative importance. In this section's empirical analysis, we are trying to capture the effect of female Congress members' disproportionate introduction of bills that—from a legislative perspective—are not terribly important and are instead written to emphasize their work and positions taken on behalf of their constituents. We thus weight each bill that is introduced equally. It should be noted, however, that the different methodologies employed here and by Volden, Wiseman, and Wittmer (2013) allow for both answers to be correct in different contexts—women may both introduce a disproportionate number of messaging bills, and thus their aggregate level of legislative "success" may appear low (suggesting a position-taking function to the introductions themselves), while also being quite successful at shepherding through the process bills introduced with clear policy or lawmaking goals in mind.

Empirical Tests

Following others in the legislative success literature (Anderson, Box-Steffensmeier, and Sinclair-Chapman 2001;[5] Cook 1979; Hasecke and Mycoff 2007; Parker and Davidson 1979), we measure legislative success at the level of the individual legislator. To test the success hypothesis, we observe the percentage of all bills sponsored by each member that advanced to five different stages of the legislative process in each chamber. First, we observed the percentage of a member's bills that received any official attention from the standing committee to which it was referred. A bill was deemed to have been the subject of committee action if the committee (or one of its subcommittees) held a hearing in conjunction with the bill or considered the bill in a mark-up session. Second, we observed the percentage of a member's bills that were reported out of committee. Third, we determine the percentage of a member's bills that were scheduled for any type of action on the floor of the bill's home chamber. Fourth, we observe the percentage of a member's bills that passed the member's home chamber. Finally, we determine the percentage of a member's bills that were ultimately enrolled as public law. Though these five stages of the legislative process do not represent all possible measures of legislative success, they are a representative cross-section of the stages through which a bill must pass in order to become law.

Figure 5.4 graphically presents men's and women's mean hit rates for each stage of the legislative process mentioned above in the House of Rep-

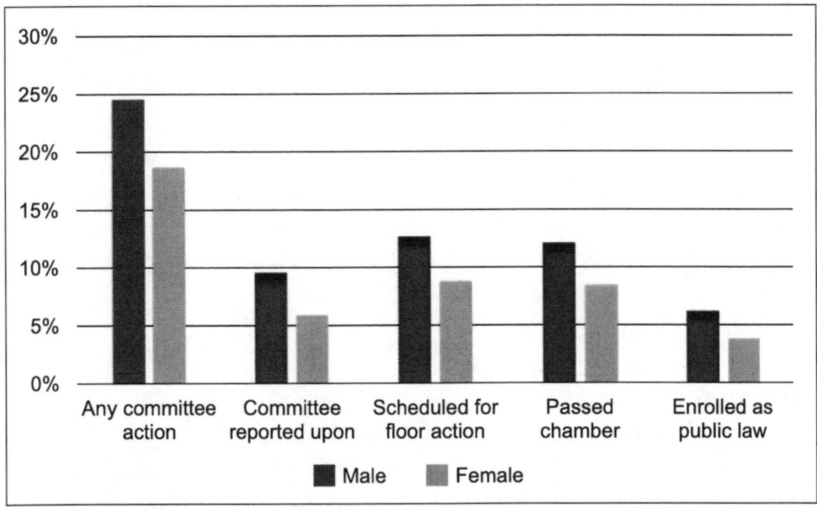

Figure 5.4. Legislative success in the House of Representatives: Percentage of bills reaching indicated state of legislative process

resentatives. One interesting thing to note about figure 5.4 is that, overall, the percentage of members' bills reaching each stage of the legislative process does not conform to our understanding of the "textbook Congress." In the textbook Congress, a bill is introduced and immediately referred to a committee, which then may choose to report the bill forward or not. If the bill is reported, it moves to floor consideration, where it may or may not pass the chamber. According to this understanding of the legislative process, the number of bills reaching each stage should be less than the number that reaches the prior stage, as actors at each stage "winnow" the number of bills still active (Krutz 2005). Thus the bars in figure 5.4 should get shorter or at least remain flat as they move from left to right. However, this is not the case: the mean percentage of bills scheduled for floor action and passing the chamber is greater than the mean percentage of bills that a committee reports forward. This is due to the fact that, in the House, most noncontroversial bills reach the floor through a procedure known as suspension of the rules, which does not require committee action; more bills reach the floor via suspension of the rules than any other route (Oleszek 2007).[6]

The primary finding reported in figure 5.4 is that for every stage of the legislative process, male House members see a greater percentage of their bills reach that stage of the process than female House members. As we move further along in the legislative process, the size of the gender difference narrows: 25 percent of male-sponsored bills get scheduled for committee action, whereas only 19 percent of female sponsored bills do, for a difference of 6 percentage points. For the three middle categories, the difference between men and women is 4 percentage points. Finally, the mean male House member sees 6 percent of his sponsored legislation become law, but the mean female House member sees only 4 percent. Nonetheless, the difference between men and women at each stage is statistically significant ($p<.001$ for all five stages). Overall, it appears that the initial sorting between female and male bills—more properly, we contend, between primarily messaging bills and primarily substantive bills—occurs in the earliest stages of the legislative process. This comports with the idea that the difference between the genders is primarily due to this difference in emphasis in what types of bills each gender sponsors.

Figure 5.5 presents the corresponding results for the Senate. There are several patterns worth noting. First, the expected "winnowing" pattern, absent in the House results of figure 5.4, is present in the Senate. This is because Senate leaders shepherd bills to the floor via alternate routes much less often than House leaders do. Second, for four of the five stages of the legislative process, senators have roughly the same "hit rates" as House members do. Individual senators introduce significantly more legislation than individual House members (figure 5.1, table 5.1), so their relatively equivalent hit rates indicate that they see a greater number of their bills advance through the legislative process as well. Third, and more directly relevant to our theory, female senators see a smaller percentage of their bills reach all five stages of the legislative process than male senators. Across the five stages of the legislative process that we examine, the magnitude of the difference follows roughly the same pattern as it does in the House. The average male senator sees 22 percent of his bills receive attention in committee, but for women the corresponding number is only 16 percent, for a difference of 6 percentage points. Across the remaining four categories, the differences are 4, 3, 3, and 2 percentage points, respectively. And once again, all of these differences are statistically significant ($p<.01$ for the first three categories, and $p<.02$ for the last two).

We again check the robustness of our results by estimating multivariate models to control for other factors that may influence the likelihood of a member's bills becoming law. The unit of analysis is the individual member of Congress. This analysis expands upon previous examinations of potential gender differences in legislative outcomes with its focus on the U.S. Congress rather than state legislatures (e.g., Bratton and Haynie 1999; Saint-Germain 1989; Thomas and Welch 1991); its longer time

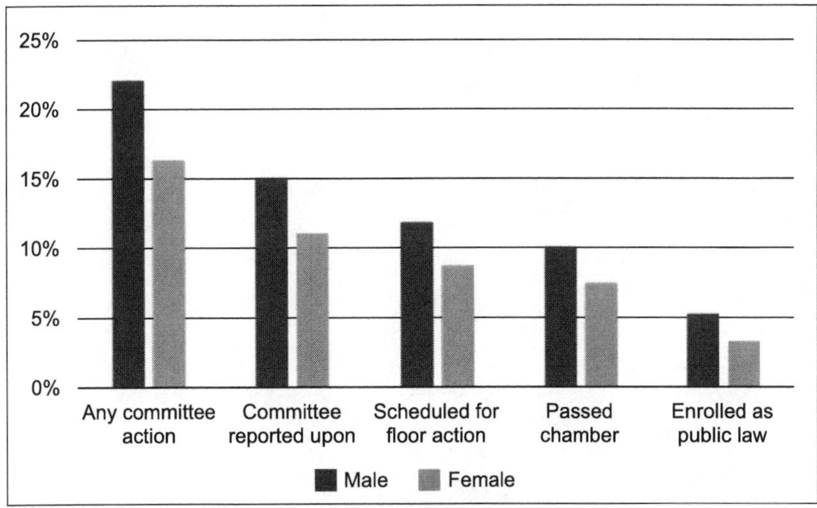

Figure 5.5. Legislative success in the Senate: Percentage of bills reaching indicated state of legislative process

frame of analysis (e.g., Jeydel and Taylor 2003); and its assessment of all sponsored legislation rather than only bills focused on certain issue areas (e.g., Thomas and Welch 1991). This brings our analysis more in line with nongendered studies of legislative success (e.g., Cook 1979; Hasecke and Mycoff 2007).

The dependent variables used are the same as we examined in the above bivariate analysis: the percentage of each member's sponsored bills that make it to each stage of the legislative process in each chamber. We thus estimate a total of ten models. Each dependent variable in this case is left-censored at zero, so we employ Tobit. We utilize the same independent variables as in the previous analyses; table 5.2 provides a description of each of them and how they were operationalized. Our principal independent variable is once again *Female*. Results are reported in table 5.5 for the House and table 5.6 for the Senate.

For the House, the results mirror those of the bivariate relationships reported in figure 5.4: *Female* is negative and significant in all five models (see table 5.5). Once again we generated predicted gender differences from each model, and once again they are not substantively different than those presented in figure 5.4. We suggest that the implication of these results is not that female House members are less legislatively effective or face widespread institutional bias, but rather that their use of bill sponsorship for position-taking purposes results in women introducing a disproportionately high number of messaging bills where "success" is more accurately defined as the introduction itself.

However, in the Senate models (table 5.6) *Female* is negative in four of the five models, but not significant in any of the five models. Thus it appears that one of the covariates accounts for much if not all of the observed bivariate relationship between gender and legislative success. One obvious suspect, given the years we employ in our analysis, is seniority. Especially in the Senate of the 1990s, women were not very senior members of the chamber—most had been elected in 1992 or later and were still accruing their earliest years of seniority throughout the rest of the decade. More broadly, these results mean that we cannot yet determine whether

TABLE 5.5. Multivariate Analysis of Legislative Success, House of Representatives

	Committee action	Reported by committee	Scheduled for floor action	Passed chamber	Became public law
Female	–.027^	–.027^	–.027^	–.025^	–.034^
	(.015)	(.014)	(.016)	(.013)	(.018)
Seniority (logged)	.016^	.052***	.040***	.030***	.033***
	(.008)	(.007)	(.009)	(.007)	(.010)
Lagged vote	.0004	.0003	–.00004	.0002	.00007
	(.0004)	(.0004)	(.0004)	(.031)	(.0005)
Ideological extremity	–.127***	–.111***	–.175	–.145***	–.138***
	(.036)	(.032)	(.037)	(.001)	(.042)
District partisanship	–.001*	–.00004	.001^	.001*	.001
	(.0006)	(.0005)	(.0006)	(.0005)	(.0007)
Majority	.123***	.206***	.206***	.190***	.151***
	(.012)	(.011)	(.012)	(.001)	(.014)
Party leader	–.060	–.084^	.041	–.010	.026
	(.051)	(.047)	(.050)	(.043)	(.054)
Appropriations Committee	–.053***	.018	.035*	.043***	.067***
	(.016)	(.014)	(.016)	(.013)	(.017)
Rules Committee	–.118***	–.106***	–.024	–.099***	–.064^
	(.030)	(.028)	(.031)	(.026)	(.035)
Committee chair	.117***	.159***	.190***	.186***	.156***
	(.026)	(.021)	(.025)	(.020)	(.026)
Committee RMM	.014	.006	–.020	.002	.015
	(.027)	(.025)	(.029)	(.023)	(.031)
Constant	.101**	–.231***	.279***	–.113***	–.300***
	(.039)	(.035)	(.040)	(.032)	(.045)
N	3431	3431	3431	3431	3431
Log likelihood	–1210	–995.0	–1299	–882.9	–1230
sigma	.293	.234	.279	.228	.279
	(.004)	(.005)	(.005)	(.004)	(.006)

female senators are introducing disproportionately more messaging bills than men.

Attracting Cosponsors

Finally, we assess a second potential by-product of a disproportionate emphasis on messaging bills: how many other members cosponsor each bill. As discussed above, cosponsorship is an act of pure position taking. By cosponsoring a bill, a member of Congress signals that he or she agrees with the policy or issue content of the bill. Messaging bills are crafted

TABLE 5.6. Multivariate Analysis of Legislative Success, Senate

	Committee action	Reported by committee	Scheduled for floor action	Passed chamber	Became public law
Female	–.031	–.012	–.001	.002	–.016
	(.025)	(.017)	(.014)	(.015)	(.012)
Seniority (logged)	–.000	.013^	.016*	.009	.001
	(.016)	(.007)	(.006)	(.007)	(.005)
Lagged vote	–.054	.046	.071	.092	.017
	(.102)	(.069)	(.059)	(.062)	(.052)
Reelect in 2	.019	.014	.011	.011	.002
	(.016)	(.011)	(.009)	(.010)	(.008)
Ideological extremity	–.165***	–.107**	–.100***	–.099**	–.058*
	(.051)	(.035)	(.030)	(.032)	(.026)
State partisanship	.497***	.327***	.279***	.267***	.198***
	(.112)	(.076)	(.066)	(.057)	(.058)
Majority	.102***	.077***	.067***	.065***	.052***
	(.017)	(.011)	(.010)	(.010)	(.009)
Party leader	–.015	–.008	.110***	.100***	.072**
	(.049)	(.033)	(.028)	(.029)	(.024)
Appropriations Committee	.025	.025*	.017^	.015	.006
	(.017)	(.011)	(.010)	(.010)	(.009)
Committee chair	.096***	.107***	.063***	.047***	.039***
	(.024)	(.016)	(.014)	(.015)	(.012)
Committee RMM	–.007	–.008	–.023	–.008	–.014
	(.024)	(.017)	(.014)	(.015)	(.013)
State size (logged)	–.015*	–.012*	–.007	–.007	.002
	(.008)	(.005)	(.004)	(.004)	(.004)
Constant	–.034	–.096^	.118***	–.196***	–.159***
	(.073)	(.050)	(.043)	(.045)	(.038)
N	800	800	800	800	800
Log likelihood	81.03	288.2	327.8	270.4	224
Sigma	.204	.136	.118	.121	.097
	(.005)	(.004)	(.003)	(.004)	(.003)

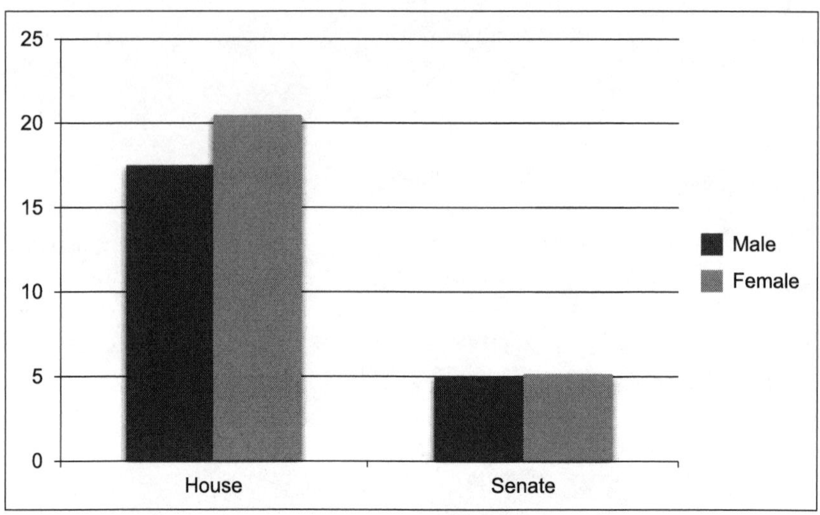

Figure 5.6. Average number of cospsonsorships on sponsored bills

for the specific purpose of communicating popular positions; as a result, messaging bills should attract more cosponsors than bills that are crafted for the purpose of becoming law.[7] If members of Congress are looking for popular messages to publicly attach their names to (the main point of cosponsoring a bill), more often than not they will find what they are looking for in a messaging bill. Since we posit that female members sponsor more messaging bills than males do, we further predict that, on average, bills sponsored by female members will secure more cosponsors than bills introduced by their male counterparts. And attracting cosponsors is beneficial to the original sponsor: as one of our interviewees explained, "It is a good strategy to get a lot of people on your bills going in, plus it's a big press hit."

To test this proposition, we again look at individual legislators. For each legislator we observe the mean number of cosponsors he or she garnered for all of his or her bills, in every Congress. Figure 5.6 presents the average of these numbers in the House and Senate, separated by male and female members. In the House, results are as predicted: female members average three more cosponsors per bill than male members, and the bivariate difference is statistically significant ($p<.000$). In the Senate, however, the difference is much smaller: female senators receive an average of only 0.15 more cosponsors per bill than male senators. This difference is not statistically significant ($p< 0.348$).

As in the previous analyses, we test the robustness of these results by estimating multivariate models for each chamber in which the dependent variable is the average number of cosponsors a member receives for his or her sponsored bills in a given Congress. This dependent variable is distributed roughly normally; as a result we use OLS to estimate it. The independent variables are identical to those used previously; they are summarized above in table 5.2. Once again the key independent variable is a dummy variable that indicates Congress members' gender. Results are presented in table 5.7.

TABLE 5.7. Mean Number of Cosponsors on Sponsored Bills

	House	Senate
Female	3.97***	.887*
	(.767)	(.390)
Seniority (logged)	2.20***	.083
	(.441)	(.162)
Lagged vote	.024	.059***
	(.023)	(.015)
Reelect in 2	—	–.179
		(.223)
Ideological extremity	5.38**	.803
	(1.92)	(.730)
District partisanship	–.017	.056***
	(.034)	(.017)
Majority	1.26*	–.103***
	(.625)	(.243)
Party leader	16.4***	5.69***
	(4.65)	(1.12)
State size (logged)	—	–.060
		(.101)
Appropriations Committee	–1.96*	–.190
	(.925)	(.217)
Rules Committee	.837	—
	(1.73)	
Committee chair	–2.25*	.389
	(1.07)	(.337)
Committee RMM	1.34	.189
	(1.54)	(.317)
Bills sponsored	–.174**	–.061***
	(.057)	(.017)
Bills sponsored squared	–.0001	.0003*
	(.001)	(.0001)
Constant	11.5	5.16***
	(2.23)	(1.14)
N	3470	800
R^2	.049	.175

For the House, results are similar to the bivariate analysis: *Female* is significant and positive. The value of the coefficient is 3.97, indicating that once other influences are controlled for, the female "advantage" in garnering cosponsorships is slightly larger than what was indicated in the bivariate analysis. Turning to the Senate, support for our hypothesis now emerges: accounting for the various potential influences on cosponsorship rates reveals a clear gender difference as the coefficient on *Female* is positive and statistically significant. Despite the very slight difference indicated by the bivariate relationship reported in figure 5.6, the OLS estimation indicates that on average, female senators receive an average 0.89 more cosponsors for each bill than male senators.

Discussion: House-Senate Differences

This chapter demonstrates that female and male members of Congress use the legislative process differently from one another. All Congress members use the legislative process both to influence national policy and to help themselves win reelection. But we show that the relative weight of each motivation is different for male and female members. Female members, due to their gendered vulnerability, concentrate their legislative efforts more on electorally oriented position-taking than male members—women sponsor more bills than men, sponsor more resolutions, and cosponsor more. More sponsorships and cosponsorships, by definition, mean more public positions.

Further, the bills that men and women sponsor are different from one another in a way not identified in previous studies of legislative activity: female Congress members introduce more messaging bills than men. This strategy is evidenced not only by the fact that a smaller percentage of female-sponsored bills become law, but also by the fact that female members receive more cosponsorships for their sponsored bills than male members, even though their bills do not progress as far in the legislative process. Moreover, in the next chapter we show that women are more responsive to their constituents' policy positions than men are. In the House of Representatives, compared to men, women introduce a larger number of bills that pertain to the substantive issue areas their voters care about. This is another piece of the same puzzle—if women concentrate more on messaging bills than men do, it makes sense that those messaging bills will be relevant to their voters' policy concerns.

Notable among the results of this chapter are chamber differences in how strongly the evidence supports some of the predictions. On one hand, female members of both chambers sponsor and cosponsor more legislation than male members. However, significant chamber differences appear when we test for the likelihood that this increase is in part a function of women introducing a disproportionate share of messaging bills. In the House, it is unequivocal both that female-sponsored bills are less likely to advance through the legislative process and that female-sponsored bills receive more cosponsors than male-sponsored bills. Taken together, these findings lend support to the claim that female representatives utilize the legislative process's position-taking benefits more than males. In the Senate, however, the evidence for both propositions is much weaker: for each hypothesis some evidence exists, but for both the case can hardly be called unimpeachable. Thus the question arises, what causes the pattern in which gender differences in the nature of bills introduced is so much more robust in the House than in the Senate?

We believe that the answer lies in the different amount of resources available to members of each chamber (Lazarus 2010). Senators enjoy several resource advantages over House members. For one, senators' staff and office allowances are, depending on the size of the state they represent, up to five times greater than House members' allowances. This allows most individual senators to also maintain a much larger presence in Washington than House members do. Second, nearly every senator is chair or ranking minority member of a committee or subcommittee, while in the House a relative few hold these positions. Most of these positions also come with still more staff. Third, the Senate's smaller size means each individual senator can claim a greater share of his or her chamber's common goods, such as the House and Senate recording studios. Finally, when running for reelection, Senators can use their position as statewide officeholders to command at least some of the resources of their state's party apparatus. House members, representing smaller districts whose shapes do not often conform to county lines or other political organizational units, often claim a much smaller share of these resources.

The sum total of all of these resource advantages means that when senators need to sponsor and cosponsor more bills and resolutions, they can do so even if they are also waging an active campaign in their state or district. Alternatively, they also have the resources to work simultaneously on moving their sponsored bills through the chamber. They do not need to make the same kinds of trade-offs between legislative and electoral activity that House members—who, with fewer staff and less resources in general, must choose carefully how best to deploy them—do. This produces a stark contrast between female members of the House and Senate. Female senators can conceivably produce both messaging bills *and* policy-oriented bills. And our mixed results suggest that female senators may be able to even introduce bills that do both. Female House members, for their part, have to pick and choose: if they want (need) to sponsor messaging bills, they might have to sacrifice some on the policy side; they also likely trade-off resources in terms of whether to draft bills or to focus on pushing those that have been introduced through the chamber.

Conclusions

Our findings go beyond prior studies of gender differences in legislative behavior; to a significant extent, prior literature on gender effects in the legislative process focuses on ideological differences between the genders, or on the fact that women emphasize women's issues in their legislative activity to a much greater extent than men do (e.g., Diamond 1977; Carroll 2001; Thomas 1994). Our examination also differs from those investigating traditional electoral vulnerability, given the inherent trade-offs these members must make between legislating (including bill introductions and cosponsorships) and campaign activities (e.g., Lazarus 2010). But looking at the issue from the standpoint of gendered vulnerability offers a different perspective.

We show in this chapter that women's gendered vulnerability leads them to focus predominantly on the position-taking aspects of legislating. Given the clear electoral benefits of such activities (e.g., Box-Steffensmeier et al. 2003; Rocca and Gordon 2010), female legislators utilize bill sponsorship and cosponsorship to send a clear message to their constituents that they are working directly for them. We thus find that female legislators in both the House and the Senate sponsor more bills and more resolutions, cosponsor more bills and resolutions, and garner more cosponsors for those bills they introduce than their male counterparts. And, as we show in the proceeding chapter, the bills they introduce—and the eventual votes they cast on bills considered on the chamber floor—hew more closely to their districts' needs. Women legislators thus work hard to show voters that they are representing them in the highest levels of government.

Our results showcase an important way in which gendered vulnerability differs from electoral vulnerability. Traditional electoral vulnerability leads members to concentrate more heavily on campaign activities, perhaps to the detriment of legislating. We suggest that gendered vulnerability induces a different pattern of behavior: one that is primarily constituent-focused, with an added dose of showing that one is working hard to faithfully represent those constituents. Legislating thus becomes an important mechanism to transmit this message to voters. Drafting bills and resolutions, as well as cosponsorships, provides clear position-taking opportunities that female legislators take distinct advantage of as compared to their male colleagues. The trade-offs that do arise concern the ultimate result of this legislative activity: bill advancement through the chamber. Female House members do not see as much of their sponsored legislation move through the legislative process as their male counterparts; female senators, however, experience relatively equal rates of success.

The patterns uncovered in this chapter have serious implications for how male and female members of Congress approach their jobs. On one hand, purely representational activities such as position taking can be beneficial to constituents. Position taking can be a valuable mechanism of substantive representation if it means that a representative pays more attention to issues that constituents care about. This is doubly so if it brings attention to issues and groups that are otherwise not well represented. Media-savvy Congress members might also bring some national attention to local issues, which can then boost the chances of the local issues receiving substantive attention in Congress at a later date. On the whole, position taking is primarily an electoral activity, but it is not wholly devoid of substantive importance.

Nonetheless, there might be some drawbacks when a group of members focus their activity so closely on the electorally beneficial aspects of legislation. For one, female members of Congress may feel more restricted in the policy areas they can legislate on than male members, because their legislation is tied more tightly to electoral concerns. As we show in chapter 6, women House members introduce bills that address the issues that their constituents are most likely to care about to a greater extent than men. It is easy to see how this strategy could be advantageous electorally. And, as we discuss more in chapter 7, it suggests women provide better representation under a traditional delegate model. On the other hand, though, male legislators, with their relative electoral safety, may possess more freedom to "dabble" legislatively in policy areas that are not necessarily salient to their district. Does this mean that female members cede influence on issues of broad national concern (unless these issues are unusually salient in the female member's electorate)? We are not in a position to answer this question definitively, but it is an important question for future research into the broader effects of gendered vulnerability.

SIX

Representing Everyone

How Gender Influences Policy Responsiveness

> You know the stories you see about the senators or the members of Congress who lose touch and move to Washington? It's not the women.
>
> —Congressional staffer, interview with authors, summer 2013

During the 103rd Congress, sixteen men sat on the on the Senate Judiciary Committee, but only two women: Dianne Feinstein (D-CA) and Carol Moseley Braun (D-IL). This committee is most famous for vetting presidential nominees to the federal judiciary, including Supreme Court nominees. However, most of the committee's work addresses issues related to the operation of the federal judiciary (civil and criminal), federal criminal law, immigration, and civil liberties. So one might expect senators on the Judiciary Committee to represent states whose citizens deal the most with the judicial system, such as states that have more urban areas and higher minority populations (these are proxies; we discuss these measures in more detail below). This was not at all true for the men on the committee during the 103rd Congress—they overwhelmingly represented states that are more rural, such as Utah, Vermont, and South Dakota, and had relatively small minority populations. On the other hand, the two women on the committee represented states that almost perfectly fit the committee's policy profile: California and Illinois.

This example reflects a common pattern. We constructed scores for each of the fifty states that measure how salient a committee's policy issues are to the people who live there. For the Judiciary Committee in the 103rd Congress, out of all fifty states Feinstein's California ranked first, and Moseley Braun's Illinois ranked third, while most of the male committee members' scores represented states falling in the bottom half. Jumping ahead to the 109th Congress—during which the Senate had fourteen women, up from only six in the Senate in the 103rd—Feinstein was the lone woman on the Senate Judiciary Committee and once again represented the state whose voters measured the highest level of need. A second Senate committee, the Environment and Public Works Committee, demonstrates the same pattern. It oversees a large number of government construction projects, which makes it especially salient to voters who work in, and those who hope to work in, the construction industry. The two highest-ranking states in terms of constituent salience were both represented on the committee—California's Barbara Boxer (D-CA) and New York's Hillary Clinton (D-NY).

Over the last three chapters, we examined Congress members' constituent- and reelection-oriented activities, and consistently we find that female members of Congress pursue these activities to a greater extent than male members of Congress. In this chapter, we turn to a more context-dependent assessment of issues and policies. While all legislators seek to represent their constituents, how and to what degree they represent the policy views that their constituents want them to varies widely. We propose that one manifestation of gendered vulnerability is that female legislators will, in the aggregate, more faithfully represent the views of their constituents than males in terms of the issues they tackle, the policies they pursue, and the votes they cast. As Dianne Feinstein, Carol Moseley-Braun, Barbara Boxer, and Hillary Clinton showcase, female members of Congress orient their legislative work toward their constituents. In other words, women are simply better substantive representatives than men. This chapter assesses this claim by investigating how well members represent their constituents in terms of their committee work, the bills they introduce, and their roll-call votes.

Gender and Representation

A core question driving legislative scholars is to what degree elected representatives work to advance the interests of their constituents. One primary mechanism for representing constituents is advocating for policies and issues that will help them; this is the epitome of substantive representation

(Pitkin 1967). However, as Richard Fenno noted, legislators think in terms of "constituencies," and they always have more than one; Fenno (1973) proposed four main constituencies legislators care about. A legislator may thus seek to curry the favor of his or her party faithful, those who have supported him or her in the past, or members of the opposite party the legislator thinks can be wooed at the next election. Legislators may also seek to represent their constituents broadly, regardless of who may have supported them previously.

Extant literature in this area focuses on how female members' policy preferences differ from that of male members. As many have argued (e.g., Mansbridge 1999; Pitkin 1967), substantive representation is many times only truly achieved through descriptive representation. Thus, the literature focuses on whether female legislators provide substantive representation for other women by focusing on "women's issues," or issues that disproportionately impact women in society. An incomplete list of these issues includes abortion (and reproductive rights policy more broadly), children and family issues, employment and economic equality, and women's health care. Overwhelmingly, studies find that female legislators are more supportive of women's issues than male legislators. This pattern holds true in state legislatures (Bratton and Haynie 1999; Saint-Germain 1989), the House of Representatives (Swers 1998, 2002,; Dolan 1997), and the Senate (Frederick 2010).

Female legislators support women's issues across all stages of the legislative process. For instance, female members introduce more bills that concern women's issues than males (Saint-Germain 1989; Thomas and Welch 1991; Swers 2002). Additionally, female legislators are more likely then male legislators to cosponsor bills dealing with women's issues (Swers 2002; Wolbrecht 2002), more likely to participate in committee proceedings on these bills (Norton 2002), more likely to discuss women's issues in floor debate (Walsh 2002), and more likely to offer floor amendments dealing with women's issues (Swers 2002). Perhaps most prominent is the roll-call vote: when chambers vote on bills that concern women's issues, female legislators are more likely to support these bills than their male counterparts (Thomas 1994; Swers 1998, 2002; Frederick 2009, 2010; Tatalovich and Schier 1993; Oldmixon 2002).

Other studies have identified policy differences between male and female legislators beyond the realm of women's issues. Some find that female legislators' increased attention to women's issues is balanced by a lower level of attention paid to other issues, including agriculture (Reingold 2000) and business and commerce (Thomas 1994; Reingold 2000). Analyses of roll calls as well as self-reports of policy opinions find female legislators are more willing to fund arts programs (Boles and Scheurer 2007), more supportive of welfare programs (Poggionne 2004), less in favor of the death penalty and prayer in schools (Epstein, Niemi, and Powell 2005), and less willing to cut taxes at the expense of government programs (Epstein, Niemi, and Powell 2005). In fact, female legislators are generally more liberal than their male colleagues, even within the same party (Swers 2002; Rocca, Sanchez, and Uscinski 2008; Welch 1985; Frederick 2010).[1]

Gendered Vulnerability and Policy Priorities

Our interest in policy differences between men and women in Congress is more nuanced than questions of "Do women support X more or less than men?" The fact that women are uniquely and consistently vulnerable in their reelection campaigns suggests that gender-based policy differences might depend on what voters want out of their representatives in Congress. Thus in this chapter we break somewhat from prior studies in this area. Extant studies generally investigate whether female legislators fulfill the goals of descriptive and especially substantive representation of women through their policy foci. They also look for absolute and constant differences between male and female legislators. For instance, past studies investigate the claim that because of their different social, familial, and personal concerns, female legislators are *always* more liberal, or *always* more supportive of women's issues than male legislators. However, we argue that there is another class of gender-based policy differences that is more conditional, and that might not be identified at all in a search for absolute differences: we posit that women, due to their gendered vulnerability, are more likely than men to reflect the concerns of their constituents in their legislative activities.

In chapter 5, we showed that women's gendered vulnerability leads to an increased volume of legislative activity. Women sponsor more bills and resolutions, and cosponsor more bills and resolutions, than their male colleagues. These activities clearly showcase their efforts on behalf of their constituents, and have been shown to lead to positive effects come election time. We also find evidence that women's bills, particularly in the House, are written with position-taking in mind: women's bills are less likely to move through the chamber but much more likely to garner cosponsors. Thus, unlike traditional electoral vulnerability, women's perception of their precarious position regarding both constituent favor and reelection leads them to utilize the electorally beneficial aspects of position-taking through legislating.

If women utilize the legislative process to curry favor with their constituents and take electorally useful positions, this should appear not only in the volume of legislative activity they undertake, but also in the *content* of that activity. Constituents desire to see their representatives working on their behalf. A necessary corollary is that the work done by members of Congress will reflect the interests and needs of their constituents. Representative Marcy Kaptur had this to say about what it means to serve in Congress: "This is what I can promise: I will always represent my constituents, working-class people. My agenda is shaped by what is happening to the people of my district, the conditions of their lives. It always has been" (Kahn 2017). One staffer we interviewed went further, suggesting that "[w]omen run because they want to make a difference and serve constituents. Men run because they want the title and power. But men are not as focused on making a difference for individual constituents." We extend this line of reasoning to argue that female legislators approach their time in office with an eye toward their constituents' specific needs and concerns, and do so to a greater degree than their male counterparts.

Later in this chapter, we show how this orientation induces Congress members—in particular, female Congress members—to introduce bills that play well with their voters. But here we pull just a few examples from the 115th Congress to illustrate the point. When Grace Meng (D-NY) introduced a bill to make feminine products such as tampons and pads tax free, the bill (HR 972) represented an actual attempt to remove taxes from these products. But, equally so, the bill was a way for Meng to take a public stance on an issue that affects her inner-city constituents who have a hard time affording basic necessities. When Susan Brooks (R-IN) introduced a bill to increase educational assistance to veterans (HR 1104) and another one to make it easier for military families to apply for federal benefits (HR 1078), she signaled her promilitary credentials to her conservative voters just as much as she actually attempted to enact these changes in the law. Rep Terri Sewell (D-AL) was speaking directly to her constituents—61 percent of whom are African American—when she introduced the Historically Black Colleges and Universities Capital Financing Improvement Act (HR 1123) and a bill to create a commission to study the idea of paying reparations to descendants of slaves (HR 40). And Rep. Martha Roby (R-AL) could not have been clearer about her intentions when she introduced the Halt Tax Increases on the Middle Class and Seniors Act (HR 1051).

We are not arguing that women are the only ones to introduce such messaging bills. But we are arguing that gendered vulnerability incentivizes women to introduce them more than men do. And so too with other actions that signal a member's policy preferences to voters—women both have to send more signals (see chapter 5) than men and make sure those signals more closely correspond to what voters actually want.

These contentions—that members tailor their policy activity to their voters' preferences, and that women do so more than men—can only be true if voters notice what members do in office and punish unwanted activity at the ballot box. Voters do, indeed, notice these things. Even though voters might seem uninformed about politics, if a member of Congress makes a misstep voters can become informed very quickly—because other actors like the media or electoral opponents have incentives to spread such information (Arnold 1990). As a result, there are identifiable links between the Congress members' actions and vote shares. For instance, a wealth of studies find that members who have ideologically extreme roll-call-voting records pay a price when they run for reelection (Canes-Wrone, Brady, and Cogan 2002; Erikson 1971; Erikson and Wright 2000; Ansolabehere, Snyder, and Stewart 2001). More recently, Carson et al. (2010) suggest that it is not necessarily ideological extremity that hurts members but excessive partisanship; however, the key point is the same: voters can and do punish members who exhibit unwanted roll-call behavior. Similar patterns of electoral retribution also appear to exist for state legislators, where voters know even less about the candidates (Hogan 2008). There is also some evidence that voters do not just respond to members' broad ideological patterns, but also to more discrete activities as well, including individual roll-call votes (Bovitz and Carson 2006), bill introductions (Parker and Goodman 2009), pork barrel spending (Sellers 2002), and even floor speeches (Box-Steffensmeier et al. 2003).

Since voters notice what goes on in Congress and react accordingly, it is no surprise that members of Congress take voter preferences into account when making legislative choices. They admit as such when asked about it in interviews (Kingdon 1989; Fenno 1978a), but there are other types of evidence as well. For instance, quasi experiments confirm that when legislators' constituencies change, members' behaviors change accordingly: when a member of the House is redistricted into a more liberal or conservative district, his or her roll-call-voting behavior becomes more liberal or conservative (Glazer and Robbins 1985). Similar patterns are found when authors look at specific sets of roll-call votes: Kastellec, Lax, and Phillips (2010) find that senators' votes on Supreme Court nominations are sensitive to state-level public opinion on the nominee. In addition to roll-call votes, the policy areas that members of Congress focus their attention on tend to be those their voters care about the most (Bishin 2009): members of Congress disproportionately introduce bills in the policy areas their constituents find the most salient (Woon 2009; Sulkin 2005) and fund pork barrel projects that their voters are most likely to appreciate (Lazarus 2009; Lazarus and Reilly 2010).

Finally, though all members are at least somewhat responsive to their constituents' preferences, electorally vulnerable members are generally *more responsive* than safe members. There has been a generation-spanning academic debate over what has come to be known as the marginality hypothesis, the proposition that electorally vulnerable members vote differently than safe members on roll calls. A complete review of this voluminous literature is well beyond the scope of this project (Fiorina 1974 provides a good synopsis up to that point). However, the most recent and methodologically sophisticated entries into this debate consistently find that vulnerable members are both less ideologically extreme (Griffin 2006; Canes-Wrone, Rabinovich, and Volden 2007; Frederick 2008) and less partisan (Carson et al. 2010) than safe members.[2]

Arising from all of this, we argue that gendered vulnerability does not just lead women to pay *more* attention to their constituents, as we showed in chapters 2–5. It also leads female members of Congress to adhere more closely to their voters' policy preferences than males. Regardless of their own personal policy preferences, the preferences that women express through their legislative activity will be more strongly constrained by what voters want. Thus, for instance, if voters in a particular constituency want liberal representation, they are more likely to get it from a female member of Congress than from a male member. This applies to specific policy areas as well: if voters in a particular constituency are particularly concerned about crime, legislators of any stripe would be wise to pay particular attention to issues surrounding crime. However, if this constituency has a female representative, then they are likely to get more attention focused on the issue of crime than if they have a male representative.

The single most telling illustration of this is the quote we lead the chapter with, a congressional staffer who observed during one of our interviews, "You know the stories you see about the senators or the members of Congress who lose touch and move to Washington? It's not the women." Another staffer offers a similar, though slightly less pointed, observation: "We spend a lot of time hearing from constituents and where our voice needs to be heard. Mainly the purpose of legislation is to try and benefit the people of the district, to do something meaningful." Former representative Anne Northup described how her district's interests and problems led her to pursue certain policy areas: "I got very, very involved in my district, and it was really a labor of love for me. Everything from infrastructure, what are the problems we have with the airport (we had huge problems with the airport), what are the problems we have the McAlpine Lock and Dam (we had huge problems with that), what are the problems with this bridge that was supposed to be built forty years ago, and what kind of leadership would it take. But also, what is going on in the minority community in our district . . . what about the health disparities. . . . [I] slowly became more and more involved in all of these issues."

The implication of our argument is that women legislators are not only better at substantively representing the interests of other women, but that they are simply better period at substantive representation than men. While generally the literature on substantive representation focuses on those who share the same descriptive characteristics as the representative, we argue that female legislators are more likely to represent the substantive interests of all of their constituents. Female legislators, due to their gendered vulnerability, will thus be more likely to reflect both the political characteristics and concerns of their district when undertaking legislative activities. We explore this effect in the context of three types of legislative behavior: committee memberships, bill introductions, and roll-call behavior.

Committee Assignments

We first examine whether congresswomen's committee assignments better reflect their constituents' needs and interests than those of men. Our theory predicts that the relationship between committee assignments and a district's level of demand for legislative action within a certain policy area will be stronger among female members than male members. Women, with an eye toward their reelection goals, will be more likely to structure their legislative activities to reflect their constituents' concerns, and nothing focuses a legislator's activity on a certain policy like membership on a committee. A seat on a given committee gives a member the opportunity to work on all of the bills members have introduced within the committee's policy jurisdiction. As a result, canny reelection- and constituent-minded legislators seek out assignments on committees that deal with policy areas of particular importance to their voters. Committee membership then gives them opportunities to shape policy, take public positions, procure federal spending, and be seen as an effective proponent of their voters' interests within that policy area.

In particular, the need for a strong reelection record drives women to seek out committee assignments that both suggest they are focused on the concerns of their constituents and provide a mechanism for directly addressing those needs via the legislative process. For example, former Representative Northup mentioned working on issues surrounding the airport in her district, as well as health care and the lock and dam. She secured a spot on the Appropriations Committee, and placements on two key subcommittees: Labor, Health and Human Services, and Education; as well as Transportation and Treasury. She eventually secured funding for two new bridges over the Ohio River, among other things (*Politics in America*, 2004, 419). Similarly, one of our interviewees noted that "in my House experience, [the member] was on the Transportation and Infrastructure Committee, and I remember that although that might not have been her personal policy passion, the priority there grew because that was an important issue back home."

Previous studies have explored how members' electoral demands influence their committee assignments, but primarily through the lens of larger theories of congressional organization. As a result, much of the literature examining which members have seats on which committee does so in the context of members' ideology or party loyalty (e.g., Cox and McCubbins 1993; Krehbiel 1991; Maltzman 1998). There have been comparatively few studies on gender disparities in committee assignments, and the most thorough of these focuses on the requests that members make to their respective party organizations, which control committee assignments (Frisch and Kelly 2006). They find few differences between men and women in the patterns by which members request committee seats. They also find that Democratic women are equally as likely as men to receive an assignment they requested, but, among Republicans, women are less likely to receive a requested assignment. Once again, however, this study focuses on absolute differences between men and women, rather than on differences that are contingent upon the constraints voters place on Congress members of each gender.

On the other hand, Adler (2002) argues that to examine the effect *voters* have on committee assignments one must look at the district, rather than any measure of legislator behavior. Adler devises district-level measures of the extent to which voters demand committee-controlled goods and services. In other words, these measures reflect constituents' level of need for the goods and services that are provided by each committee. In doing so, Adler notes that nearly any committee assignment could help a member of Congress win reelection if given to the right member of Congress and used skillfully. This is a powerful critique of previous scholarship, which tended to categorize committees into three types: "constituency committees" that allow members of Congress to direct goods to specific groups of voters; "control committees" that are simultaneously the most powerful committees and the most desirable to sit on; and "policy committees" that work on policy areas of broad national importance, but are neither directly helpful toward reelection nor especially powerful (Deering and Smith 1997; Fenno 1973). Under Adler's formulation, sitting on Foreign Affairs—traditionally considered a policy committee—can be helpful to a member of Congress representing a district with a heavily immigrant population. Similarly, sitting on the Judiciary Committee—also a policy committee, which has jurisdiction over most crime legislation—can be helpful to a member whose constituents are particularly concerned about crime. Even committee assignments that at first glance seem incompatible with a member's district can be bent to the member's advantage. Shirley Chisholm, the nation's first female African American member of Congress, represented an urban New York district. When she first arrived in Congress, Democratic leaders assigned her to the Agriculture Committee, which on the surface has no relevance to most of her constituents. Many interpreted the move as an effort to impede her legislative and electoral career. However, she used Agriculture's jurisdiction over food aid to the needy to expand the food stamp program and create a new aid program for women, infants, and children. Both programs were important to the relatively poor district she represented, and helped establish her reputation as an advocate for her constituents (Chisholm 1970).

Adler thus argues that most if not all committees should be composed of members whose constituents express the highest levels of demand for the goods and services provided by each committee. In other words, when it comes to measurable aspects of House districts and states that indicate the extent to which a committee's jurisdiction is salient to a constituency, committee members should be outliers, rather than broadly representative of the entire chamber. Using a Monte Carlo simulation procedure, he presents convincing evidence that members generally sit on committees that work to serve the demands of their specific constituents.[3]

We build on Adler's work and examine whether female committee members are more likely to be outliers with respect to constituent needs than their male committee members. Committee work is a powerful tool members use to represent their constituents. We argue that female legislators' heightened desire to faithfully represent their constituents leads them to pursue committee assignments for reelection and constituent purposes. We therefore predict that women are more likely than men to sit on committees that are best suited to addressing the needs and demands of their constituents.

To test this proposition, we utilize Adler's (2002) methodology. He utilized a Monte Carlo simulation to test whether members of a standing committee are representative of the chamber as a whole in terms of the extent to which constituents have an interest in (we will use the word "demand") the policy areas within the committee's jurisdiction (see Adler 2002, 50–52, for an extended discussion of the choice of this method; see also Groseclose 1994). We focus on standing committees in both the House and the Senate between the 103rd and 110th Congresses. Monte Carlo simulations allow us to re-create the membership of each committee by repeatedly drawing a series of random samples of members, each of which is the same size as the actual committee during each Congress. For example, during the 103rd Congress, the House Agriculture Committee had forty-eight members. We thus drew a random sample of forty-eight representatives (out of the entire 435 who served during the 103rd Congress) to create a simulated House Agriculture Committee. But instead of doing this just once, we repeated the process 10,000 times to create 10,000 simulated 103rd Congress House Agriculture Committees. Indeed, we used this process to create 10,000 randomly drawn simulations of each standing committee included in our analysis (more than ten in each chamber), for each Congress. The simulations were conducted without replacement.

Adler used the simulation process to determine whether the actual committee members have higher-demand constituencies than the members of the corresponding simulated committees. He did this by adopting a measure of district demand for the policy area each committee covers; we discuss these demand measures in more detail below. Adler observed the median levels of demand for each of the randomly drawn simulated committees (i.e., he collected a dataset comprising the 10,000 medians, one for each simulated committee), and compared those measures to the median level of demand of the corresponding actual committee. This procedure allowed him to test the null hypothesis that committee composition is unrelated to constituent demand. That is, if the actual committee's median level of demand is higher than the median level of demand for 95 percent of the simulated committees, he rejected the null hypothesis of there being no relationship between committee composition and constituency demand at the 95 percent confidence level.

We adapt this procedure to test our prediction that female legislators are more likely than their male colleagues to join committees that best serve their constituents. To operationalize districts' and states' levels of demand for the committees' goods and services, we turn to Adler's measures. Table 6.1a provides a complete list of the district or state-level measures that were used to create the demand measure for each House committee, while table 6.1b does the same for the Senate committees. To create a single need measure that reflects the scope of issues under each committee's jurisdiction, Adler standardized each component variable (meaning that the raw measures were transformed such that each has a mean of zero and a standard deviation of one), and then added them together; we likewise created a single summary measure of demand for each committee.[4] We then calculated, using these demand measures for each member, the median constituent need score for each simulated committee, as well as the male and female contingents of the actual committees.

We therefore do not compare the simulated medians to the full committee median. Rather, we separately compare the simulated medians to the median of the male contingent on the committee, and then to the female contingent on the committee. Our theory predicts that female legislators are more likely than their male colleagues to join those committees that best serve their constituents, and thus allow them to better substantively represent their districts and the people who live in them. We thus formally expect that the median score of women actually on the committee will be higher (i.e., reflect more constituent need for that policy) than the corresponding median score of simulated committees. Stated differently, we expect that committee females will represent outliers in terms of constituent need, as compared to the medians of our simulated committees. We further hypothesize that we will *not* see a similar relationship when we compare the median for men actually on the committee and the median scores for the simulated committees. We operationalize this by observing the number of committees in which the female contingent's median demand level is significantly greater than 95 percent of the 10,000 simulated committees and the male contingent median demand level is not. Committees that fall into this category we count as confirming our hypothesis. Committees where the opposite is true (where the male contingent's median is greater than 95 percent of the simulated committee's medians, but the female contingent's median is not) are evidence against

TABLE 6.1A. House Committees and Demand Measures

Committee	Demand Measures
Agriculture	Percentage of district population employed in farming, fishing, and wildlife
	Percentage of district population living in rural farming areas
Armed Services	Number of military installations in district
	Number of major military installations in district
	Size of the district's military (noncivilian) workforce
Banking, Finance and Urban Affairs	Percentage of district population living in urban areas
	Percentage of district population that is African American
	Percentage of district population that is unemployed
	District contains one of the fifty largest cities
	Size of the district's banking assets
	Percentage of district population employed in finance, insurance, and real estate
Education and Labor	Percentage of district population employed in blue–collar industries
	Percentage of district workforce that is unionized
	Percentage of population attending public elementary and high schools
	Median family income (multiplied by –1 to reflect that lower income reflects higher need)
Energy and Commerce	Percentage of district population employed in wholesale and retail trade
	Percentage of district population employed in transportation or public utilities
Foreign Affairs	Percentage of district population that is foreign born
Government Operations	Percentage of district population employed by the federal government
	District is within 100 miles of Washington, DC
Judiciary	Percentage of district population living in urban areas
	Percentage of district population that is African American
	District contains one of the fifty largest cities
Merchant Marine and Fisheries	District borders a coastal area or the Great Lakes
	District contains a Merchant Marine, Coast Guard, or state maritime academy
	District is in a city with one of the twenty-five most active ports
Natural Resources (named Interior and Insular Affairs prior to 1993)	Amount of district acreage owned by the National Park Service and Bureau of Land Management
	Population per square mile of district (multiplied by -1 to reflect that smaller population density reflects higher need)
Post Office and Civil Service	Percentage of district population employed by the federal government
Transportation and Public Works	Percentage of district population employed in transportation and public utilities
	Percentage of district population employed in construction
	Relative flood-potential level of district
	Percentage of district population that is unemployed
Veterans' Affairs	Percentage of district population who are veterans
	Number of beds in district VA hospital

Note: Adapted from Adler 2002, table 1, 56–59.

TABLE 6.1B. Senate Committees and Demand Measures

Committee	Demand Measures
Agriculture	Percentage of state population employed in farming, fishing, and wildlife
	Percentage of state population living in rural farming areas
Armed Services	Number of military installations in state
	Number of major military installations in state
	Size of the state's military (noncivilian) workforce
Banking, Housing and Urban Affairs	Percentage of state population living in urban areas
	Percentage of state population that is African American
	Percentage of state population that is unemployed
	Size of the state's banking assets
	Percentage of state population employed in finance, insurance, and real estate
	Population per square mile of state
Health, Education, Labor and Pensions	Percentage of state population employed in blue-collar industries
	Percentage of state workforce that is unionized
	Percentage of state population attending public elementary and high schools
	Median state family income (multiplied by -1 to reflect that lower income reflects higher need)
Energy and Natural Resources	Amount of state acreage owned by the National Park Service and Bureau of Land Management
	Population per square mile of state (multiplied by -1 to reflect that smaller population density reflects higher need)
Foreign Affairs	Percentage of state population that is foreign born
Government Operations	Percentage of state population employed by the federal government
Judiciary	Percentage of state population living in urban areas
	Percentage of state population that is African American
	Population per square mile of state
Environment and Public Works	Percentage of state population employed in transportation and public utilities
	Percentage of state population employed in construction
	Relative flood-potential level of state
	Percentage of state population that is unemployed
Commerce, Science and Transportation	Percentage of state population employed in transportation and public utilities
	Percentage of state population employed in construction
	Percentage of state population identifying employment as wholesale or retail trade
	Port activity within state
Veterans' Affairs	Percentage of state population who are veterans
	Number of beds in VA hospitals across the state

Note: Adapted from Adler 2002, table 1, 56–59.

the hypothesis. Committees where both the male and female contingents' medians are above or below also do not provide support for our hypothesis.

Table 6.2 reports the findings for the House, while table 6.3 reports the findings for the Senate. Each square in the grid represents a committee-Congress. A "+" in a particular square indicates that the actual female committee median reflects a significantly higher constituent demand score than the simulated committee medians *and* that we do *not* see a similar relationship for committee males. That is, a "+" indicates observations that confirm our hypothesized relationship. Conversely, a "-" captures instances where the actual male committee median is significantly higher than the constituent demand score for the simulated committee medians *and* there is not a similarly significant relationship for committee females—observations that offer disconfirming evidence. Blank entries mean that either both committee females and committee males are outliers, or that neither group is an outlier. For the purposes of this analysis, we utilize a cut-point of $p<.05$, or the finding that fewer than 500 of the simulated committee medians produced a constituent need score greater than the actual female committee median. The appendix provides the full results, expressed as p-values, of the comparisons for each committee in each Congress of the simulated committee medians to the actual committee median, female median, and male median. As interested readers will see in the appendix, with member-

TABLE 6.2. Comparison of Female and Male Committee Medians to Simulated Committee Medians for the House of Representatives, 103rd–110th Congresses

	103rd	104th	105th	106th	107th	108th	109th	110th
Committee								
Agriculture								
Armed Services				–				
Banking	+	+	+	+	+			+
Commerce		–	+					
Education								
Foreign	–	–						
Governmental Affairs					+	–	–	–
Judiciary	+	+	+	+	+	+	+	
MMF		–	–	–	–	–	–	–
Resources								
POCS	+	–	–	–	–	–	–	–
Transportation	+	+	+	+	+	+	+	+
Veterans	+	+		+				

Notes: The Merchant Marine and Fisheries Committee (MMF) was folded into the Resources Committee as of the 104th Congress

The Post Office and Civil Service Committee (POCS) was dissolved as of the 104th Congress

Constituent data does not exist for the Governmental Affairs committee as of the 108th Congress

ship on the Agriculture Committee in both chambers reflecting this finding particularly well, there are instances where both committee males and committee females are outliers in terms of constituent need. The tables below report these findings as null, however, since we are interested in those times in which only committee females are outliers in terms of constituent demand. The main results we provide in this chapter thus present the strongest possible test of our theory.

Overall, our results provide fairly strong evidence that female members take advantage of committee memberships to serve as representatives for their constituents to a much greater extent than men do. Examining table 6.2, we see that of the eighty-seven total simulation tests conducted for the House of Representatives, in twenty-seven instances (31% of the observations) our expectations are confirmed: in these instances, committee females are outliers relative to the chamber, while their male counterparts are not. In contrast, there are only four cases (5%) where the male committee contingent is an outlier while the female committee contingent is not. In the remaining observations, either both genders are outliers in comparison to the chamber or neither are. Moreover, there are some interesting patterns within committees: female committee members are consistently constituent preference outliers (while males are not) on the House Banking, Judiciary, and Transportation Committees. For Armed Services and Foreign Affairs, however, the only significant results show committee males as outliers. In contrast, only three Congresses show significant results for the Veterans Affairs Committee, and in all three instances female committee members are again the constituent need outliers.

Turning to the results for the Senate in table 6.3, we find even more convincing evidence of women being stronger constituent need outliers than men. Of the seventy-seven total simulation tests conducted for the Senate, our hypothesis is confirmed in forty-five, or 58 percent, of the tests. In contrast, in only seven instances (9.1%) are committee males constituent need outliers where women are not. The disconfirming observations, moreover, are limited almost exclusively to the Energy and Natural Resources Committee. Strikingly, committee females are outliers in every Congress for the Commerce, Science and Transportation Committee and the Environment and Public Works Committee, and in every Congress but one for the Judiciary Committee as well as the Banking, Housing, and Urban Affairs Committee. In fact, female senators were constituent need outliers on every standing committee but two during both the 109th and 110th Congresses. Perhaps most notable, particularly in contrast to the findings for the House, female committee members on the Armed Services and Foreign Affairs Committees—two areas where female legislators may be plagued by gender trait stereotypes held by voters—are again outliers in the majority of Congresses. Only with the Governmental Affairs and Energy and Natural Resources Committees do we not see at least some confirmation of our primary hypothesis.

Overall, we find that female members of Congress, and particularly the Senate, seek out committee assignments that best help them advocate for their constituents' interests and concerns, and do so to a considerably greater extent than men do. The result is that female members are thus also better positioned to help influence policy change in these areas. As many of our interviewees noted, the areas where members of Congress can have the most impact are those that fall within the jurisdiction of the committees they sit on. And our results suggest that female members are much more cognizant than their male colleagues of their constituents' interests, as opposed to other potential committee procurement goals (see Fenno 1973).

Policy representation extends simply beyond sitting on relevant committees, however, to the legislative activities members undertake. We now turn our attention to bill introductions and then roll-call votes to investigate potential gender-based differences in terms of policy congruence between legislative activity and a member's constituents.

TABLE 6.3. Comparison of Female and Male Committee Medians to Simulated Committee Medians for the Senate, 103rd–110th Congresses

	103rd	104th	105th	106th	107th	108th	109th	110th
Committee								
Agriculture	n/w	n/w					–	+
Armed Services	+	+				+	+	+
BHUA		+	+	n/w	+	+	+	+
Commerce, Science and Transportation	+	+	+	+	+	+	+	+
Energy and Natural Resources	n/w	n/w	–	–	–	–	–	–
Environment and Public Works	+	+	+	+	+	+	+	+
Foreign Affairs			+	+	+	+	+	+
Governmental Affairs	n/w	n/w					–	–
HELP						+	+	
Judiciary	+	+	+	+	+		+	+
Veterans	n/w	n/w					+	+

Notes: The Governmental Affairs Committee was dissolved as of the 109th Congress
"n/w" = No women served on the committee during that Congress

Bill Introductions

> You probably find that women do introduce legislation that has more of a direct effect on their constituents.
>
> —Congressional staffer, interview with authors, summer 2013

Chapter 5 explores potential gender differences in legislative activity in terms of the *volume* of legislative activity members undertake. In accordance with our theory, we find that women not only introduce more bills overall than their male colleagues, but (particularly in the House) the bills they introduce appear to be disproportionately made up of messaging bills. We thus also find confirmation that female legislators agree with Mayhew's premise that "the electoral payment is for positions rather than for effects" (1974, 132). However, while women may introduce more bills, and more bills that are targeted at reelection efforts, to what degree do women introduce bills that are directly linked to the needs of their districts?

The core assumption underlying Mayhew's claim is that legislators will take positions on issues their constituents care about; not simply any position will do. Districts vary as to which constituent needs matter most. Some districts are urban while others are rural; some contain large military installations while others house a sizable technology sector. The higher a district's need in a certain area grows, the more likely a legislator should introduce bills and focus other position-taking activities on that topic. Previous studies consistently find links between representatives' actions and constituent priorities. For example, Woon (2009) finds a fairly clear link between constituent demand and the likelihood that a senator will introduce more bills on a certain topic; he also finds, however, that committee membership is the best predictor of whether senators will introduce bills in specific policy areas. Hansen and Treul (2015) recently find that representation of lesbians, gays, and bisexuals is more likely by representatives with larger numbers of LGB constituents. Similarly, studies find that minority groups experience increased substantive representation as their numbers within a district grow (e.g., Bishin 2009; Browning, Marshall, and Tabb 1986; Haider-Markel, Joslyn, and Kniss 2000).[5]

As laid out above, we argue that this constituent-specific policy activity will be more likely among women than men, due to women's heightened electoral concerns. The desire to be reelected causes women to pay more attention to their constituents' needs, and this in turn leads them to be better substantive representatives. Bill introductions, even for messaging bills, still involve a substantial commitment of time and resources (Schiller 1995); a member must thus consciously choose to focus on an issue to draft a bill, while accordingly decreasing her attention on another policy area. A large number of previous studies have addressed the question of gender differences in substantive representation from the vantage point of whether women better represent women. These studies, building on broader representational theories, investigate whether women are more likely, in part because of their gender, to introduce bills that address women's issues. Their results consistently confirm this prediction: female members introduce more bills that concern women's issues than males (Saint-Germain 1989; Thomas and Welch 1991; Swers 2002).

However, female representatives do not only represent women, and women themselves are not a monolithic entity. Rather, female representatives—indeed, all representatives—represent a broad swath of constituents with a variety of interests. We thus hypothesize that one implication of women's gendered vulnerability is that they will seek to substantively represent the interests of all of their constituents more closely than their male colleagues do in terms of their bill sponsorship activities. We thus expect to see that, as district needs grow in a particular area, female representatives will be more likely than their male colleagues to introduce bills related to those needs.

We test this hypothesis by reexamining the bill introduction data utilized in chapter 5, but examining the bills members introduce within each of five specific policy areas: agriculture, crime, labor, health care, and defense. We then estimate models predicting the number of bills a member introduces in these areas. The models are similar to those in chapter 5 (see table 5.2 for an explication of variables and their coding). We again control for seniority (logged), ideological extremity, district ideology, and whether the member serves on the relevant committee of jurisdiction; we also add in a control for the overall number of bills sponsored by each member.

All else being equal, we expect that members representing districts with higher constituent demand indicators should introduce more bills in that policy area; we posit this relationship will be stronger for female members than for males. To capture this relationship, we introduce a constituent demand indicator for each policy area. We then interact the constituent demand indicator with *Female*. If the bills that women introduce are more closely tied to their constituents' interests, then the coefficients on the interaction terms should be positive and significant. This would indicate that the number of bills a woman introduces within a policy area rises more sharply with voters' level of demand than the number of bills introduced by a male legislator—even if both are being at least somewhat responsive to their districts. For agriculture bills, we use as our constituent demand indicator the percentage of the member's district living in rural farming areas. To capture district demand for crime-related bills, we utilize the percentage of the district that lives in an urban area. We operationalize district demand for defense-related policies as the number of active military members living in the district. Constituent demand for health-care-related bills is measured as the percentage of the district over age sixty-five. Finally, we operationalize district demand for labor-oriented policies as the percentage of the district living in a household with at least one union member. A summary of these district demand measures appears in table 6.4.

Table 6.5 reports the policy-specific bill introduction models for the Senate while table 6.6 reports them for the House. We find very little support for our theory in the Senate. In all of the policy areas except Labor, the coefficient for *Demand* is positive and significant, but the coefficients for the interaction are not. These results suggest that, among senators, males and females target their bill introductions in these five issue areas to constituent demand to a roughly equal extent.

Conversely, in the House (see table 6.6), we see that in three policy areas—agriculture, health care, and defense—the interaction between *Female* and *Demand* is significant and positive at $p<.05$, and this relationship is similarly significant and positive at $p<.10$ with crime bills. These findings suggest facially that female legislators introduce more bills in these policy areas than male legislators do when the level of district demand is high. It is difficult, however, to understand the substantive effects of this relationship, particularly given the use of an interaction term in the estimation. We therefore graphically present in figures 6.1a–d the predicted probability of the number of bills in each policy domain that both male and female legislators will introduce as the level of district demand increases from its minimum level to its maximum; in each figure, the dotted line represents the predicted probability for males and the solid line represents the predicted probability for females.

The predicted probabilities for agriculture-related bill introductions

TABLE 6.4. Policy Demand Measures in Estimations of Bill Introduction

Policy Area	Measure
Agriculture	% of residents living in rural farm areas
Crime	% of residents living in urban areas
Labor	% of residents belonging to a labor union (state-wide)
Health Care	% of residents over the age of 65
Defense	% of residents serving in the military

in figure 6.1a reflects the relationship between the number of agriculture bills a member introduces and the percentage of voters in the district who live in rural farm areas. Even when district demand is at its highest, males at most introduce less than one agriculture-related bill. Alternatively, the number of bills female representatives introduce spikes once the percentage employed in farming exceeds 3 percent; those with districts with the highest amount of demand are predicted to introduce twice as many bills as males that address agriculture-related issues. What is most notable about these results is the fact that no female represents a district with more than 6 percent living in a rural farm area, while some males represent districts where the percentage in rural farming areas hits 10 percent, or almost double the level of constituent need.

Figure 6.1b addresses crime bills. Here, the picture is more nuanced,

TABLE 6.5. Policy–Specific Bill Introduction in the Senate

	Crime	Agriculture	Labor	Health Care	Defense
Female	–.259	–.747*	.262	1.10**	.461
	(.220)	(.322)	(.552)	(.428)	(.615)
Demand	.751***	14.9***	–.0002	12.4***	13.9***
	(.215)	(2.05)	(.009)	(1.36)	(3.64)
Demand*female	–.492	21.0	–.017	–5.91^	–32.7
	(.115)	(16.0)	(.024)	(3.28)	(64.6)
Lagged vote	–.085	.416	1.60*	1.95***	1.32*
	(.520)	(.743)	(.755)	(.356)	(.605)
In–cycle	.027	.168	.283*	.204***	.089
	(.071)	(.108)	(.114)	(.055)	(.096)
Committee	.947***	.575***	1.00***	.404***	.481***
	(.071)	(.126)	(.132)	(.063)	(.097)
NOMINATE	–.173^	–.513***	–.249	–.376***	–.267^
	(.099)	(.146)	(.172)	(.077)	(.138)
State ideology	–.332	.600	.841	.388	.088
	(.548)	(.945)	(1.02)	(.440)	(.829)
Seniority	.025	–.126*	–.159*	–.012	.214***
	(.042)	(.063)	(.071)	(.035)	(.061)
Party leader	.219	–.552*	1.33***	–.049	.375
	(.306)	(.280)	(.324)	(.157)	(.274)
State Size	.014	.187**	.145*	–.182***	.052
	(.044)	(.064)	(.063)	(.028)	(.048)
Bills sponsored	.022***	.006^	.011**	.028***	.015***
	(.002)	(.004)	(.004)	(.001)	(.003)
Constant	–.471	–1.13^	–1.82**	–2.50***	–1.51**
	(.428)	(.617)	(.665)	(.314)	(.511)
N	499	499	499	499	499
Log likelihood	-861.4	-599.6	-565.6	-993.4	-770.2

though it still provides support for our theory. For both males and females, a higher percentage of urban dwellers leads to an increase in crime-related bill introductions. However, the upward trend for female legislators is more pronounced, particularly once the percentage of urban residents cross the 50 percent threshold.

Figure 6.1c, reflecting defense-related bill introductions, reveals little change in the number of bills a male representative introduces as the number of active-duty military members rises. Alternatively, the probability of a female representative introducing defense-related bills steadily increases as the number of active military constituents grows. However, we do note that the overall substantive effect is rather small as most members will never introduce a defense-related bill; those that do, according to our analysis, are most likely to be females with high levels of district demand.

Finally, figure 6.1d, which presents the predicted probability of the number of bills a representative will introduce related to health care, presents the starkest confirmation of our theory. There is almost no change in the probability of the number of health-care-related bills introduced

TABLE 6.6. Policy–Specific Bill Introduction in the House

	Crime	Agriculture	Labor	Health Care	Defense
Female	–.311	.019	–.533	–.107	–.156
	(.288)	(.189)	(.411)	(.193)	(.120)
Demand	.469***	11.5***	.005	1.51*	1.58
	(.113)	(1.32)	(.005)	(.664)	(2.21)
Demand*female	.571^	15.8*	.010	4.41**	11.4*
	(.327)	(6.32)	(.015)	(1.45)	(4.86)
Lagged vote	–.002	–.003	.003	–.002	–.006*.
	(.002)	(.003)	(.003)	(.002)	(.003)
Committee	1.05***	1.23***	1.19***	.739***	.686***
	(.064)	(.109)	(.083)	(.050)	(.075)
NOMINATE	.252***	–.192^	–.376***	–.286***	–.116
	(.007)	(.104)	(.087)	(.054)	(.077)
District ideology	.008**	–.007^	–.018***	.006**	–.014***
	(.003)	(.004)	(.003)	(.002)	(.003)
Seniority	–.106*	.254***	.097	.161***	.333***
	(.044)	(.066)	(.059)	(.035)	(.052)
Party leader	–.377	–1.60	.283	–.607^	–1.28*
	(.391)	(1.02)	(.305)	(.333)	(.556)
Bills sponsored	.038***	.038***	.020***	.034***	.025***
	(.002)	(.004)	(.003)	(.001)	(.002)
Constant	–1.12***	–1.80***	–.369***	–.734***	.048
	(.210)	(.357)	(.273)	(.169)	(.241)
N	2168	2168	2168	2168	2168
Log likelihood	–2317	–1316	–1694	–3173	–2086

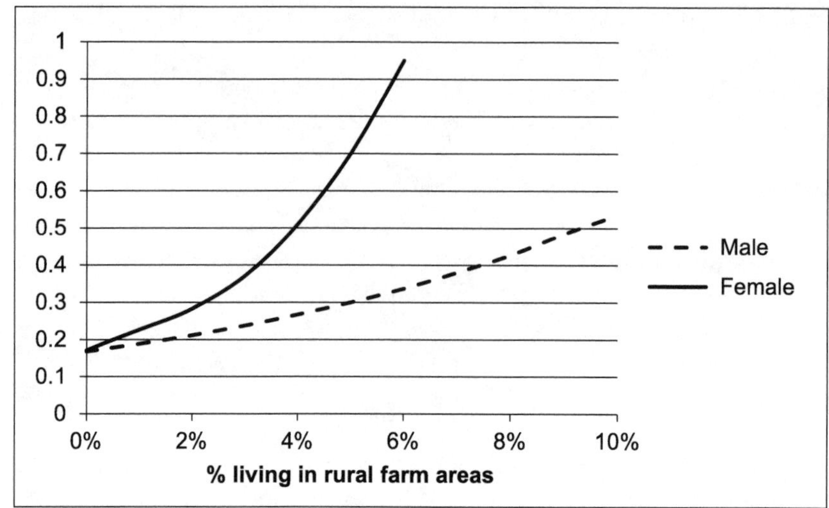

b

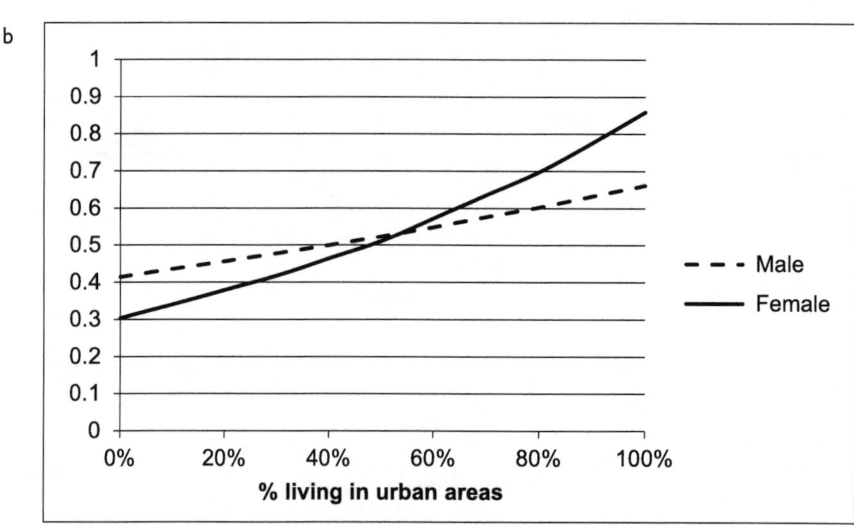

Figure 6.1. Policy-specific bill introduction among male and female members of the House

c

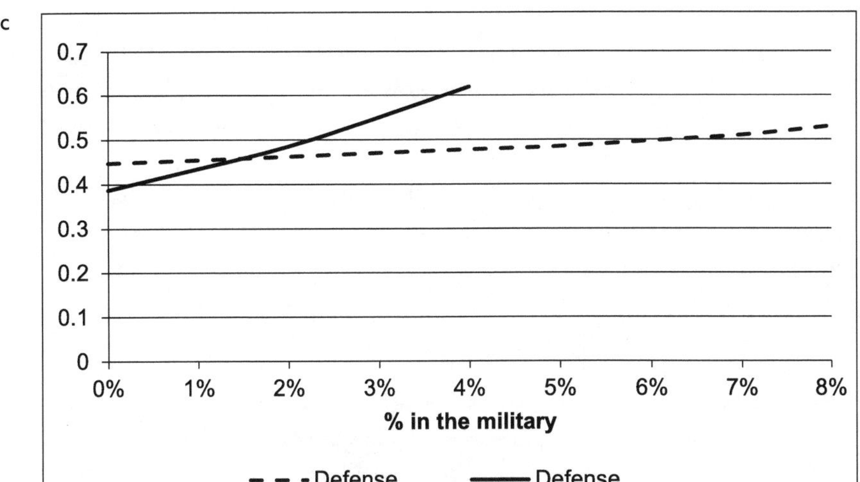
0.7
0.6
0.5
0.4
0.3
0.2
0.1
0
0%
1%
2%
3%
4%
5%
6%
7%
8%
% in the military
Defense
Defense

d

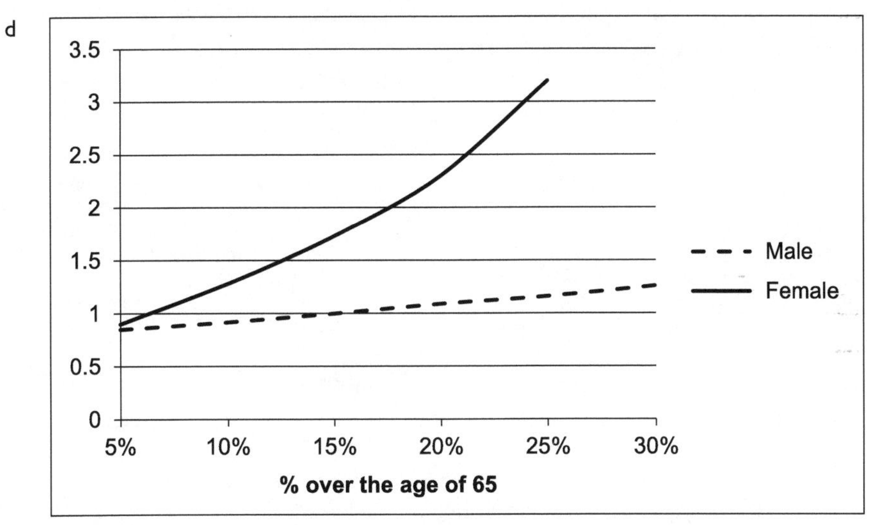
3.5
3
2.5
2
1.5
1
0.5
0
5%
10%
15%
20%
25%
30%
% over the age of 65
Male
Female

by male legislators as the percentage of voters over the age of sixty-five increases; all else being equal, males introduce one health care bill. Comparatively, the number for women increases steadily as the percentage of the elderly climbs. Women with the highest level of constituent demand are predicted to introduce three times as many health care bills as women with the lowest demand—and three times as many bills as their male colleagues who represent districts with the highest possible percentage of elderly constituents.

Overall, while confirmation of our theory is limited solely to the House of Representatives, we find clear evidence that female representatives' legislative activities more closely hew to the needs of their districts. As constituent demand increases in a particular policy area, female representatives are increasingly likely to introduce bills that address these issues. Female representatives more closely align their legislative priorities with those of their constituents. The Senate findings are admittedly surprising, particularly given the close correlation between constituent demand and committee assignments for female senators. One potential answer was mentioned by a number of interviewees—that given the paucity of women chairs of committees in the Senate, but also the propensity for these committees to offer large packages of legislation, women's names may not be seen as frequently. A distinct but related suggestion was that, particularly in the Senate, active members will introduce amendments in committee as a way to get their legislative priorities enacted; our data only capture stand-alone bills. This paradox presents an interesting question for future research.

Roll Call Behavior

> [Other members I worked for] would go to the floor and they would vote for the Republican line every time. There was no prep work involved; it was whatever the party said they were able to do and it was an easy vote. With [female Representative X] that was not the case. There was a lot of deliberation, and almost every vote . . . goes to what her district wants. There was an electoral aspect to that.
>
> —Congressional staffer, interview with authors, summer 2013

The final area of substantive representation we explore concerns members' roll-call votes. Similar to the bills members introduce, roll-call votes give members clear opportunities to take positions on issues, and show their constituents that they are actively working to advance their interests.

Electorally motivated members must be concerned with whether their constituents perceive them to be representing their constituents' interests (Mayhew 1974). A number of studies show that roll-call voting is closely tied to constituents' ideologies or policy preferences. For instance, Glazer and Robbins (1985) take advantage of decennial redistricting to show that House members whose districts become more liberal (conservative) subsequently become more liberal (conservative) in their voting behavior. Moreover, members with greater electoral concerns are less likely to deviate from their district's preferences, as such deviations can lead to increased electoral risks. Thus several studies highlight that the degree of correspondence between constituent preferences and member voting behavior varies with members' electoral vulnerability, as traditionally measured by lagged vote share (Ansolabehere, Snyder, and Stewart 2001; Canes-Wrone, Rabinovich, and Volden 2007; Erikson and Wright 2000; Griffin 2006).[6] Thus, even more so than bill introductions, roll-call votes capture the degree to which members actively substantively represent their constituents.

We argue that since female members face a more difficult reelection environment, they will vote with their district's preferences to a greater extent than their male colleagues. A number of studies have examined gender differences in roll-call voting by investigating whether female legislators are more likely than male legislators to support legislation on topics of interest to women (Reingold 1992), or vote differently on roll-call votes generally (Gehlen 1977; Leader 1977; Welch 1985; but see Reingold 2000). We instead propose that, due to their gendered vulnerability, female members more generally hew closer to their district's preferences in roll-call voting than male members.

The study of the relationship between members' roll-call voting and district preferences has typically been most closely associated with investigations of the marginality hypothesis (see, e.g., Griffin 2006). This hypothesis proposes that members who are electorally vulnerable in the traditional sense (i.e., those who are elected from marginal districts) are more likely to vote with their constituencies than other members of Congress. Following this literature, we construct a measure of the degree to which a member's roll-call voting corresponds with his or her voters' ideological preferences. We begin with members' DW-NOMINATE scores (Poole and Rosenthal 2006) as our measure of member ideology, and the state or district's presidential vote in the most recent election as the measure of district ideology. For each chamber, we regress members' DW-NOMINATE score on the percentage of the district's presidential vote that went to the Democratic presidential candidate, and a set of Congress-level dummy variables. We then recover the error term for each observation, the difference between

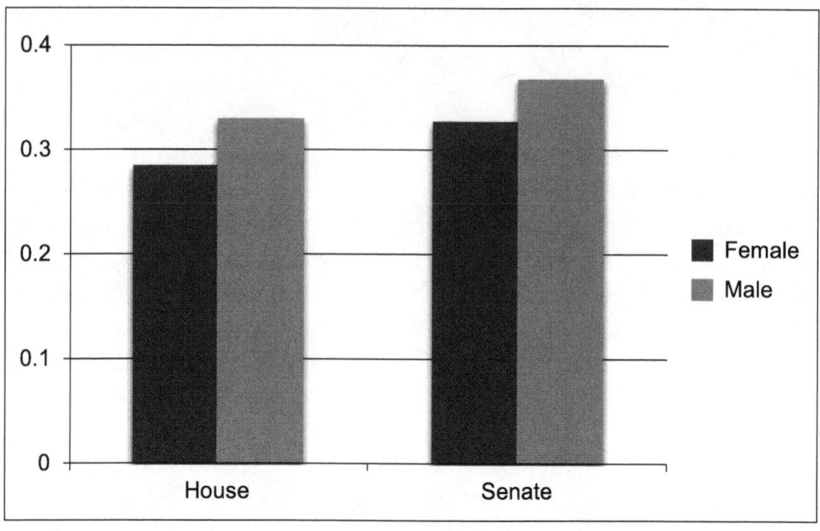

Figure 6.2. Mean male and female deviation scores—House and Senate

the member's actual DW-NOMINATE score and the score predicted by the regression, and take its absolute value. Since a larger value on this error term is associated with a bigger difference between the district and the member, we call this score the *deviation score*. We predict that, on average, women have smaller deviation scores than men.

The bivariate results in figure 6.2 support our hypothesis: female members' deviation scores are lower than male members' scores in both the House and the Senate. To account for possible confounding factors, we use OLS to estimate members' deviation scores in a model in which the primary independent variable is, once again, the dummy variable *Female*. We use the same primary controls as we have throughout this book, with one exception. We omit the variable indicating ideological extremity, as it is derived from the same NOMINATE scores we use to obtain the deviation measure. Thus *ideological extremity* and *deviation score* are determined by the same roll-call votes.

Results are presented in table 6.7. Robust standard errors are in parentheses. Results indicate that, as predicted, the deviation between member roll-call voting and district/state preferences is smaller for female members than it is for male members. Figures 6.3 and 6.4 graphically illustrate these findings using kernel density plots for members' roll call deviation scores. In both chambers, females' mean deviation scores are significantly smaller than those for males; the results are strongest in the Senate. For House members, the male deviation score mean is .32, as compared to .29 for females; this difference is significant at $p<.01$. For senators, the mean deviation score jumps from .32 for females to .38 for males, and is again significant at $p<.01$.

Once again, other factors influence members' deviation scores as well. In the House, senior members deviate less than junior members, while we find no difference according to seniority in the Senate. In both chambers, electorally vulnerable members deviate more than safe members, and members representing highly partisan districts deviate less than members representing relatively moderate districts. Party leaders also have higher deviation scores than the rank and file. Other chamber differences appear with respect to committee membership and position: members of the Rules Committee and committee ranking minority members in the

TABLE 6.7. Roll-Call Deviation from District

	Senate	House
Female	–.080***	–.015*
	(.017)	(.007)
Seniority (logged)	.001	–.008*
	(.007)	(.004)
Lagged vote	–.489***	–.110***
	(.074)	(.021)
In-cycle	–.009	—
	(.011)	
District partisanship	–1.16***	–.748***
	(.071)	(.027)
Majority	.032**	–.080***
	(.012)	(.005)
Party leader	.045*	.068***
	(.023)	(.020)
Appropriations Committee	–.010	–.015*
	(.011)	(.006)
Rules Committee	—	.025*
		(.010)
Committee chair	–.061***	.005
	(.017)	(.015)
Committee RMM	–.012	.033**
	(.017)	(.011)
State Size	.005	—
	(.005)	
Constant	1.30***	.915***
	(.052)	(.017)
N	800	3470
R^2	.412	.384

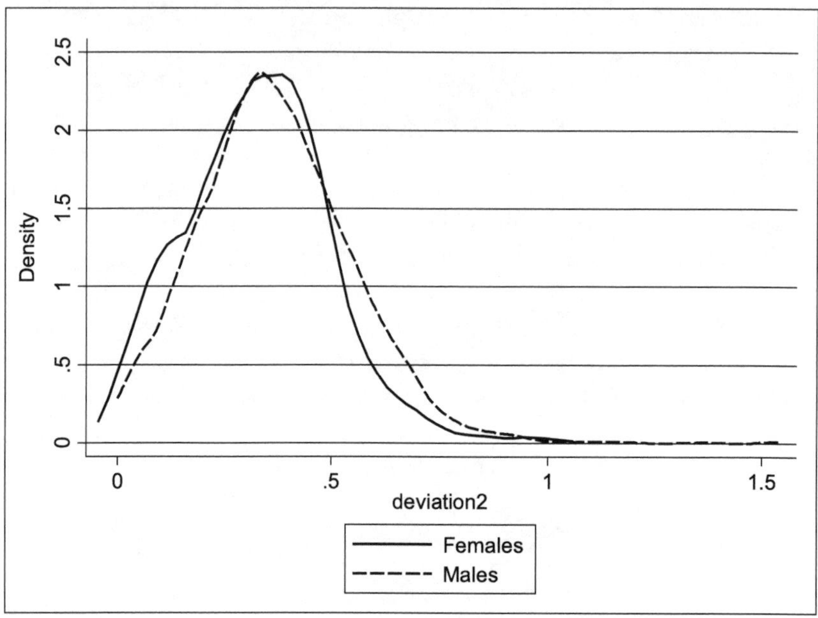

Figure 6.3. Kernel density plots of male and female roll call deviation scores in the House of Representatives

House have higher deviation scores, while members of the House Appropriations Committee deviate less. Alternatively, in the Senate, committee chairs deviate less, but we find no effect for those senators serving on the Appropriations Committee or serving as a committee ranking minority member. Overall, in both chambers female members hew more closely to their constituents' preferences when determining how to vote on legislation pending on the floor.

Conclusion

This chapter turns our attention away from the question of which activities legislators prioritize to their issue and policy priorities. We argue that women's gendered vulnerability leads them to adopt a different strategy of policy prioritization than their male colleagues: one that more faithfully represents their constituents' interests and needs. We find strong support for the notion that women utilize committee assignments, bill introductions (at least in the House), and roll-call votes to advance the desires of

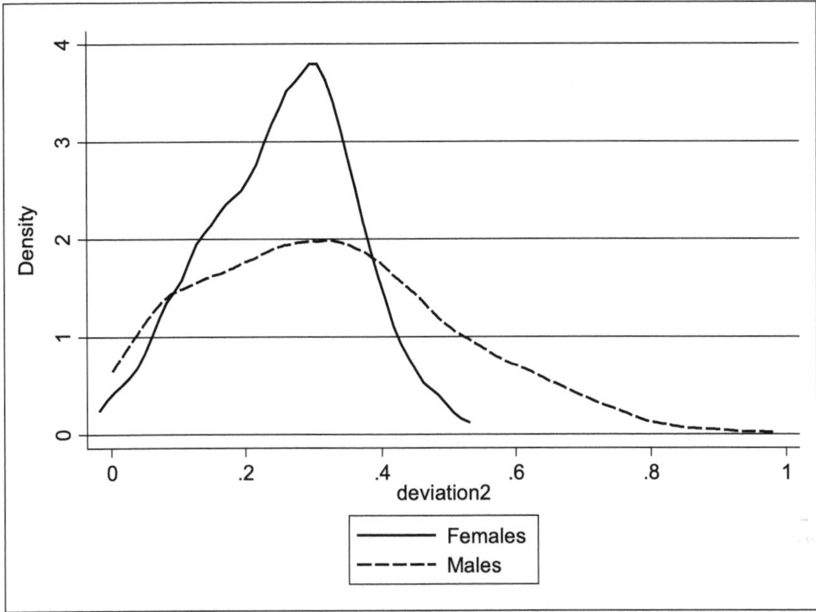

Figure 6.4. Kernel density plots of male and female roll call deviation scores in the Senate

their constituents to a greater degree than men. In other words, we find that women act as better substantive representatives for all of their constituents.

The normative implications of our findings are striking: female legislators more clearly represent their constituents than males do. Thus, while women must be highly—if not overly—concerned with how their actions and issue prioritizations influence their reelection prospects, the result is that women do a better job of reflecting their constituents' interests in the legislative priorities they pursue. Most studies focus simply on the question of whether women better represent women. We find here that women better represent everyone. We turn in the conclusion to a more detailed exploration of the implications of this finding, as well as those throughout the book, for both the concept of gendered vulnerability and the legislative behavior of both men and women once elected to office.

SEVEN

Conclusion

"Nevertheless, She Persisted"

The Story of Women in Elected Office

In February 2017, Senator Elizabeth Warren of Massachusetts was formally silenced on the Senate floor under Senate Rule 19; she was accused of making disparaging remarks against another senator, Jeff Sessions, who was being considered at the time for the position of U.S. attorney general. She was found to "impugn" Sessions when she read Coretta Scott King's 1986 letter to the Senate Judiciary Committee that argued against Sessions' confirmation to the U.S. district court; he was ultimately not confirmed. Perhaps most notably, Senate Majority Leader Mitch McConnell gave the following explanation for why this rarely invoked rule was utilized: "She was warned. She was given an explanation. Nevertheless, she persisted" (see Hawkins 2017).

We have argued throughout this book that not just Warren, but female politicians in general embody this persistence. They must—it is an adaptive trait women have almost evolutionarily developed that allows them to successfully navigate an electoral arena that is much more precarious for them than it is for men. In turn, this same persistence has important implications for female politicians' behavior once in office. Female politicians in both the United States and abroad recognize this dangerous arena. U.S. Representative Barbara Lee (2015) referred to it when she argued that female politicians in the United States face continuing obstacles on their road to elected office, many stemming from broader societal biases:

> How do these deeply entrenched barriers manifest in the political sphere? They turn into roadblocks on the path to power, allowing women to sometimes get a seat at the table, but not at the head of the table. We see the height of those barriers in how hard women have to work to reach the same goals as men. They're present in how women have to do more and be more to be considered qualified. It is made clear by the fact that, even with the accomplishments they earned in their own right—a US Senate seat, the role as a leading diplomat of the free world—they are often defined by their husbands.

Similarly, the first female president of Chile, Michelle Bachelet, suggested that female politicians face "cultural expectations, demands, and if I may say, even some social punishment" as they try to balance the demands of careers versus family (Torregrosa 2012). Bachelet further noted that female politicians must contend with biases about their ability to hold elected office: "People would say, 'She's very nice, but she's not capable, she doesn't have the character to be president'—and worse" (Torregrosa 2012). Christine Todd Whitman, the former governor of New Jersey, argues that party recruitment efforts can also reflect unconscious gender biases: "The party apparatus, while they talk about supporting women, it's more talk than real action. I don't think it's all sexism, but when the people you spend your time with all look like you, you tend to support those people" (Tamari 2014).

Anecdotes and studies alike reflect the notion that women perceive themselves to be less qualified and potentially more vulnerable to attack, particularly in the political world. For example, Kathy Boockvar, a former congressional candidate, stated, "I can't tell you how many times that I've encouraged a woman to run for something—whatever it is, from township supervisor, to state representative, to Congress—and the first response is, 'I'm not qualified'" (Tamari 2014). Similarly, Senator Kirsten Gillibrand stated, "I felt almost embarrassed to say 'I want to run for Congress. . . . I just felt, 'Am I smart enough? Am I tough enough? Can I do this job?' A lot of us doubt ourselves. And it's something we have to overcome" (Forbes 2014). In a different interview Gillibrand noted, "Well, for a lot of women, when they're first running for office, they feel that it's arrogant or conceited that they think they should be elected to something. I certainly felt that way" (Schnall 2015).

But even though barriers to elected office for women continue to exist, women who run also win; in fact, they win at equal rates to men. This presents a conundrum—female candidates clearly overcome these obstacles to be as successful as they are. Additionally, gender socialization coupled with gender biases experienced in the electoral arena create the perception among female legislators that they are uniquely vulnerable to challenge. We thus ask, how do the persistent electoral and social biases facing female incumbents affect them while they are in office? Put another way, what strategies do female legislators adopt to successfully persist?

We show that female legislators pursue a legislative orientation focused on mitigating potential attacks and proving to one's constituents (and colleagues) that they deserve to be in office—and returned come reelection time. Women thus focus more than men on constituent-oriented activities and those with high reelection payoffs. Importantly, these behavioral differences occur on two distinct dimensions: women not only undertake more of these constituent-based activities but they also do them in a way that more accurately reflects their constituency's specific needs and interests. This novel conception of gender differences in legislative behavior moves beyond simply examining certain issue areas or types of activities to offer a comprehensive explanation for clear distinctions in how men and women approach legislating. Our theory successfully explains differences between male and female behavior across four different areas of legislative activity: constituency service, distributive benefits, legislative activity, and policy representation.

Gendered Vulnerability: The Findings

Chapter 2 more fully explicates our theory of gendered vulnerability. We explore both the antecedents to gendered vulnerability—electoral conditions that disfavor female candidates and persistent gender socialization effects—as well as the implications of gendered vulnerability for female legislators. Most prominently, we argue that gendered vulnerability induces women to approach their legislative work in qualitatively different ways than men, with a particular emphasis on constituent- and reelection-oriented activities. Utilizing data on all legislators (in the House and Senate) serving in the 103rd through 110th Congresses, we show in the following four chapters strong support for our theory. Importantly, we also highlight how gendered vulnerability at times manifests itself differently in the House as compared to the Senate.

In chapter 3, we examine nonlegislative constituency work. A key priority for members of Congress is to serve their constituents back home. While many people think about the legislative work members do, members also work to help constituents directly with individualized issues. Members further concentrate on keeping in touch with their constituents, whether through mailed communications (also known as franked mail) or visits back to the district. Chapter 3 presents the first-ever study of gender differences in constituency activities that uses data on the activities themselves, rather than members' self-reports of their activities (or, more accurately, their perceptions of their activities). We argue that women, due to their gendered vulnerability, will concentrate more heavily on these constituency-based activities than men. Our results generally confirm this hypothesis, though we also find some notable chamber differences. In the House, female members utilize their franked mail privileges to a much greater degree than their male counterparts. Whether we examine these constituent communications in terms of dollars spent, the total number of pieces of franked mail sent, or the per capita number of pieces sent, women simply communicate more with the voters back home. Alternatively, in the Senate, an increased focus on constituents results in female senators, relative to male senators, placing more of their staff in the home state—where the work typically focuses solely on constituency services as opposed to the legislative orientation of DC staff.

Chapter 4 turns to the procurement of distributive benefits, otherwise known as "pork." Pork provides an opportunity for legislators to secure funds that are sent directly to one's district, and so the member can quite easily claim credit for this achievement. Pork thus offers one of the best credit-claiming mechanisms for legislators, particularly in terms of highlighting their work on behalf of their constituents. We argue that women take more advantage of this constituent-oriented, credit-claiming opportunity than men. We examine earmark distribution in both chambers as part of the Fiscal Year 2008 Appropriations bills, as well as the distribution of stimulus funds under the American Recovery and Reinvestment Act of 2009. We find clear evidence that female representatives and female senators more successfully procure earmarks for their districts than their male counterparts. Senators' joint earmarking requests also result in more funds sent to a state if one member of the delegation is female. We further find that female House members' districts received more stimulus funds than those of their male colleagues. We do not find a gender difference with respect to stimulus funds in the Senate, but this may be a function of how we attempted to capture senators' influence on the funding decisions.

Chapter 4 also begins to explore the substantive implications of our theory of gendered vulnerability. We posit that women, due to their gendered vulnerability, more heavily prioritize constituent-oriented activities than men; these activities also generally provide clear reelection payoffs. However, our theory is not only that women will concentrate on these activities more, but also that the *content* of their actions will more clearly reflect their constituents' needs and demands. The stimulus funds distributed by the ARRA provide a useful arena to test this hypothesis: since the ARRA's purpose was to stimulate economic recovery, districts with higher poverty rates should have, all else being equal, received more funds than those that were more economically stable. We suggest this effect will be further magnified if the district is also represented by a woman. The results are clear: female representatives representing economically distressed districts procured more stimulus funds than males representing similar constituencies.

Chapters 5 and 6 then turn to the work of legislating. Chapter 5 examines the volume of legislative activity that members undertake, while Chapter 6 investigates the substantive content of that legislative activity. Legislating provides one of the clearest opportunities for members to show their constituents they are working hard for their interests. Members both write and cosponsor bills and resolutions that reflect their voters' needs; by doing so, members take public positions on issues while also showcasing their efforts on behalf of their constituents. The theory of gendered vulnerability proposes that women will be more likely to both sponsor and cosponsor bills and resolutions, and we find exactly that in both the House and the Senate. However, we also argue that females' emphasis on the position-taking aspects of legislating leads to an important side effect: the introduction of an increased proportion of messaging bills as opposed to substantive policy bills. We investigate this phenomenon in two ways, finding support for both: first, bills introduced by women representatives are less likely to move successfully through the legislative process than those introduced by men; while, second, bills introduced by women members in both chambers garner more cosponsors than those offered by men. The dual implication is that women more heavily utilize the position-taking benefits of legislating to show their constituents they are working to represent them—and this emphasis serves them extremely well come election time, but this emphasis on position-taking may result in fewer of women's sponsored bills becoming law. The Senate results suggest, however, that the increased resources granted to senators in general may mitigate female senators' need to make trade-offs between introducing messaging and policy bills.

However, while chapter 5 suggests women are more active in the legislative arena overall, is this heightened activity actually reflecting their constituents' needs? As suggested above, the theory of gendered vulnerability holds that not only will women do more, but those efforts will be more directly targeted to the needs of their constituents, and thus more closely reflect the substantive issues most relevant to their districts. Chapter 6 thus investigates the policy content of legislators' work in three different ways. First, we examine committee assignments. The bulk of legislative work is done within Congress's standing committees, and so members who wish to influence particular areas of policy should seek out assignments on the relevant committees. We argue that women will be more likely to do so than men. We find that in both the House and the Senate, female committee members are, in general, more likely than males to represent districts that directly benefit from the goods and services provided by the committees they sit on. Second, we assess the policy content of the bills introduced by members of Congress. Here, chamber differences emerge: female House members, but not female senators, are more likely than their male counterparts to introduce bills in specific policy areas as the level of district demand increases. Third, we examine members' roll-call votes; we expect that women's roll-call votes will more closely hew to their district's preferences than those of men. Once again, we find that women more accurately reflect their constituents' interests than men, and this finding holds true in both the House and the Senate.

The empirical results presented in chapters 3 through 6 thus reveal clear gender differences in legislative behavior. Importantly, our analyses go beyond most previous studies of potential gender differences to examine both the panoply of activities members engage in as well as the multitude of issues they address on a day to day basis. We examine four distinct areas of legislative activity, while also seeking to understand whether potential gender differences manifest themselves across the legislative spectrum. Our findings clearly indicate that gender matters: women, compared to men, more heavily emphasize constituent-oriented activities—which are also those activities that generally offer the most electoral benefits—while also more closely reflecting their constituents' interests through these activities. And this effect is not limited to women's issues. Rather, it appears across the board, ranging from education to agriculture to defense. Further, our analyses and findings also show that these gender differences are not limited to a single chamber. Rather, they are felt in both the House and the Senate.

We also depart from most previous studies of gender in legislative behavior—and studies of legislative behavior writ large—by examining both the House and the Senate. Investigating both chambers allows us to understand the ways in which gendered vulnerability potentially manifests itself in different ways. Perhaps most notably, while we do uncover some important chamber differences, the consistent finding is that gendered vulnerability influences legislator perceptions as well as legislative behavior in the House and the Senate.

We thus believe that the preceding chapters strongly illuminate our central thesis: women, due to their gendered vulnerability, approach the legislative process in a qualitatively different way than men. Women's perception of vulnerability—grounded in gender socialization and crystallized during the election process—leads them to focus on constituent-oriented and electorally beneficial activities that continually showcase that they deserve to be in Congress. And this orientation is twofold: not only do female legislators engage in these activities more than males, they also do so in a way that is more in line with their constituents' wishes. The ultimate implication is that women provide better substantive representation than men to *all* of their constituents. Even though our empirical explorations are limited to the United States Congress, our theory potentially describes all elected officials. So it may be the case that women's increased attention to constituents extends far beyond the Capitol Building into each of the fifty state capitols, and into local governments as well.

The Implications of Gendered Vulnerability: Are Women Better Representatives Than Men?

We find that women, compared to men, spend more time interacting with constituents personally both in the district and (anecdotally) in Washington, devote more of their staff's attention to casework, send more mail, bring to constituents spending for more federal projects, make more public statements for constituents to consume, are better about keeping those public positions within policy areas their constituents find salient, and are better able to keep their voting records close to (a reasonable proxy of) their constituents' preferences. In ways both big and small, important and frivolous, female members of Congress simply do a better job than men of keeping their constituents in mind.

Does this make women better representatives than men? The answer to that question requires us to consider what makes for a good representative in the first place. Edmund Burke (1968 [1790]) famously proposed two mutually exclusive views of representation: acting as a trustee or a delegate. Under the trustee model of representation, an elected official acts in the best interests of the country as a whole, rather than in constituents' more narrow interest. A representative acting in this mode might take an action that seems to go against her constituents' preferences if she perceives that doing so is the better course for a larger number of people. On the other hand, a representative acting as a delegate explicitly follows the preferences of his or her constituents. Taken to its logical conclusion, this theory of representation implies that a delegate has no individual autonomy, but is elected simply to be an advocate for the aggregate opinions of voters. However, one does not need to go that far to see that a representative who acts as a delegate is much more beholden to voters, and much more reflective of voter preferences, than one who acts as a trustee.

One set of representational acts involves the extent to which members of Congress communicate with their constituents. Members send many different types of messages to voters, and do so in a number of ways. Members communicate policy positions first and foremost, but they also make sure that voters are kept appraised of bills the member is shepherding through Congress, how the member has voted on recent high-profile bills, which high-powered officials the member might have had a meeting with, the spending projects the member is working to bring to the district, local activities or other opportunities for members to interact with constituents, and, for individual constituents, prior casework that the member might have performed. And this information gets to constituents via e-mail, letters, press releases, and other ways as well. Taking all of this together, we find in every place we look that female members have more newsworthy items that they might communicate with voters about (e.g., more sponsored bills, more spending projects) and that female members spend more time communicating these things to voters (they send more letters and possibly spend more time in the district).

Does this make female members of Congress better representatives than men? Here it may not matter whether one thinks about representation through the lens of the delegate or the trustee model of representation. For delegates, the core elements of the theory require that representatives learn *from* their voters (so they can faithfully represent voters' views while in office); it is only a short distance to assume that the reverse is beneficial as well—that representation is enhanced when the representative communicates his or her actions and intentions to constituents early and often. This communication allows voters to better evaluate what representatives are doing in their official capacity and to decide, come election time, whether the representative deserves another term in office. For trustees, this communication can be equally important for voters. Even though representatives in this mold are not beholden to voters' preferences, they still must be selected for office by voters. So voters need information about what members are doing in office just as much in this line of thinking as they do in the delegate perspective. Both perspectives seem to suggest that members who communicate more with their voters are giving those voters a clearer choice when they run for reelection, and are therefore better at fulfilling their representational duties. Regardless of what theory of representation one chooses, women thus appear to make better representatives than men in this respect.

A second set of representative acts is much closer to the central debate between the delegate and the trustee models: policy representation. The most prominent way members represent their voters' policy interests is in their voting records on the floor of the chamber. But there are other ways as well, including sponsoring bills in, and seeking membership on, committees that have jurisdiction over policy areas their voters care about. It is in this area we once again find clear differences between men and women—female representatives consistently hew closer to their voters' policy interests than male representatives do.

Whether or not this makes women normatively better representatives depends on whether one believes that representatives should be trustees or delegates. If you think representatives are or should be delegates, then women are without doubt better representatives than men. Through their floor votes, bill introductions, and committee memberships, female members of Congress present their constituents' interests to their respective chambers much more faithfully than male representatives do. Advocates for the delegate model would view women legislators as model legislators, ensuring that the needs of their constituents are represented and their voices counted during the most important debates of the day; this is the essence of Hanna Pitkin's (1967) conception of substantive representation.

On the other hand, if you think representatives are or should be trustees, women appear to falter compared to men. The trustee model holds that (1) members are to consider the good of the whole nation above the good of their constituents, and (2) members should give their own judgment considerable leeway—if not outright precedence—when deciding issues of substance. The devout trustee aficionado would hold that women are overly beholden to the whims of their constituents, and this prevents them from fulfilling both of these conditions. However, it must be noted that we find only that men reflect their constituents' wishes less than women; it is an open question whether the policies they pursue do in fact meet the first, necessary criteria.

Finally, a third set of representative acts that we examine exists wholly outside the trustee-delegate framework. Here we are speaking of constituent service—primarily casework, but the term also applies to members' garnering federal spending for projects that benefit local voters and also simply making one's self available for meeting with constituents either in Washington, DC, or in the district. These are important aspects of representatives' responsibilities to voters. However, the trustee-delegate framework is so closely tied to whether members adhere to voters' policy preferences that it does not have much to say about whether representatives owe constituents any type of service outside of strict policy responsiveness. As a result, we can simply say that irrespective of the view of representation one takes, women are better than men at performing constituent service. Or, at the very least, they provide their constituents with *more* of these services. Either way, the additional service that women provide—the extra caseworkers, the higher levels of spending they procure—make them better representatives of their voters' interests in this respect as well.

In the end, the question of whether one group of representatives is better than another group is multifaceted. In this case, the answer clearly points to women for at least two of the three dimensions of representation we identify. It is relatively straightforward to conclude that since women outperform men in constituent services and communicate with their voters more than men do, that this makes them better representatives in these respects. This is true even though some of these acts come with fierce debates as to their normative desirability. Perhaps most prominently, pork barrel spending is deeply unpopular with the American public. But what counts as pork is also deeply subjective—a widened road or federally funded hospital wing in someone else's district may be pork of the worst kind, but in the observer's own district those projects are vital improvements to local infrastructure. The same could be said of travel back to the district—members are excoriated for not spending enough time in Washington, DC, or for missing votes on the floor of their chambers. But when a member spends several days in the district showing voters how they qualify for federally subsidized low-income loans or hosting a jobs fair for the long-term unemployed, absence from DC becomes more excusable. And, by almost every measure we examine, women engage in these activities more than men do. So, by these measures, women do indeed appear to be better representatives. Whether women are better representatives because of their closer adherence to voters' policy preferences is more open to debate. Common wisdom seems to side with the delegate model of representation: good representatives are ones who do what voters want them to do. And women clearly do that more than men do.

However, there are some potential downsides to a strong constituent-oriented focus. First, as we discuss in chapter 5, female House members (but, notably, not female senators) see fewer of their bills enacted into law, even though their sponsored bills garner more cosponsors and hew more closely to their voters' interests. We argue that this difference is in part a function of women representatives' outsized emphasis on introducing messaging bills. The question, however, is whether important substantive changes are not occurring. Does women's focus on the position-taking function of legislating stifle policy innovation or lead to women's voices being reflected less than their numbers would suggest? Alternatively, might these impediments be mitigated as the number of women in elected office increases, as does their presence in the ranks of senior chamber and committee leadership?

Second, women more faithfully reflect their constituents' interests, both in terms of securing federal funding (chapter 4) and legislative activity (chapter 6). But what does that mean in terms of what women advocate for and accomplish? While increased diversity is generally seen as broadening the debate, do the pressures women feel from voters potentially lead them to emphasize certain issues over others? Or might female legislators be more hesitant to support certain policies because of a concern about how their voters will perceive their actions? Is a potential result that women may be ceding legislative leadership on some issues to men?

On the other hand, might women's focus on constituent views lead to less partisanship and polarization? As one interviewee noted, "[Female representative] just could not go down and do what the party wanted; she did not vote the party line every time she wanted to. . . . She really wanted to be a good [party member] but she just couldn't do it because of her district." Another interviewee made a similar argument, this time about a female senator from the opposite party: "She wasn't here to just be a rubber stamp and say 'yes' to whatever the party was putting forward. She was here and carved out a role and believed that her role in the process was to bring a specific perspective and that would be from the state but also her experiences that got her here." Representative Marcy Kaptur points with pride to her emphasis on her constituents over party ties: "My agenda is shaped by what is happening to the people of my district, the conditions of their lives. It always has been. And I'm heavily led by that, which is why I've opposed presidents in both parties. I stood up to Bill Clinton, especially on jobs and trade. And after George W. Bush was elected, he came to my district first. *First!* I was opposed to the economic regime he was imposing on places that I represent. In the early 2000s, he brought the president of Mexico with him to try to embarrass me, and all I can tell you is it *didn't work.* The people of my district stood with me. And they continue to stand with me" (as told to Kahn 2017). Representative Kaptur acknowledges both her emphasis of district needs over party ties, as well as the support that focus gains her with her constituents; as of 2017, Representative Kaptur is the longest-serving woman in the House.

It may thus be that an unintended side effect of a strong constituent orientation is increased bipartisanship, as members put aside partisan differences to try to solve issues facing those in their districts. And there is evidence to support this speculation. Volden, Wiseman, and Wittmer (2013) find that minority women House members outpace their male colleagues in terms of building coalitions to enact legislation. Senator Barbara Mikulski (D-MD) has long held monthly women-senator-only dinners where one of the primary rules is no partisan discussions (Bash 2012). *Time Magazine*, in an article entitled "The Last Politicians," told the story of how the twenty women then serving in the Senate met for dinner to successfully devise a plan to end the government shutdown of 2013 (Newton-Small 2013). And women legislators routinely suggest that more women leads to more bipartisanship. For example, former senator Olympia Snowe (R-ME) predicted that bipartisanship will increase as the number of women increases since women are "more relationship-oriented and more collaborative" (Snowe 2013, 100). Senator Susan Collins (R-ME) had this to say about the end of the 2013 shutdown: "I don't think it is a coincidence that women were so heavily involved in trying to end this stalemate. Although we span the ideological spectrum, we are used to working together in a collaborative way" (quoted in Weisman and Steinhauer 2013). On the House side, Representative Shelley Moore Capito (R-WV) explains, "We have a women's caucus in Congress—both Republicans and Democrats—and when we meet, we go right to bipartisan issues where we can find common ground" (Wong 2010). A further benefit of female legislators' increased substantive representation may therefore be increased bipartisanship within Congress.

However, while there are more women in Congress than ever before, they still make up only 19 percent of the House and 21 percent of the Senate as of January 2017. And many of these women have only recently been elected, particularly on the Republican side, where only twenty-one of 241 House Republicans are women in the 115th Congress. As a result, women are generally not as senior as their male colleagues, and not as likely to hold leadership (Nancy Pelosi notwithstanding), committee chair, or ranking member positions. Many of our interviewees brought up this issue of the lack of seniority and leadership positions among women; as one explained, "Women are disproportionately not in leadership where they can control what takes place [legislatively]." In fact, in the current 115th

Congress (2017–2018) there are only two female committee chairs in each of the two chambers: Senator Lisa Murkowski, chair of the Senate Energy and Natural Resources Committee; Senator Susan Collins, chair of the Aging Committee; Representative Virginia Foxx, chair of the Education and the Workforce Committee; and Representative Susan Brooks, chair of the Ethics Committee. Part of the issue is the relative lack of elected women Republicans: during the 113th Congress, when the Democrats controlled the Senate, women held a record nine committee chair positions. Senator Patty Murray voiced the following concern at the start of the 114th Congress, when Republicans regained control of the Senate: "As women were chairing these committees [in the 113th Congress], you saw a lot of bipartisan agreements. So if you just look at it from that perspective, I'm worried, going forward, that we will not have those same things that women bring to the table to help get agreements in a way that works for everyone" (quoted in Stolberg 2015). The question thus arises of how many women will be necessary for these potential bipartisan side effects to be truly felt.

Alternatively, a number of our interviewees suggested that one side effect of the gender socialization forces we highlight is that women are more interested in getting it done, and less interested in reaping rewards. Thus, is it possible that women are more willing to sacrifice having their name on a bill in exchange for seeing the policies they care about enacted? One interviewee argued, "With respect to success in legislating, you probably find that women do introduce legislation that has more of a direct effect on their constituents, but also that they're going to be so much more interested in simply getting it done that they are more likely to subsume it and not necessarily be directly credited for getting it done. So they will hand it over to the chairman of the committee, whoever that may be, it'll become his, and it'll get packaged, and he'll be the one that carries the ball over the finish line." A second interviewee made a similar point: "I think there is a chair bias. . . . Dave Camp and [Patrick] Tiberi are more likely to get something passed than [Lynn] Jenkins and Diane Black even though they are fabulous members working really hard on tax stuff. It is just that they are not the chair of the subcommittee or the committee." She also noted, "I can't remember a lot of [female senator's] individual issue bills going all the way, but I did have a whole list of amendments and pieces that she can claim as hers that we did that were part of the process." The broader effects of women's legislative activities may thus be somewhat obscured by women's desire to simply solve the problem, rather than a need to claim authorship.

Going Forward

Our theory breaks with previous scholarship by taking a more holistic view of what it means to elect women to the U.S. Congress. We argue and show that gendered vulnerability is felt by all female legislators, and the resultant behavioral effects extend from the most junior House members to the most senior senators. We find consistently that females engage in the process of legislating and representing their constituents in a manner distinct from their male colleagues, and this difference transcends specific issue areas or particular aspects of legislating.

That said, we also recognize that our study is a first step in understanding how gendered vulnerability operates and influences political behavior. We see three fertile areas for future exploration. First, our focus was admittedly on between-group differences with respect to male and female legislators. We believe it was necessary to show how gendered vulnerability emerges and operates, and to establish that this gendered vulnerability applies to all women in the U.S. Congress. However, in-group variations among female legislators may exist, and provide an important area for future research: Are there distinctions in how gendered vulnerability influences Democratic vs. Republican women, or women who represent various regions on the country? An attendant question is one of long-term effects for particular women. Do senior women experience gendered vulnerability more or less than junior women? Do women experience it more (or less) after the occurrence of a particularly close (or easy) reelection contest?

Second, a growing literature examines the application of critical mass theory to both state legislatures as well as national legislatures in other countries. Extending this literature to the U.S. Congress raises the question, might the effects of gendered vulnerability fluctuate as the number of women in the chamber grows? In particular, is there a "tipping point," or a certain percentage of female members, at which we might expect that gender-based behavior differences no longer exist? Or do the social and electoral forces that contribute to the existence of gendered vulnerability mitigate the potential effects of reaching such a tipping point?

Finally, the theory of gendered vulnerability, in principle, applies generally to all female officeholders. Thus there is room to uncover its effects in places other than the United States Congress. For instance, we may find that female officeholders in other offices, such as governors, state legislators, and even elected judges, are similarly more attentive to voter concerns. We suggest that the social and electoral forces we highlight apply to all females considering electoral office, regardless of the level of the office or the branch within which it exists, though this remains an open question. Differences may also emerge in how the behavioral outputs of gendered vulnerability manifest themselves.

Overall, we believe women's outsized attention to constituent interests is positive. It should be, as we show in the preceding chapters, that members who represent poverty-stricken districts will work harder to secure economic stimulus funds, that members with a large number of elderly constituents will focus more on health care, and that members whose districts are largely rural, farming communities will spend more time on agricultural issues. Otherwise, we run the risk that these constituencies, whoever they may be, will not be represented and their voices will be left unheard. Further, we are heartened by the possibility that such a focus on constituent issues may decrease partisan polarization, whether pursued by females or males. And, finally, while gender parity in the U.S. Congress is still a ways off, we agree that as more and more women are elected to office, and as women gain more seniority and leadership positions, the positive effects of their emphasis on substantive representation will be felt nationwide.

Appendix

Full Results for Committee Membership Simulations

TABLE A.1A

Committee	103rd-comm	103rd-comm men	103rd-comm women	104th-comm	104th-comm men	104th-comm women	105th-comm	105th-comm men	105th-comm women
Agriculture	0.0000	0.0000	0.0000	0.0000	0.0000	0.0000	0.0000	0.0000	0.0000
Armed Services	0.0000	0.0000	0.0000	0.0000	0.0000	0.0068	0.0000	0.0000	0.0005
Banking	0.3533	0.4179	0.0000	0.2620	0.3548	0.0000	0.3047	0.4044	0.0000
Commerce	0.3979	0.1496	0.9994	0.0518	0.0483	0.9533	0.1407	0.2671	0.0002
Education	0.2668	0.1657	0.9738	0.2701	0.2049	1.0000	0.1833	0.0534	1.0000
Foreign	0.0000	0.0000	0.8759	0.0105	0.0094	0.9113	0.0090	0.0248	0.0023
Governmental Affairs	0.8253	0.6700	0.9913	0.9143	0.8011	0.9938	0.4551	0.3916	0.9760
Judiciary	0.0359	0.0786	0.0226	0.0218	0.0780	0.0001	0.4317	0.7191	0.0000
MMF*	0.0425	0.0425	0.0425	n/a	n/a	n/a	n/a	n/a	n/a
Resources	0.0000	0.0000	0.0000	0.0000	0.0000	0.0000	0.0000	0.0000	0.0000
POCS**	0.4988	0.9572	0.0000	n/a	n/a	n/a	n/a	n/a	n/a
Transportation	0.0359	0.2429	0.0000	0.2465	0.6813	0.0000	0.6246	0.9361	0.0000
Veterans	0.2334	0.3042	0.0582	0.8017	0.8145	0.0004	0.8825	0.8627	1.0000

TABLE A.1B

Committee	106th-comm	106th-comm men	106th-comm women	107th-comm	107th-comm men	107th-comm women	108th-comm	108th-comm men	108th-comm women
Agriculture	0.0000	0.0000	0.0000	0.0000	0.0000	0.0000	0.0000	0.0000	0.0000
Armed Services	0.0000	0.0000	0.2417	0.0000	0.0000	0.0038	0.0000	0.0000	0.0000
Banking	0.3805	0.7786	0.0000	0.0484	0.3052	0.0000	0.0252	0.0361	0.0008
Commerce	0.1373	0.1642	0.0923	0.2453	0.5923	0.0870	0.7268	0.6298	0.9252
Education	0.1804	0.0975	0.6649	0.4140	0.1625	1.0000	0.8257	0.5629	0.9998
Foreign	0.0038	0.0087	0.0000	0.0018	0.0094	0.0000	0.0044	0.0050	0.0000
Governmental Affairs	0.2088	0.1736	0.9449	0.2068	0.2068	0.0000	n/a	n/a	n/a
Judiciary	0.4770	0.5302	0.0001	0.6101	0.6309	0.0001	0.2312	0.3105	0.0242
MMF*	n/a	n/a	n/a	n/a	n/a	n/a	n/a	n/a	n/a
Resources	0.0000	0.0000	0.0000	0.0000	0.0000	0.0000	0.0000	0.0000	0.0000
POCS**	n/a	n/a	n/a	n/a	n/a	n/a	n/a	n/a	n/a
Transportation	0.0836	0.4249	0.0000	0.5811	0.7352	0.0000	0.5097	0.6825	0.0000
Veterans	0.1064	0.2324	0.0000	0.8439	0.8051	1.0000	0.0002	0.0002	0.0002

TABLE A.1C

Committee	109th-comm	109th-comm men	109th-comm women	110th-comm	110th-comm men	110th-comm women
Agriculture	0.0000	0.0000	0.0000	0.0000	0.0000	0.0000
Armed Services	0.0000	0.0000	0.0000	0.0000	0.0000	0.0000
Banking	0.0050	0.0146	0.0000	0.0403	0.0927	0.0000
Commerce	0.4133	0.2113	0.8444	0.7540	0.6407	0.8453
Education	0.5042	0.3948	0.9728	0.2412	0.2412	0.0838
Foreign	0.0026	0.0045	0.0000	0.0020	0.0044	0.0000
Governmental Affairs	n/a	n/a	n/a	n/a	n/a	n/a
Judiciary	0.1988	0.4397	0.0000	0.0019	0.0005	0.0146
MMF*	n/a	n/a	n/a	n/a	n/a	n/a
Resources	0.0000	0.0000	0.0000	0.0000	0.0001	0.0000
POCS**	n/a	n/a	n/a	n/a	n/a	n/a
Transportation	0.5752	0.6733	0.0000	0.5645	0.6655	0.0014
Veterans	0.0010	0.0023	0.0010	0.0017	0.0017	0.0000

TABLE A.2A

Committee	103rd-comm	103rd-comm men	103rd-comm women	104th-comm	104th-comm men	104th-comm women	105th-comm	105th-comm men	105th-comm women
Agriculture	nw**	nw	nw	nw	nw	nw	0.1163	0.0870	0.6682
Armed Services	0.3576	0.3576	0.0000	0.4750	0.6378	0.0000	0.4019	0.2642	0.9137
BHUA	0.0260	0.0403	0.0000	0.0199	0.0546	0.0000	0.1640	0.2793	0.0000
Commerce, Science, Transportation	0.7363	0.7989	0.0000	0.9259	0.9259	0.0000	0.6525	0.6525	0.0000
Energy and Nat Resources	nw	nw	nw	nw	nw	nw	0.0004	0.0004	0.7005
Environ and& Public Works	0.3114	0.5186	0.0000	0.2568	0.5406	0.0000	0.5853	0.7120	0.0000
Foreign Affairs	0.2222	0.1155	0.8086	0.2777	0.2607	0.8539	0.2796	0.2854	0.0000
Governmental Affairs*	nw	nw	nw	nw	nw	nw	0.4415	0.2007	0.9991
HELP	0.8258	0.7222	1.0000	0.4398	0.2511	1.0000	0.9386	0.7007	1.0000
Judiciary	0.4114	0.5798	0.0000	0.3297	0.3297	0.0000	0.0605	0.0680	0.0000
Veterans	nw	nw	nw	nw	nw	nw	0.6242	0.7075	0.1810

TABLE A.2B

Committee	106th-comm	106th-comm men	106th-comm women	107th-comm	107th-comm men	107th-comm women	108th-comm	108th-comm men	108th-comm women
Agriculture	0.0775	0.0801	0.5252	0.1436	0.1436	0.1991	0.0080	0.0080	0.0080
Armed Services	0.1727	0.1727	0.3132	0.1757	0.1757	0.5026	0.1827	0.1827	0.0002
BHUA	nw	nw	nw	0.4985	0.6405	0.0000	0.6636	0.7988	0.0002
Commerce, Science, Trans	0.6197	0.6197	0.0000	0.6681	0.8632	0.0000	0.8199	0.9265	0.0000
Energy and Nat Resources	0.0007	0.0003	0.3065	0.0033	0.0003	0.9225	0.0007	0.0003	0.8106
Environ and Public Works	0.2900	0.7934	0.0000	0.7193	0.7193	0.0000	0.7141	0.7794	0.0000
Foreign Affairs	0.2857	0.3132	0.0000	0.4028	0.5385	0.0000	0.5029	0.5826	0.0000
Governmental Affairs*	0.2483	0.1040	0.9997	0.5756	0.5756	0.5756	0.6358	0.6358	0.9990
HELP	0.9975	0.9948	0.9999	0.7299	0.7299	0.5038	0.9567	0.9567	0.0000
Judiciary	0.0608	0.1295	0.0000	0.2711	0.2711	0.0000	0.0350	0.0350	0.0000
Veterans	0.6401	0.7227	0.2018	0.4005	0.5213	0.1593	0.5061	0.5684	0.1155

TABLE A.2C

Committee	109th-comm	109th-comm men	109th-comm women	110th-comm	110th-comm men	110th-comm women
Agriculture	0.0114	0.0114	0.2068	0.0617	0.0935	0.0101
Armed Services	0.1960	0.2409	0.0002	0.0688	0.0688	0.0252
BHUA	0.5127	0.6955	0.0002	0.7762	0.7762	0.0016
Commerce, Sci, Trans	0.8357	0.9466	0.0000	0.8964	0.9738	0.0177
Energy and Nat Resources	0.0566	0.0000	0.8243	0.0029	0.0003	0.4372
Environ and Public Works	0.0576	0.1335	0.0000	0.0313	0.1095	0.0000
Foreign Affairs	0.2523	0.2523	0.0000	0.1367	0.1367	0.0000
Governmental Affairs*	n/a	n/a	n/a	n/a	n/a	n/a
HELP	0.7865	0.8810	0.0000	0.8342	0.8342	0.5664
Judiciary	0.1614	0.3656	0.0000	0.2595	0.2595	0.0000
Veterans	0.6502	0.8180	0.0002	0.1076	0.5412	0.0002

Notes

CHAPTER 1

1. Howie Carr, a columnist for the *Boston Herald*, used the "Granny" moniker several times, including in an August 1, 2012, column entitled "Keeping Up with Granny Ain't Easy . . .".

CHAPTER 2

1. Pete Wilson resigned from the Senate to run for governor of California in 1990, creating a special election in 1992. As a result, both of the state's Senate seats would be up at the same time in 1992.

2. Full results from the 2014 and 1983 studies can be viewed online at http://nova.wpunj.edu/hainese/hainesdeauxlofaro/

3. The Citizen Political Ambition Study surveys a sample of "potential" candidates for elected office; the samples are constructed by identifying citizens employed in those professions most likely to lead to political careers, such as lawyers, political activists, and educators. The surveys have been conducted three times: 2001, 2008, and 2011. The surveys in 2001 and 2011 utilized distinct samples, while the 2008 survey reflects a follow-up survey of those originally included in the 2001 study. In all three cases, the surveys were conducted by Jennifer Lawless and Richard Fox.

4. The 2008 CAWP Recruitment Study surveyed both state legislators and mayors. For state legislators, they sent surveys to all female state legislators serving in the fifty states and a random sample of male legislators, and for mayors, they sent surveys to all female mayors of cities with 30,000 persons or more and a random sample of male mayors. Table 2.3 reports numbers solely from the state legislator responses.

5. Suffolk University–USA Today poll of 1,000 national likely voters. Surveys were conducted via landline and cell phone interviews, September 24–28, 2015.

6. In addition, minority women potentially face even more hurdles. For example, Clayton and Stallings (2000) highlight how black female candidates must confront both gender and racial stereotypes in their quest for office.

7. Quinnipiac University poll of 1,144 registered voters conducted via telephone interviews. Interviews were conducted October 29–November 2, 2015.

8. Associated Press–NORC Gender Discrimination in the U.S. survey. Survey of 1,096 respondents using both online and telephone interviews; survey was conducted between August 11 and August 14, 2016.

9. Bloomberg poll of 1,000 of adults via landline and cell phone interviews. Survey conducted June 10–13, 2016.

10. It should be noted that these questions about descriptive and substantive representation are not simply limited to legislative bodies, but have also been explored in terms of courts (see, e.g., Peresie 2005; Steffensmeier and Hebert 1999) and executive agencies (see, e.g., Meier and Nicholson-Crotty 2006; Riccucci and Saidel 1997).

CHAPTER 3

1. We focus on the resources devoted to constituent service rather than the service itself because, unfortunately, it is very difficult to directly observe and measure constituent service. Virtually no scholars have even tried. The biggest problem is that there is no requirement that congressional offices keep records of their casework. Most offices do keep some type of a list of people they have performed services for. But offices usually do not keep track of the type of help a constituent received or the number of times they have helped each individual or family. As a result, it is more common to look for other indicators of how much attention a member pays to her district.

2. Fiorina (1981) and Cain, Ferrejohn, and Fiorina (1987) offer several critiques of the district-level studies (in particular, Johannes and McAdams 1981). The most important of these is that the studies suffer from severe endogeneity. On one hand, how well or how much a member serves constituents should influence how he or she does at the polls. But on the other hand, members' *expectations* about how they will do at the polls should influence how much time and attention they pay to their constituents. This leads to problems estimating the relationship between the two variables. As Romero (2006) puts it, "[I]f electorally vulnerable incumbents behave prospectively their efforts can appear ineffectual because high expected vote shares will be associated with low resource allocations, and low expected vote shares will be associated with high resource allocations. This uncontrolled, negatively signed influence thus cancels the positive influence resource allocations have on the district vote" (245). This endogeneity artificially inflates standard errors in estimates of member vote share and, according to Fiorina, leads McAdams and Johannes to inappropriately reject the hypothesis of constituency service influence.

For their part, McAdams and Johannes (1981, 1988) argue that the Fiorina camp's positive empirical results do not show that casework is helpful; rather, the results are an artifact of the way Fiorina et al. construct their variables. Fiorina (1977) and Cain, Ferejohn, and Fiorina (1987) estimate dependent variables indicating whether the respondent voted for the incumbent, or the respondent's evaluation of the incumbent as indicated in a thermometer score. The independent variables were taken from questions about whether respondents had ever received assistance from their member of Congress; and if they had received assistance, whether they were satisfied with that assistance. McAdams and Johannes argue that all of these variables, both independent and dependent, depend on respondents' imperfect memory and—at the end of the day—how much the respondent likes the incumbent. As a result, the entire research program "invok[es] an endogenous system of generalized affect. People who like the congressman and vote for him also recognize him, agree with him (or think they do), and say all sorts of other good things about him. Some of this requires factual misperception" (1981, 593). In other words, the people in Fiorina's studies who say that they received casework and were satisfied by it may not have actually done so; they might just like the member of Congress and as a result be willing to say good things about him or her. As a result, McAdams and Johannes argue that Fiorina et al. inappropriately find evidence of casework influence when none is actually there.

3. These studies solve the "generalized affect" problem discussed in note 2, chapter 3 above by merging the NES results with district-level data on members' actual levels of district service. This gives researchers independent variables that are independent from affect, and thus measured independently of the dependent variable(s). This makes these more recent articles more convincing than the prior work.

4. This is the same type of endogeneity that McAdams and Johannes (1988) argue that Fiorina (1977) suffers from.

5. One reason for this is that House members are resource-poor compared to senators—they do not have as many staff or as large an allowance so they have to rely on relatively cheap forms of communication more than senators do. A second reason is that senators receive more TV and radio exposure than House members, owing to both their greater prominence in national politics and the simple fact that state borders are more congruent with major media markets than are most House district borders.

6. We are indebted to Parker and Goodman (2009, 2013) for generously sharing data with us, which we use to examine both House members' franking in this section and House members' travel to the district in the next section.

7. When House members pay for travel out of their allowance, those payments are reported publicly. However, the travel reports are listed together with all the other disbursements out of members' office allowances, sorted by date among hundreds of thousands of other line items that are not electronically searchable (in most libraries, including those of the authors' home university, these still exist on microfiche). Moreover, members often report both legs of a trip separately, and sometimes do not bother reporting the return trip at all. This makes it difficult to accurately determine how many days each member spent in-district. Worse, if someone else paid for the travel, the member would likely not report it at all. In the Senate, this information is not housed in any single publicly available location, which is why we only examine House travel activity in this section.

8. More systematically, the female senators in our dataset represent bigger states (11 million residents) on average than male senators do (4.5 million).

9. As House districts are nominally equal in population, the intent behind giv-

ing each House member a different amount of money is to address their varying costs in travel back and forth between the district and Washington, DC. Nonetheless, this is the same pot of money the House members pay their staffers out of.

CHAPTER 4

1. In three of the studies, this correlation exists most strongly or even exclusively among liberal voters, or the voters in districts electing liberal members (Sidman and Mak 2006; Sellers 1997; Alvarez and Schousen 1993).

2. We credited each requesting member with having received a single earmark, and evenly divided the money the earmark was worth between the requesting members.

3. In models we do not report, we also tested the proposition that the covariates operate differently for women and men by interacting several of them with *Female*. Two of the interaction terms were significant. First, *female*seniority* was positively related to both dependent variables, indicating that seniority was more important in the distribution of earmarks among females than it was among males. Additionally, *female*lagged vote* was negative and significant in both models. This means that female members' earmarking success was more strongly tied to their electoral vulnerability—in the traditional sense of the term—than was male members' success.

4. We also tested the proposition that, just as with stimulus funds, women are more responsive to their districts in procuring earmarks. First, hypothesizing that liberal voters are more supportive of pork barrel spending more generally (Sidman and Mak 2006), we reestimated the models in tables 1 and 2 and included an interaction term *female*presvotedem*. If female members are more responsive to the ideological preferences of their voters in procuring earmarks, the coefficient on *female*presvotedem* should be positive, significant, and larger than the coefficient on *presvotedem*. However, the interaction term is not significant in any of the reestimations. The second way we test this proposition is by creating several categories of earmarks based on the policy or issue that the earmark spending addressed. The categories we created were defense, crime, transportation, health care, water projects, education, agriculture, and energy policy. Then for each category we identified a measure of the salience of each policy area to individual districts. Thus, for instance, the measure of salience for agriculture spending was the percentage of the population living in rural farm areas, and the measure of salience for defense spending was the percentage of the population enlisted in the military. Then, we estimated multivariate models in which both earmark and funding totals within these categories were the dependent variable, and the independent variables included female, the salience measure, and the interaction between the two. If the interaction is significant, this would indicate that female members are more responsive to their constituents' particular interests than male members. However, of the eight categories we investigated, we found significant evidence of this pattern only for agriculture spending.

5. States coded as battleground states are Florida, Indiana, Missouri, Montana, North Carolina, North Dakota, and Ohio.

6. The most likely explanation for this counterintuitive finding is known in

the economics literature as Wagner's Law. In brief, it states that the size of government grows with, among other things, industrialization of the economy. Thus it predicts that government will spend more heavily in times and places where income is highest.

CHAPTER 5

1. One bill did become law, but it had to get there through the Senate legislative process: it was subsumed by a Senate bill sponsored by Mike DeWine that covered similar substantive issues.

2. Though most resolutions are used in this manner, others are related to the technical aspects of legislative procedure. For instance, members are appointed to committees, conference committees are sometimes requested, and officers of each chamber are appointed via resolution. Resolutions with no position-taking content are excluded from the analysis presented later in the chapter.

3. There are, of course, alternate paths through the legislative process in both chambers. However, the same incentives apply: If the sponsor does not necessarily want the bill to pass, why should anyone else make the effort to push the bill through via, say, a discharge petition?

4. Previous examinations of the differences between men and women in legislative success offer mixed results: some studies find gender does not significantly explain legislative success rates (e.g., Bratton and Haynie 1999; Jeydel and Taylor 2003; Thomas 1994), while others find women legislators are more successful at seeing their favored bills enacted (Saint-Germain 1989; Thomas and Welch 1991). However, with the exception of Jeydel and Taylor (2003), all prior investigations into this question examine state legislatures rather than the U.S. Congress.

5. Anderson, Box-Steffensmeier, and Sinclair-Chapman (2001) argue that this method of operationalizing legislative success, which they call the "hit rate," is inappropriate because it sets up unfair comparisons between legislators who introduce different numbers of bills. However, our theory makes no predictions about members' baseline *levels* of success, but predicts success rates. In particular, we want to see whether members' different levels of bill introduction influence their *rates* of success.

6. To consider a piece of legislation in this manner, a member makes a motion to "suspend the rules and pass the bill." From that point, debate is limited to forty minutes, no amendments can be offered to either the motion or the underlying bill, and the motion must receive the approval of two-thirds of the voting members to pass. Once the motion passes, the bill is usually considered to have passed (Oleszek 2007).

7. Several scholars (e.g., Kessler and Krehbiel 1996) argue that cosponsorship acts not as a signal to voters or any other electoral actors, but as a signal to other legislators. This perspective, for one, predicts that there is no relationship between electoral vulnerability and cosponsorship activity. Moreover, it also predicts that female bills should receive *fewer* cosponsors, on average, than male bills. If cosponsorship is primarily an intrachamber signal there's no reason for a member to cosponsor a bill whose sponsor does not intend for it to go anywhere in the legislative process. To the extent that female-sponsored bills are intended for

electoral signaling, they should get fewer cosponsors. Thus a test of this hypothesis also offers an indirect but critical test between two conceptions of cosponsorship.

CHAPTER 6

1. On the other side of the coin, there are several limitations to these gender-based policy differences (Reingold 2008). First is that not every study examining the issue finds significant gender differences in policy preferences, be they self-reported (Reingold 2000) or expressed through legislative activity (Vega and Firestone 1995). Even where differences are significant, women are not always consistently more liberal than men (e.g., Hogan 2008). Second, gender differences—especially in broad ideological measures such as DW-NOMINATE—appear to decline over time (Dodson 2006; Swers 2002; Vega and Firestone 1995), especially within the Democratic Party. Thus, some recent studies of the gender gap in legislative behavior identify one only within the Republican Party (Boles and Scheurer 2007; Evans 2005; Frederick 2009; Swers 2002). Finally, gender's influence on policy preferences, even when statistically significant, is not as substantively impactful as other variables, particularly party. Thus many of the above findings refer primarily to differences within parties: Democratic and Republican women, respectively, are more liberal than their male same-party counterparts.

2. The most important methodological improvement is the introduction of two-stage least squares. Early studies used single-stage models to estimate roll-call behavior, with voter preferences, vulnerability, and an interaction between the two as the key independent variables. More recent studies use 2SLS to purge this equation of the endogenous effect that roll-call behavior can have on electoral vulnerability.

3. Frisch and Kelly (2006) take advantage of Adler's district measures to examine the actual requests members make to get on certain committees. For a majority of committees, they find a significant correlation between whether a member requested that committee and district characteristics that indicate demand for a particular service provided by it.

4. Following Adler, we also treat lower values of district median income and population in square miles as representing higher need, and so multiply those standardized variables by -1 to correctly account for their influence on the level of constituent demand for certain committee jurisdictions.

5. Unfortunately, at least in relation to racial minorities, there is also some evidence, particularly within states, that growing minority populations can have a backlash effect (e.g., Brown 1995; Hero and Tolbert 1996; Radcliff and Saiz 1995; but see Krueger and Mueller 2001 for a discussion of how party politics may overcome these problems).

6. The literature that examines the "marginality hypothesis" is long and has generally produced weak results. However, most of these weak results came from studies that examined the relationship between marginality and party loyalty (see, e.g., Fiorina 1974). Only more recently has this literature turned its attention to the relationship between marginality and congruence with voter preferences. On this question, results have been consistently positive.

References

Abramowitz, Alan I. 1975. "Name Familiarity, Reputation, and the Incumbency Effect in a Congressional Election." *Western Political Quarterly* 28: 668–84.

Aday, Sean, and James Devitt. 2001. "Style over Substance: Newspaper Coverage of Elizabeth Dole's Presidential Bid." *International Journal of Press/Politics* 6: 52–73.

Adler, E. Scott. 2002. *Why Congressional Reforms Fail: Reelection and the House Committee System.* Chicago: University of Chicago Press.

Alexander, Deborah, and Kristi Anderson. 1993. "Gender as a Factor in the Attribution of Leadership Traits." *Political Research Quarterly* 46: 527–45.

Alvarez, R. Michael, and Jason L. Saving. 1997. "Congressional Committees and the Political Economy of Federal Outlays." *Public Choice* 92: 55–73.

Alvarez, R. Michael, and Matthew M. Schousen. 1993. "Policy Moderation or Conflicting Expectations? Testing the Intentional Models of Split-Ticket Voting." *American Politics Quarterly* 24: 410–38.

Anagnoson, J. Theodore. 1980. "Politics in the Distribution of Federal Grants: The Case of the Economic Development Administration." In *Political Benefits*, ed. Barry Rundquist. Lexington, MA: Lexington Books.

Anagnoson, J. Theodore. 1982. "Federal Grant Agencies and Congressional Election Campaigns." *American Journal of Political Science* 26: 547–61.

Anderson, William D., Janet M. Box-Steffensmeier, and Valeria Sinclair Chapman. 2001. "Navigating Rough Waters: Modeling Member Effectiveness in the U.S. House of Representatives." Paper presented at the Annual Meeting of the American Political Science Association, Washington, DC, August 31–September 3.

Ansolabehere, Stephen, James Snyder, and Charles Stewart. 2001. "The Effects of Party and Preferences on Congressional Roll-Call Voting." *Legislative Studies Quarterly* 26:533–72.

Anzia, Sarah, and Christopher Berry. 2011. "The Jackie (and Jill) Robinson Effect: Why Do Congresswomen Outperform Congressmen?" *American Journal of Political Science* 55: 478–93.

Arnold, R. Douglas. 1979. *Congress and the Bureaucracy*. New Haven: Yale University Press.

Arnold, R. Douglas. 1990. *The Logic of Congressional Action*. New Haven: Yale University Press.

Auspurg, Katrin, Thomas Hinz, and Carsten Sauer. 2017. "Why Should Women Get Less? Evidence on the Gender Pay Gap from Multifactorial Survey Experiments." *American Sociological Review* 82: 179–210.

Baitlinger, Gail. 2015. "Meet the Press or Meet the Men? Examining Women's Presence in American News Media." *Political Research Quarterly* 68: 579–92.

Balcerzak, Ashley. 2017. "Women (Candidates) under Attack (Really!) by Outside Groups. (Men, Not so Much)." Center for Responsive Politics, http://www.opensecrets.org/news/2017/03/women-candidates-under-attack. Accessed March 13, 2017.

Balla, Steven J., Eric D. Lawrence, Forrest Maltzman, and Lee Sigelman. 2002. "Partisanship, Blame Avoidance, and the Distribution of Legislative Pork." *American Journal of Political Science* 46:515–25.

Barnello, Michelle A., and Kathleen A. Bratton. 2007. "Bridging the Gender Gap in Bill Sponsorship." *Legislative Studies Quarterly* 32: 449–74.

Bash, Dana. 2012. "Mikulski Makes History While Creating 'Zone of Civility' for Senate Women." *CNN.com*, March 17.

Bash, Dana, and Abigail Crutchfield. 2016. "Longest-Serving Female Lawmaker Says Goodbye." *CNN.com*, December 15.

Bauer, Nichole M. 2015. "Emotional, Sensitive, and Unfit for Office? Gender Stereotype Activation and Support for Female Candidates." *Political Psychology* 36: 691–708.

Bauer, Nichole M. 2017. "The Effects of Counterstereotypic Gender Strategies on Candidate Evaluations." *Political Psychology* 38: 279–95.

Baxter, Sandra, and Marjorie Lansing. 1980. *Women and Politics: The Invisible Majority*. Ann Arbor: University of Michigan Press.

Bennett, James T., and Thomas J. DiLorenzo. 1982. "The Political Economy of Political Philosophy: Discretionary Spending by Senators on Staff." *American Economic Review* 72: 1153–61.

Berch, Neil. 2004. "Women Incumbents, Elite Bias, and Voter Response in the 1996 and 1998 U.S. House Elections." *Women & Politics* 26: 21–33.

Berke, Richard L. 1999. "As Political Spouse, Bob Dole Strays from Campaign Script." *New York Times*, May 17.

Bernstein, R. 1986. "Why Are There So Few Women in the House?" *Western Political Quarterly* 39: 155–64.

Bers, Trudy Haffron. 1978. "Local Political Elites: Men and Women on Boards of Education." *Western Political Quarterly* 31 (3): 381–91.

Bickers, Kenneth, Diana Evans, Robert Stein, and Robert Wrinkle. 2007. "The New and Old Electoral Connection: Earmarks and Pork Barrel Politics." Paper presented at the Annual Meeting of the Midwest Political Science Association, Chicago, April 12.

Bickers, Kenneth, and Robert Stein. 1996. "The Electoral Dynamics of the Federal Pork Barrel." *American Journal of Political Science* 40:1300–1326.

Bishin, Ben. 2009. *Tyranny of the Minority: The Subconstituency Politics Theory of Representation*. Philadelphia: Temple University Press.

Blair, Diane D., and Jeanie R. Stanley. 1991. "Personal Relationships and Legislative Power: Male and Female Perceptions." *Legislative Studies Quarterly* 16:495–507.

Boatright, Robert G. 2014. *Congressional Primary Elections*. New York: Routledge.

Boles, Janet K., and Katherine Scheurer. 2007. "Beyond Women, Children, and Families: Gender, Representation, and Funding for the Arts." *Social Science Quarterly* 88: 39–50.

Bond, Jon R., Cary Covington, and Richard Fleisher. 1985. "Explaining Challenger Quality in Congressional Elections. *Journal of Politics* 47: 510–29.

Bovitz, Gregory L., and Jamie L. Carson. 2006. "Position-Taking and Electoral Accountability in the U.S. House of Representatives." *Political Research Quarterly* 59: 297–312.

Bowles, Hannah Riley, Linda Babcock, and Lei Lai. 2007. "Social Incentives for Gender Differences in the Propensity to Initiate Negotiations: Sometimes It Does Hurt To Ask." *Organizational Behavior and Human Decision Processes* 103: 84–103.

Boxer, Barbara. 2016. *The Art of Tough: Fearlessly Facing Politics and Life*. New York: Hachette Books.

Box-Steffensmeier, Janet M., David C. Kimball, Scott R. Meinke, and Katherine Tate. 2003. "The Effects of Political Representation on the Electoral Advantages of House Incumbents." *Political Research Quarterly* 56: 259–70.

Box-Steffensmeier, Janet M., Laura W. Arnold, and Christopher J.W. Zorn. 1997. "The Strategic Timing of Position Taking in Congress: A Study of the North American Free Trade Agreement." *American Political Science Review* 91: 324–38.

Bratton, Kathleen A. 2002. "The Effect of Legislative Diversity on Agenda-Setting: Evidence from Six State Legislatures." *American Politics Research* 30:115–42.

Bratton, Kathleen A. 2005. "Critical Mass Theory Revisited: The Behavior and Success of Token Women in State Legislatures." *Politics and Gender* 1: 97–125.

Bratton, Kathleen A., and Kerry L. Haynie. 1999. "Agenda Setting and Legislative Success in State Legislatures: The Effects of Gender and Race." *Journal of Politics* 61: 658–79.

Braun, Carol Moseley. 1999. "Interview #1: The Road to the United States Senate." Interview conducted by Betty K. Koed. https://www.senate.gov/artandhistory/history/oral_history/MoseleyBraunCarol.htm. Accessed March 5, 2017.

Brescoll, Victoria L., and Eric Luis Uhlmann. 2008. "Can An Angry Woman Get Ahead? Status Conferral, Gender, and Expression of Emotion in the Workplace." *Psychological Science* 19: 268–75.

Broverman, Inge K., Susan Raymond Vogel, Donald M. Broverman, Frank E. Clarkson, and Paul S. Rosenkrantz. 1972. "Sex-Role Stereotypes: A Current Appraisal." *Journal of Social Issues* 28: 59–78.

Brown, Carrie Budoff. 2017. "I Felt I Had to Speak Out and Say Something." *Politico: Women Rule Podcast*, March 7. http://www.politico.com/story/2017/03/women-rule-deb-fischer-valerie-jarrett-235742. Accessed March 8, 2017.

Brown, Robert. 1995. "Party Cleavage and Welfare Effort in the American States." *American Political Science Review* 89: 23–33.

Browning, Rufus P., Dale Rogers Marshall, and David H. Tabb. 1986. "Protest Is Not Enough: A Theory of Political Incorporation." *PS: Political Science and Politics* 19: 576–81.

Burke, Edmund. (1790) 1968. *Reflections on the Revolution in France*. London: Penguin Books.

Burns, Nancy, Kay Lehman Schlozman, and Sidney Verba. 2001. *The Private Roots of Public Action: Gender, Equality and Political Participation*. Cambridge: Harvard University Press.

Burrell, Barbara C. 1994. *A Woman's Place Is In The House: Campaigning for Congress in the Feminist Era*. Ann Arbor: University of Michigan Press.

Butler, Daniel M., and Jessica Robinson Preece. 2016. "Recruitment and Perceptions of Gender Bias in Party Leader Support." *Political Research Quarterly* 69: 842–51.

Bystrom, Dianne G. 2010. "Advertising, Web Sites, and Media Coverage: Gender and Communication Along the Campaign Trail." In *Gender and Elections: Shaping the Future of American Politics*, 2nd ed., eds. Susan J. Carroll and Richard L. Fox. New York: Cambridge University Press.

Bystrom, Dianne G., Mary C. Banwart, Lynda Lee Kaid, and Terry Robertston. 2004. *Gender and Candidate Communication: VideoStyles, WebStyles, NewsStyles*. New York: Routledge.

Cain, Bruce, John Ferejohn, and Morris Fiorina. 1987. *The Personal Vote: Constituency Service and Electoral Independence*. Cambridge: Harvard University Press.

Campbell, James E. 1982. "Cosponsoring Legislation in the U.S. Congress." *Legislative Studies Quarterly* 7: 415–28.

Canes-Wrone, Brandice, David W. Brady, and John F. Cogan. 2002. "Out of Step, Out of Office: Electoral Accountability and House Members' Voting." *American Political Science Review* 96 (1): 127–40.

Canes-Wrone, Brandice, Julia Rabinovich, and Craig Volden. 2007. "Who Parties? Floor Voting, District Ideology, and Electoral Margins." In *Party, Process, and Political Change in Congress*, ed. David W. Brady and Mathew D. McCubbins. Palo Alto: Stanford University Press.

Canes-Wrone, Brandice, William Minozzi, and Jessica Bonney Reveley. 2011. "Issue Accountability and the Mass Public." *Legislative Studies Quarterly* 36: 5–35.

Carey, John M., Richard G. Niemi, and Lynda W. Powell. 1998. "Are Women State Legislators Different?" In *Women and Elective Office: Past, Present, and Future*, ed. Sue Thomas and Clyde Wilcox. New York: Oxford University Press.

Carroll, Susan J. 1984. "Woman Candidates and Support for Feminist Concerns: The Closet Feminist Syndrome." *Western Political Quarterly* 37: 307–23.

Carroll, Susan J. 1985. "Political Elites and Sex Differences in Political Ambition: A Reconsideration." *Journal of Politics* 47: 1231–43.

Carroll, Susan J. 1994. *Women as Candidates in American Politics*, 2nd edition. Bloomington, IN: Indiana University Press.

Carroll, Susan J, ed. 2001. *The Impact of Women in Public Office*. Bloomington: Indiana University Press.

Carroll, Susan J. 2003. *Women and American Politics: New Questions, New Directions*. New York: Oxford University Press.

Carroll, Susan J., and Kira Sanbonmatsu. 2013. *More Women Can Run: Gender and Pathways to the State Legislatures*. New York: Oxford University Press.

Carson, Jamie, Gregory Koger, Matthew J. Lebo, and Everett Young. 2010. "The Electoral Costs of Party Loyalty in Congress." *American Journal of Political Science* 54: 598–616.

Cech, Erin, Brian Rubineau, Susan Silbey, and Caroll Seron. 2011. "Professional Role Confidence and Gendered Persistence in Engineering." *American Sociological Review* 76: 641–66.

Chang, Kenneth. 2015. "The Long Strange Trip to Pluto, and How NASA Nearly Missed It." *New York Times*, July 18.

Charness, Gary, and Aldo Rustichini. 2011. "Individual Behavior and Group Membership." *Games and Economic Behavior* 72: 77–85.

Chernick, Howard A. 1979. "An Economic Model of the Distribution of Project Grants." In *Fiscal Federalism and Grants-in-Aid*, ed. P. Mieszkowski and W. H. Oakland. Washington, DC: Urban Institute.

Chisholm, Shirley. 1970. *Unbought and Unbossed*. New York, NY: Houghton Mifflin.

Christensen, Wendy. 2016. "Why Bill Was the Face of Hillary's Historic Nomination." *Pacific Standard*, August 2. https://psmag.com/why-bill-was-the-face-of-hillary-clintons-historic-nomination-21d5b9d4bd38#.wzmiwjrux

Clayton, Dewey M., and Angela M. Stallings. 2000. "Black Women in Congress: Striking the Balance." *Journal of Black Studies* 30: 574–603.

Coates, Jennifer. 1993. *Women, Men and Language: A Sociolinguistic Account of Gender Differences in Language*. London, UK: Longman.

Cohn, Peter. 2006. "Moving Target." *National Journal* 38: 60–61.

Conover, Pamela Johnston, and Virginia Gray. 1983. *Feminism and the New Right: Conflict Over the American Family*. New York: Praeger.

Cook, Timothy. 1979. "Legislature vs. Legislator: A Note on the Paradox of Congressional Support." *Legislative Studies Quarterly* 4: 43–52.

Correll, Shelley J. 2001. "Gender and the Career Choice Process: The Role of Biased Self-Assessments." *American Journal of Sociology* 106:1691–1730.

Correll, Shelley J., and Cecilia L. Ridgeway. 2003. "Expectation States Theory." In *The Handbook of Social Psychology*, ed. John Delamater, 29–51. New York: Kluwer Academic Press.

Costantini, Edmond. 1990. "Political Women and Political Ambition: Closing the Gender Gap." *American Journal of Political Science* 34: 741–70.

Cover, Albert D. 1980. "Contacting Congressional Constituents: Some Patterns of Perquisite Use." *American Journal of Political Science* 24: 125–35.

Cover, Albert D., and Bruce S. Brumburg. 1982. "Baby Books and Ballots: The Impact of Congressional Mail on Constituent Opinion." *American Political Science Review* 76: 647–59.

Cox, Gary W., and Mathew McCubbins. 1993. *Legislative Leviathan: Party Government in the House*. Berkley: University of California Press.

Cox, Gary W., and William Terry. 2008. "Legislative Productivity in the 93rd–105th Congresses." *Legislative Studies Quarterly* 33: 1–16.

Crowder-Meyer, Melody. 2013. "Gender Recruitment Without Trying: How Local Party Recruiters Affect Women's Representation." *Politics & Gender* 9: 390–413.

Darcy, R., and Sarah Slavin Schramm. 1977. "When Women Run Against Men." *Public Opinion Quarterly* 41: 1–12.

Deaux, Kay, and Laurie L. Lewis. 1984. "Structure of Gender Stereotypes: Interrelationships Among Components and Gender Label." *Journal of Personality and Social Psychology* 46: 991–1004.

DeCoskey, Renee. 2016. "Reports That Yoko Ono and Hillary Clinton Had an Affair Are False." *Business2Community.com*. http://www.business2community.com/government-politics/reports-yoko-ono-hillary-clinton-affair-false-01686704#AeEf8vjy578E62h0.97. Accessed March 4, 2017.

Deering, Christopher J., and Steven S. Smith. 1997. *Committees in Congress*. Washington, DC: Congressional Quarterly Press.

Deutchman, Iva Ellen. 1992. "Ungendered but Equal: Male Attitudes toward Women in State Legislatures." *Polity* 24: 417–32.

Devitt, James. 1999. "Framing Gender on the Campaign Trail." Report for the White House Project Education Fund.

Diamond, Irene. 1977. *Sex Roles in the State House*. New Haven: Yale University Press.

Ditonto, Tessa. 2017. "A High Bar or a Double Standard? Gender, Competence, and Information in Political Campaigns." *Political Behavior* 39: 301–25.

Ditonto, Tessa, A. Hamilton, and D. Redlawsk. 2014. "Gender Stereotypes, Information Search, and Voting Behavior in Political Campaigns." *Political Behavior* 36: 335–58.

Dittmar, Kelly. 2010. "Negotiating Gender: Campaign Practitioners' Reflections on Gender, Strategy, and Campaigns." Paper prepared for presentation at the 2010 American Political Science Association Annual Meeting, Washington, D.C. Available at SSRN: https://ssrn.com/abstract=1669795

Dodson, Debra L. 2006. *The Impact of Women in Congress*. New York: Oxford University Press.

Dodson, Debra L., and Susan J. Carroll. 1991. *Reshaping the Agenda: Women in State Legislatures*. New Brunswick, NJ: CAWP, Rutgers University.

Dolan, Julie. 1997. "Support for Women's Interests in the 103rd Congress: The Distinct Impact of Congressional Women." *Women & Politics* 18: 81–92.

Dolan, Kathleen. 2005. "Do Women Candidates Play to Gender Stereotypes? Do Men Candidates Play to Women? Candidate Sex and Issues Priorities on Campaign Websites." *Political Research Quarterly* 58: 31–44.

Dolan, Kathleen. 2010. "The Impact of Gender Stereotyped Evaluations on Support for Women Candidates." *Political Behavior* 32: 69–88.

Dolan, Kathleen. 2014. *When Does Gender Matter? Women Candidates and Gender Stereotypes in American Elections*. New York: Oxford University Press.

Dolan, Kathleen, and Kira Sanbonmatsu. 2009. "Gender Stereotypes and Attitudes Toward Gender Balance in Government." *American Politics Research* 37: 409–28.

Dolan, Kathleen, and Lynne E. Ford. 1997. "Change and Continuity among Women State Legislators: Evidence from Three Decades." *Political Research Quarterly* 50: 137–51.

Dovi, Suzanne. 2002. "Preferable Descriptive Representatives: Will Just Any Woman, Black, or Latino Do?" *American Political Science Review* 96: 729–43.

Dunaway, Johanna, Regina G. Lawrence, Melody Rose, and Christopher R. Weber. 2013. "Traits Versus Issues: How Female Candidates Shape Coverage of Senate and Gubernatorial Races." *Political Research Quarterly* 66: 715–26.

Duerst-Lahti, Georgia, and Cathy Marie Johnson. 1990. "Gender and Style in Bureaucracy." *Women and Politics* 10: 67–120.

Eagly, Alice H., and Blair T. Johnson. 1990. "Gender and Leadership Style: A Meta-Analysis." *Psychological Bulletin* 108: 233–56.

Edwards, S. Tyler, E. Frank Stephenson, and Melissa M. Yeoh. 2012. "A Public Choice Analysis of Congressional Franking." *Public Finance Review* 40: 534–51.

Ellickson, Mark C., and Donald E. Whistler. 2000. "A Path Analysis of Legislative Success in Professional and Citizen Legislatures: A Gender Comparison." *Women & Politics* 21: 77–103.

Emanuel, Rahm. 2008. "Don't Get Rid of Earmarks." *New York Times*, August 24. http://www.nytimes.com/2007/08/24/opinion/24emanuel.html. Accessed October 22, 2010.

Epstein, Laurily K., and Kathleen Frankovic. 1982. "Casework and Electoral Margins: Insurance Is Prudent." *Polity* 14: 691–700.

Epstein, Michael J., Richard G. Niemi, and Lynda W. Powell. 2005. "Do Women and Men State Legislators Differ?" In *Women and Elective Office: Past, Present, and Future*, 2nd ed., ed. Sue Thomas and Clyde Wilcox. New York: Oxford University Press.

Erikson, Robert S. 1971. "The Advantage of Incumbency in Congressional Elections." *Polity* 3:395–405.

Erikson, Robert S., and Gerald C. Wright. 2000. "Representation of Constituency Ideology in Congress." In *Continuity and Change in House Elections*, ed. David W. Brady, John F. Cogan, and Morris P. Fiorina. Palo Alto, CA: Stanford University Press.

Eulau, Heinz, and Paul D. Karps. 1977. "The Puzzle of Representation: Specifying Components of Responsiveness." *Legislative Studies Quarterly* 2: 233–54.

Evans, Jocelyn Jones. 2005. *Women, Partisanship, and the Congress*. New York: Palgrave Macmillan.

Falk, Erika. 2008. *Women for President: Media Bias in Eight Campaigns*. Champaign: University of Illinois Press.

Feldman, Paul, and James Jondrow. 1984. "Congressional Elections and Local Federal Spending." *American Journal of Political Science* 28: 147–64.

Fenno, Richard. 1973. *Congressmen in Committees*. Glenview, IL: Scott Foresman.

Fenno, Richard. 1978a. *Homestyle: House Members in Their Districts*. New York: HarperCollins.

Fenno, Richard. 1978b. "U.S. House Members in Their Constituencies: An Exploration." *American Political Science Review* 56:310–324.

Ferejohn, John F. 1974. *Pork Barrel Politics: Rivers and Harbors Legislation, 1947–1968*. Palo Alto, CA: Stanford University Press.

Ferraro, Geraldine. 2004. *Ferraro: My Story*. Evanston, IL: Northwestern University Press.

Fiala, George. 2013. "Fashionable Nydia Inaugurated with Love." *Red Hook Star Review* (Brooklyn, NY), January 29.

Fiorina, Morris P. 1974. *Representation, Constituencies, and Roll Calls*. Lexington, MA: Heath-Lexington.

Fiorina, Morris P. 1977. *Congress: Keystone of the Washington Establishment*. New Haven: Yale University Press.

Fiorina, Morris P. 1981. "Some Problems in Studying the Effects of Resource Allocation in Congressional Elections." *American Journal of Political Science*. 25: 543–567.

Flammang, J.A. 1985. "Female Officials in the Feminist Capital: The Case of Santa Clara County." *Western Political Quarterly* 38: 94–118.

Forbes, Moira. 2014. "Sen. Kirsten Gillibrand on Why Ambition Is Not a Dirty Word." *Forbes*, November 12.

Foschi, Martha. 1996. "Double Standards in the Evaluation of Men and Women." *Social Psychology Quarterly* 59: 237–54.

Foschi, Martha, Lai, and Sigerson. 1994. "Gender and Double Standards in the Assessment of Job Applicants." *Social Psychology Quarterly* 57: 326–39.

Fowler, Linda L., and Jennifer L. Lawless. 2009. "Looking for Sex in All the Wrong Places: Press Coverage and the Electoral Fortunes of Gubernatorial Candidates." *Perspectives on Politics* 7: 519–36.

Fox, Richard L. 1997. *Gender Dynamics in Congressional Elections*. New York: Sage.

Fox, Richard L., and Jennifer L. Lawless. 2004. "Entering the Arena? Gender and the Decision to Run for Office." *American Journal of Political Science* 48: 264–80.

Fox, Richard L., and Jennifer L. Lawless. 2005. "To Run Or Not To Run For Office: Explaining Nascent Political Ambition." *American Journal of Political Science* 49: 642–59.

Fox, Richard L., and Jennifer L. Lawless. 2010. "If Only They'd Ask: Gender, Recruitment and Political Ambition." *Journal of Politics* 72: 310–36.

Fox, Richard L., and Jennifer L. Lawless. 2011. "Gendered Perceptions and Political Candidacies: A Central Barrier to Women's Equality in Electoral Politics." *American Journal of Political Science* 55: 59–73.

Frantzich, Stephen. 1979. "Who Makes Our Laws? The Legislative Effectiveness of Members of the U.S. Congress." *Legislative Studies Quarterly* 4: 409–28.

Frederick, Brian. 2008. "Constituency Population and Representation in the U.S. House." *American Politics Research* 36: 358–81.

Frederick, Brian. 2009. "Are Female House Members Still More Liberal in a Polarized Era? The Conditional Nature of the Relationship between Descriptive and Substantive Representation." *Congress & the Presidency* 36: 181–202.

Frederick, Brian. 2010. "Gender and Patterns of Roll Call Voting in the U.S. Senate." *Congress & the Presidency* 37: 103–24.

Frisch, Scott A. 1998. *The Politics of Pork: A Study of Congressional Appropriation Earmarks*. New York: Garland Press.

Frisch, Scott A., and Sean Q. Kelly. 2006. *Committee Assignment Politics in the U.S. House of Representatives*. Norman: University of Oklahoma Press.

Frisch, Scott A., and Sean Q. Kelly. 2011. *Cheese Factories on the Moon: Why Earmarks Are Good for American Democracy*. Boulder, CO: Paradigm Publishers.

Fulton, Sarah A. 2010. "What Underlies the Gendered Quality Gap? The Role of Perceptions in Shaping the Supply of Female Candidates." Paper presented at the 2010 American Political Science Association Annual Meeting, August.

Fulton, Sarah A., Cherie D. Maestas, L. Sandy Maisel, and Walter J. Stone. 2006. "The Sense of a Woman: Gender, Ambition, and the Decision to Run for Congress." *Political Research Quarterly* 59: 235–48.

Gaddie, Ronald Keith, and Charles S. Bullock III. 2000. *Elections to Open Seats in the U.S. House: Where the Action Is*. Lanham, MD: Rowman & Littlefield.

Garand, James C., and Kelly M. Burke. 2006. "Legislative Activity and the 1994

Republican Takeover: Exploring Changing Patterns of Sponsorship and Cosponsorship in the U.S. House." *American Politics Research* 34: 159–88.
Gehlen, Frieda L. 1977. "Women Members of Congress: A Distinctive Role." In *Portrait of Marginality: The Political Behavior of the American Woman*, ed. Marianne Githens and Jewell Prestage. New York: Longman.
Gertzog, Irwin N. 1995. *Congressional Women: Their Recruitment, Integration and Behavior*. 2nd edition. New York: Greenwood Publishing Group.
Gillibrand, Kirsten. 2015. *Off the Sidelines*. New York: Random House.
Givhan, Robin. 2006. "Muted Tones of Quiet Authority: A Look Suited to the Speaker." *Washington Post*, November 10.
Givhan, Robin. 2007. "Hillary Clinton's Tentative Dip into New Neckline Territory." *Washington Post*, July 19. http://www.washingtonpost.com/wp-dyn/content/article/2007/07/19/AR2007071902668.html. Accessed March 5, 2017.
Glazer, Amihai, and Marc Robbins. 1985. "Congressional Responsiveness to Constituency Change." *American Journal of Political Science* 29: 259–73.
Goldberg, Philip. 1968. "Are Women Prejudiced Against Women?" *Transaction* 5: 28–30.
Goodman, Craig, and David C. W. Parker. 2010. "Who Franks? Explaining the Allocation of Official Resources." *Congress & the Presidency* 37:257–78.
Gorman, Elizabeth H. 2005. "Gender Stereotypes, Same-Gender Preferences, and Organizational Variation in the Hiring of Women: Evidence from Law Firms." *American Sociological Review* 70: 702–28.
Green, Matthew, and Kristen Hudak. 2009. "Congress and the Bailout: Explaining the Bailout Votes and the Electoral Effect." *Legislative Studies Section Newsletter* 32 (1).
Grenell, Alexis. 2016. "Hillary Clinton, National Mother? How the Democratic Nominee Is Subverting an Age-Old Sexist Standard in Our Politics." *New York Daily News*, September 12.
Griffin, John D. 2006. "Electoral Competition and Democratic Responsiveness: A Defense of the Marginality Hypothesis." *Journal of Politics* 68: 911–21.
Groseclose, Timothy. 1994. "Testing Committee Composition Hypotheses for the US Congress." *Journal of Politics* 56: 440–58.
Guhne, Joni. 1992. "Former Congresswoman Holt Looks Back Fondly Mostly." *Baltimore Sun*, July 23.
Haider-Markel, Donald P., Mark R. Joslyn, and Chad J. Kniss. 2000. "Minority Group Interests and Political Representation: Gay Elected Officials in the Policy Process." *Journal of Politics* 62: 568–77.
Haines, Elizabeth L., Kay Deaux, and Nicole Lofaro. 2016. "The Times They Are a-Changing . . . or Are They Not? A Comparison of Gender Stereotypes, 1983–2014." *Psychology of Women Quarterly* 40: 353–63.
Hall, Joshua C., Todd M. Nesbit, and Ricky Thorson. 2012. "The Determinants of Congressional Franking: Evidence from the 110th Congress." *Journal of Applied Economics and Policy* 31: 25–34.
Hall, Richard L. 1996. *Participation in Congress*. New Haven: Yale University Press.
Hall Jamieson, Kathleen. 1995. *Beyond the Double Bind: Women and Leadership*. New York: Oxford University Press.

Hansen, Eric R., and Sarah A. Treul. 2015. "The Symbolic and Substantive Representation of LGB Americans in the U.S. House." *Journal of Politics* 77: 955–67.

Harward, Brian M., and Kenneth W. Moffett. 2010. "The Calculus of Cosponsorship in the U.S. Senate." *Legislative Studies Quarterly* 35: 117–43.

Hasecke, Edward B., and Jason D. Mycoff. 2007. "Party Loyalty and Legislative Success: Are Loyal Majority Party Members More Successful in the U.S. House of Representatives?" *Political Research Quarterly* 60: 607–17.

Hawkins, Derek. 2017. "The Silencing of Elizabeth Warren and an Old Senate Rule Prompted by a Fistfight." *Washington Post*, February 8.

Hayes, Danny. 2011. "When Gender and Party Collide: Stereotyping in Candidate Trait Attribution." *Politics & Gender* 7: 133–65.

Hayes, Danny, and Jennifer L. Lawless. 2015. "A Non-Gendered Lens? Media, Voters, and Female Candidates in Contemporary Congressional Elections." *Perspectives on Politics* 13: 95–118.

Hearn, Josephine. 2007. "Two More Reps. Complain about Treatment of Women in Hispanic Caucus." *Politico*, February 1. http://www.politico.com/story/2007/02/two-more-reps-complain-about-treatment-of-women-in-hispanic-caucus-002583

Hedlund, Ronald D., Patricia K. Freeman, Keith E. Hamm, and Robert M. Stein. 1979. "The Electability of Women Candidates: The Effects of Sex Role Stereotypes." *Journal of Politics* 41: 513–24.

Heidom, Rich, Jr. 1994. "Margolies-Mezvinsky: Voted Out of Office but Hardly Defeated." *Philadelphia Inquirer*, December 24, B01.

Hennings, Valerie M., and R. Urbatsch. 2015. "There Can Be Only One (Woman on the Ticket): Gender in Candidate Nominations." *Political Behavior* 37: 749–66.

Hero, Rodney E., and Caroline J. Tolbert. 1996. "A Racial/Ethnic Diversity Interpretation of Politics and Policy in the States of the U.S." *American Journal of Political Science* 40: 851–71.

Herreria, Carla. 2017. "Senator Identified Simply As 'Woman' in Selfie with Male Colleagues." *Huffington Post*, January 24. http://www.huffingtonpost.com/entry/senator-amy-klobuchar-woman-getty-photo_us_588179c4e4b096b4a230fadf. Accessed March 13, 2017.

Herrnson, Paul S., J. Celeste Lay, and Atiya Kai Stokes. 2003. "Women Running 'As Women': Candidate Gender, Campaign Issues, and Voter-Targeting Strategies." *Journal of Politics* 65: 244–55.

Hill, Kim Q., and Patricia A. Hurley. 2002. "Symbolic Speeches in the U.S. Senate and Their Representational Implications." *Journal of Politics* 64: 219–31.

Hogan, Robert. 2008. "Sex and the Statehouse: The Effects of Gender on Legislative Roll-Call Voting." *Social Science Quarterly* 4: 955–68.

Holman, Mirya R., Jennifer L. Merolla, and Elizabeth J. Zechmeister. 2016. "Terrorist Threat, Male Stereotypes, and Candidate Evaluations." *Political Research Quarterly* 69: 134–47.

Huddy, Leonie, and Nayda Terkildsen. 1993. "Gender Stereotypes and the Perception of Male and Female Candidates." *American Journal of Political Science* 37: 119–47.

Hutchinson, Louise. 1973. "Marjorie Holt: How She Made It To Congress." *Chicago Tribune*, January 23.

Inter-Parliamentary Union. 2017. "World Classification: Women in National Parliaments." Data collected as of January 1, 2017. http://www.ipu.org/wmn-e/classif.htm

Jennings, M. Kent, and Norman Thomas. 1968. "Men and Women in Party Elites: Social Roles and Political Resources." *Midwest Journal of Political Science* 12: 469–92.

Jewell, Malcolm Edwin, and Marcia Lynn Whicker. 1994. *Legislative Leadership in the American States*. Ann Arbor: University of Michigan Press.

Jeydel, Alana, and Andrew J. Taylor. 2003. "Are Women Legislators Less Effective? Evidence from the U.S. House in the 103rd–105th Congress." *Political Research Quarterly* 56: 19–27.

Johannes, John R., and John C. McAdams. 1981. "The Congressional Incumbency Effect: Is It Casework, Policy Compatibility, or Something Else? An Examination of the 1978 Election." *American Journal of Political Science* 25: 512–42.

Kahn, Kim Fridkin. 1993. "Gender Differences in Campaign Messages: The Political Advertisements of Men and Women Candidates for U.S. Senate." *Political Research Quarterly* 46: 481–502.

Kahn, Kim Fridkin. 1994. "The Distorted Mirror: Press Coverage of Women Candidates for Statewide Office." *Journal of Politics* 56: 154–73.

Kahn, Kim Fridkin. 1996. *The Political Consequences of Being A Woman: How Stereotypes Influence the Conduct and Consequences of Political Campaigns*. New York: Columbia University Press.

Kahn, Kim Fridkin, and Edie N. Goldenberg. 1991. "Women Candidates in the News: An Examination of Gender Differences in U.S. Senate Campaign Coverage." *Public Opinion Quarterly* 55: 180–99.

Kahn, Mattie. 2017. "Interview with Marcy Kaptur." *Elle.com*, March 2.

Kanthak, Kristin, and George A. Krause. 2010. "Valuing Diversity in Political Organizations: Gender and Token Minorities in the U.S. House of Representatives." *American Journal of Political Science* 54: 839–54.

Kanthak, Kristin, and Jonathan Woon. 2015. "Women Don't Run? Election Aversion and Candidate Entry." *American Journal of Political Science* 59: 595–612.

Kaplan, Rebecca. 2014. "New Hampshire Republican: Rep. Ann McLane Kuster 'Is Ugly as Sin.'" *CBS News*, October 13.

Kastellec, Jonathan P., Jeffrey R. Lax, and Justin Phillips. 2010. "Public Opinion and Senate Confirmation of Supreme Court Nominees." *Journal of Politics* 72: 767–84.

Kathlene, Lyn. 1990. "A New Approach to Understanding the Impact of Gender on the Legislative Process." In *Feminist Research Methods: Exemplary Readings in the Social Sciences*, ed. Joyce McCarl Nielsen. Boulder: Westview Press.

Kathlene, Lyn. 1991. "Gender, Public Policy, and the Legislative Process: Delineating the Gendered Perspectives and Outcomes of Policymaking in the 1989 Colorado State House." Dissertation for the University of Colorado at Boulder.

Kathlene, Lyn. 1994. "Power and Influence in State Legislative Policymaking: The Interaction of Gender and Position in Committee Hearing Debates." *American Political Science Review* 88: 560–76.

Kay, Katty, and Claire Shipman. 2014. "The Confidence Gap." *The Atlantic*, May. https://www.theatlantic.com/magazine/archive/2014/05/the-confidence-gap/359815/. Accessed March 5, 2017.

Kelly, Rita Mae, Michelle A. Saint-Germain, and Jody D. Horn. 1991. "Female Public Officials: A Different Voice?" *Annals of the American Academy of Political and Social Science* 515: 77–87.

Kessler, Daniel, and Keith Krehbiel. 1996. "Dynamics of Cosponsorship." *American Political Science Review* 90: 555–66.

Kingdon, John. 1989. *Congressmen's Voting Decisions, 3rd ed.* Ann Arbor: University of Michigan Press.

Kirkpatrick, Jeane J. 1974. *Political Woman*. New York: Basic Books.

Klobuchar, Amy. 2015. *The Senator Next Door: A Memoir from the Heartland*. New York: Henry Holt and Company.

Koch, Jeffrey W. 1999. "Candidate Gender and Assessments of Senate Candidates." *Social Science Quarterly* 80: 84–96.

Koch, Jeffrey W. 2002. "Gender Stereotypes and Citizens' Impressions of House Candidates' Ideological Orientations." *American Journal of Political Science* 46: 453–62.

Koger, Gregory. 2003. "Position-Taking and Cosponsorship in the U.S. House." *Legislative Studies Quarterly* 28: 225–46.

Krehbiel, Keith. 1991. *Information and Legislative Organization*. Ann Arbor: University of Michigan Press.

Krislov, Samuel. 1974. *Representative Bureaucracy*. Englewood Cliffs, NJ: Prentice Hall.

Kropf, Martha E., and John A. Boiney. 2001. "The Electoral Glass Ceiling: Gender, Viability and the News in U.S. Senate Campaigns." *Women & Politics* 23: 81–105.

Krueger, Brian S., and Paul D. Mueller. 2001. "Moderating Backlash: Racial Mobiliation, Partisan Coalitions, and Public Policy in the American States." *State Politics & Policy Quarterly* 1: 165–79.

Krutz, Glen S. 2005. "Issues and Institutions: 'Winnowing' in the U.S. Congress." *American Journal of Political Science* 49: 313–26.

Lake, Celinda, Alysia Snell, Cate Gormley, Flora Lethbridge-Cejku, and Bob Carpenter. 2013. *An Examination of the Impact of Media Coverage of Women Candidates Appearance.* http://www.nameitchangeit.org/page/-/Name-It-Change-It-Appearance-Research.pdf

Lawless, Jennifer L. 2004a. "Women, War, and Winning Elections: Gender Stereotyping in the Post-September 11th Era." *Political Research Quarterly* 53: 479–90.

Lawless, Jennifer L. 2004b. "Politics of Presence? Congresswomen and Symbolic Representation." *Political Research Quarterly* 57: 81–99.

Lawless, Jennifer L., and Danny Hayes. 2016. *Women on the Run: Gender, Media and Political Campaigns in a Polarized Era*. New York: Cambridge University Press.

Lawless, Jennifer L., and Kathryn Pearson. 2008. "The Primary Reason for Women's Underrepresentation? Reevaluating the Conventional Wisdom." *Journal of Politics* 70: 67–82.

Lawless, Jennifer L., and Richard L. Fox. 2004. "Why Don't Women Run for

Office?" *Brown Policy Report*, January. Providence, RI: Taubman Center for Public Policy, Brown University.

Lawless, Jennifer L., and Richard L. Fox. 2008. "Why Are Women Still Not Running for Public Office?" *Issues in Governance Studies* 14 (May) Washington, DC: Brookings.

Lawless, Jennifer L., and Richard L. Fox. 2010. *It Still Takes a Candidate: Why Women Don't Run for Office*. New York: Cambridge University Press.

Lawless, Jennifer L., and Richard L. Fox. 2012. *Men Rule: The Continued Under-Representation of Women in U.S. Politics*. Washington, DC: Women & Politics Institute.

Lawless, Jennifer L., Richard L. Fox, and Gail Baitinger. 2014. "Women's Underrepresentation in U.S. Politics: The Enduring Gender Gap." In *Women and Elective Office*, 3rd ed., ed. Sue Thomas and Clyde Wilcox. New York: Oxford University Press.

Lawrence, Regina G., and Melody Rose. 2009. *Hillary Clinton's Race for the White House: Gender Politics and Media on the Campaign Trail*. Boulder, CO: Lynne Rienner.

Lawrence, Regina G., and Melody Rose. 2011. "Bringing Out the Hook: Exit Talk in Coverage of Hillary Clinton's Presidential Campaign." *Political Research Quarterly* 64: 870–83.

Lazarus, Jeffrey. 2009. "Party, Electoral Vulnerability, and Earmarks in the U.S. House of Representatives." *Journal of Politics* 71: 1050–61.

Lazarus, Jeffrey. 2010. "Doing Well by Doing Good: Electorally Motivated Legislative Activity in the House and Senate." Presented at the 2010 Annual Meeting of the American Political Science Association, Washington, DC, September 2–5.

Lazarus, Jeffrey. 2013. "Issue Salience and Bill Introduction in the House and Senate." *Congress & the Presidency* 40: 215–29.

Lazarus, Jeffrey, Jeff Glas, and Kyle T. Barbieri. 2012. "Earmarks and Elections to the U.S. House of Representatives." *Congress & the Presidency* 39: 254–69.

Lazarus, Jeffrey, and Shauna Reilly. 2010. "The Electoral Benefits of Distributive Spending." *Political Research Quarterly* 63: 343–55.

Leader, Shelah Gilbert. 1977. "The Policy Impact of Elected Women Officials." In *The Impact of the Electoral Process*, ed. Louis Maisel and Joseph Cooper. Beverly Hills, CA: Sage.

Lee, Barbara. 2015. "The Real Reasons We've Never Had a Woman President." *Boston Globe Magazine*, October 20.

Lee, Frances E. 2003. "Geographic Politics in the U.S. House of Representatives: Coalition Building and Distribution of Benefits." *American Journal of Political Science* 47: 714–28.

Leeper, Mark Stephen. 1991. "The Impact of Prejudice on Female Candidates: An Experimental Look at Voter Inference." *American Politics Quarterly* 19: 248–61.

Lepore, Meredith. 2012. "Female CEOs in Washington See A Ridiculously Large Income Gap." *The Grindstone*, March 30. http://www.thegrindstone.com/2012/03/30/office-politics/female-ceos-in-washington-see-a-ridicously-large-income-gap-191/. Accessed March 10, 2017.

Leslie, Sarah-Jane, Andrei Cimpian, Meredith Meyer, and Edward Freeland. 2015. "Expectations of Brilliance Underlie Gender Distributions Across Academic Disciplines." *Science* 347: 262–65.
Levitt, Steven D., and James M. Snyder Jr. 1995. "Political Parties and the Distribution of Federal Outlays." *American Journal of Political Science* 39 (4): 958–80.
Levitt, Steven D., and James M. Snyder Jr. 1997. "The Impact of Federal Spending on House Election Outcomes." *Journal of Political Economy* 105 (1): 30–53.
Maltzman, Forrest. 1998. *Competing Principals: Committees, Parties, and the Organization of Congress*. Ann Arbor: University of Michigan Press.
Mann, Thomas E, and Raymond E. Wolfinger. 1980. "Candidates and Parties in Congressional Elections." *American Political Science Review* 74: 617–32.
Mansbridge, Jane. 1999. "Should Blacks Represent Blacks and Women Represent Women? A Contingent 'Yes.'" *Journal of Politics* 61: 628–57.
Mayhew, David R. 1974. *Congress: The Electoral Connection*. New Haven: Yale University Press.
Mayhew, David R. 1977. "The Case of the Vanishing Marginals: The Bureaucracy Did It." *American Political Science Review* 71: 177–81.
Mayhew, David R. 2000. *America's Congress: Actions in the Public Sphere, James Madison Through Newt Gingrich*. New Haven: Yale University Press.
McAdams, John C., and John R. Johannes. 1981. "Does Casework Matter? A Reply to Professor Fiorina." *American Journal of Political Science* 25: 581–604.
McAdams, John C., and John R. Johannes. 1988. "Congressmen, Perquisites, and Elections." *Journal of Politics* 50: 412–39.
McCarthy, Kate. 2012. "Chicago Sun Times Asks Whether Woman Can Be Parent AND Candidate." *Name It, Change It Blog*, September 6, http://www.nameitchangeit.org/blog/entry/chicago-sun-times-asks-whether-woman-can-be-parent-and-candidate
McCaskill, Claire. 2015. *Plenty Ladylike: A Memoir*. New York: Simon & Schuster.
McCaskill, Noland D. 2017a. "GOP Lawmaker: "'Poorly Dressed' Democratic Women Wore 'Bad-Looking White Pantsuits.'" *Politico.*, March 1. http://www.politico.com/story/2017/03/kevin-cramer-democratic-women-white-pantsuits-235578?cmpid=sf. Accessed March 4, 2015.
McCaskill, Noland D. 2017b. "Rep. Cramer Digs In, Accuses Female House Democrats of Hissing at Trump." *Politico*, March 3. http://www.politico.com/story/2017/03/kevin-cramer-female-house-democrats-235655. Accessed March 5, 2017..
Meeks, Lindsey. 2013. "All the Gender That's Fit to Print: How the *New York Times* Covered Hillary Clinton and Sarah Palin in 2008." *Journalism and Mass Communication Quarterly* 90: 520–39.
Meier, Kenneth J., and Jill Nicholson-Crotty. 2006. "Gender, Representative Bureaucracy, and Law Enforcement: The Case of Sexual Assault." *Public Administration Review* 66: 850–60.
Mendelberg, Tali, and Christopher F. Karpowitz. 2016. "Power, Gender and Group Discussion." *Political Psychology* 37: 23–60.
Merritt, Sharyne. 1980. "Sex Differences in Role Behavior and Policy Orientations of Suburban Officeholders: The Effect of Women's Employment." In *Women in Local Politics*, ed. Debra Stewart. Metuchen, NJ: Scarecrow Press.

Mezey, Susan Gluck. 1978. "Does Sex Make a Difference? A Case Study of Women in Politics." *Western Political Quarterly* 31: 492–501.

Mikesell, John L. 1987. "A Note on Senatorial Mass Mailing Expenditure and the Quest for Reelection." *Public Choice* 53: 257–65.

Milyo, Jeffrey, and Samantha Schosberg. 2000. "Gender Bias and Selection Bias in House Elections." *Public Choice* 105: 41–59.

Mo, Cecilia Hyunjung. 2015. "The Consequences of Explicit and Implicit Gender Attitudes and Candidate Quality in the Calculations of Voters." *Political Behavior* 37: 357–95.

Molinari, Susan. 1998. *Representative Mom: Balancing Budgets, Bill, and Baby in the U.S. Congress.* New York, NY: Doubleday.

Morris, Celia. 1992. *Storming the Statehouse: Running for Governor with Ann Richards and Dianne Feinstein.* New York, NY: Charles Scribner's Sons.

Morris, Randa. 2013. "Sexist Reporter Reminds Female Candidate She Has Children." *Addicting Info*, August 5. http://addictinginfo.com/2013/08/05/sexist-reporter-reminds-female-candidate-that-she-has-children-ten-questions-they-should-save-for-next-time/. Accessed March 11, 2017.

Moss-Racusin, Corinne A., John F. Dovidio, Victoria L. Brescoll, Mark J. Graham, and Jo Handelsman. 2012. "Science Faculty's Subtle Gender Biases Favor Male Students." *Proceedings of the National Academy of Sciences* 109: 16474–79.

Mueller, Carol. 1986. "Nurturance and Mastery: Competing Qualifications for Women's Access to High Public Office?" *Research in Politics and Society* 2: 211–32.

Mundy, Liza. 2015. "The Secret History of Women in the Senate." *Politico Magazine*, January/February.

National Public Radio. 2014. "The Congresswoman Whose Husband Called Her Home." *National Public Radio*, May 10. http://www.npr.org/sections/itsallpolitics/2014/05/10/310996960/the-congresswoman-whose-husband-called-her-home. Accessed March 4, 2017.

Newton-Small, Jay. 2013. "The Last Politicians." *Time Magazine*, October 28.

Niven, David. 1998a. "Party Elites and Women Candidates: The Shape of Bias." *Journal of Women, Politics & Policy* 19: 57-80.

Niven, David. 1998b. *The Missing Majority: The Recruitment of Women as State Legislative Candidates.* New York: Greenwood Publishing Group.

Niven, David, and Jeremy Zilber. 2001a. "Do Women and Men in Congress Cultivate Different Images? Evidence from Congressional Web Sites." *Political Communication* 18: 395–405.

Niven, David, and Jeremy Zilber. 2001b. "How Does She Have Time For Kids and Congress? Views on Gender and Media Coverage From House Offices." *Women & Politics* 23: 147–65.

Norrander, Barbara, and Clyde Wilcox. 1998. "The Geography of Gender." In *Women and Elective Office: Past, Present, and Future*, eds. Sue Thomas and Clyde Wilcox. New York: Oxford University Press.

Norton, Noelle H. 2002. "Transforming Policy from the Inside: Participation in Committee." In *Women Transforming Congress*, ed. Cindy Simon Rosenthal. Norman: University of Oklahoma Press.

Nyhan, Brendan, Eric McGhee, John Sides, Seth Masket, and Steven Green. 2012.

"One Vote Out of Step? The Effects of Salient Roll Call Votes in the 2010 Election." *American Politics Research* 40: 844–79.

Oldmixon, Elizabeth A. 2002. "Culture Wars in the Congressional Theater: How the U.S. House of Representatives Legislates Morality, 1993–1998." *Social Science Quarterly* 83: 775–88.

Oleszek, Walter J. 2007. *Congressional Procedures and the Policy Process*. Washington, DC: Congressional Quarterly Press.

Page, Susan. 2016. "Why Are You Yelling? The Questions Female Candidates Still Face." *USA Today*, June 5.

Palmer, Barbara, and Dennis Simon. 2005. "When Women Run Against Women: The Hidden Influence of Female Incumbents in Elections to the U.S. House of Representatives, 1956–2002." *Politics and Gender* 1: 39–63.

Palmer, Barbara, and Dennis Simon. 2006. *Breaking the Political Glass Ceiling: Women and Congressional Elections*. New York: Routledge.

Palmer, Barbara, and Dennis Simon. 2010. *Breaking the Political Glass Ceiling: Women and Congressional Elections*, 2nd ed. New York: Routledge.

Parker, David C. W., and Craig Goodman. 2009. "Making a Good Impression: Resource Allocation, Home Styles, and Washington Work." Working paper on file with authors.

Parker, David C. W., and Craig Goodman. 2013. "Our State's Never Had Better Friends: Resource Allocation, Home Styles, and Dual Representation in the Senate." *Political Research Quarterly* 66: 370–84.

Parker, Glenn, and Roger Davidson. 1979. "Why Do Americans Love Their Congressmen So Much More Than Their Congress?" *Legislative Studies Quarterly* 4: 53–60.

Parker, Glenn R., and Suzanne L. Parker. 1985. "Correlates and Effects of Attention to District by U.S. House Members." *Legislative Studies Quarterly* 10: 223–42.

Payne, Paul. 2008. "Thompson, Woolsey Defend Federal Earmarks." *Santa Rosa Press Democrat*, May 28, http://www.pressdemocrat.com/article/20080528/NEWS/805280319. Accessed October 22, 2010.

Peresie, Jennifer L. 2005. "Female Judges Matter: Gender and Collegial Decisionmaking in the Federal Appellate Courts." *Yale Law Journal* 114: 1759–90.

Pew Research Center. 2010. "Earmarks Could Help Candidates in Midterms; Palin and Tea Part Connections Could Hurt." http://people-press.org/report/642/. Accessed November 3, 2010.

Phelan, Julie E., Corinne A. Moss-Racusin, and Laurie A. Rudman. 2008. "Competent Yet Out in the Cold: Shifting Criteria for Hiring Reflect Backlash Toward Agentic Women." *Psychology of Women Quarterly* 32: 406–13.

Phillips, Anne. 1995. *The Politics of Presence*. New York: Oxford University Press.

Pitkin, Hanna. 1967. *The Concept of Representation*. Berkeley: University of California Press.

Pogash, Carol. 1986. "Mayor Dianne Feinstein's Twelve Rules for Getting Ahead." *Working Women Magazine*, January.

Poggione, Sarah. 2004. "Exploring Gender Differences in State Legislators' Policy Preferences." *Political Research Quarterly* 57: 305–14.

Poole, Keith T., and Howard Rosenthal. 2006. *DW-NOMINATE Data: 98th to 110th Congress*. Extracted from www.voteview.com.

Preece, Jessica Robinson, Olga Bogach Stoddard, and Rachel Fisher. 2016. "Run, Jane, Run! Gendered Responses to Political Party Recruitment." *Political Behavior* 38: 561–77.

Radcliff, Benjamin, and Martin Saiz. 1995. "Race, Turnout, and Public Policy in the American States." *Political Research Quarterly* 48: 775–94.

Ragsdale, Lyn, and Timothy E. Cook. 1987. "Representatives' Actions and Challengers' Reactions: Limits to Candidate Connections." *American Journal of Political Science* 31: 45–81.

Reingold, Beth. 1992. "Concepts of Representation among Female and Male State Legislators." *Legislative Studies Quarterly* 17: 509–37.

Reingold, Beth. 1996. "Conflict and Cooperation: Legislative Strategies and Concepts of Power Among Female and Male State Legislators." *Journal of Politics* 58: 464–85.

Reingold, Beth. 2000. *Representing Women: Sex, Gender, and Legislative Behavior in Arizona and California.* Chapel Hill: University of North Carolina Press.

Reston, Maeve. 2014. "In Iowa GOP's Joni Ernst Broke a Gender Barrier on Her Own Terms." *Los Angeles Times*, November 5.

Reuben, Ernesto, Paola Sapienza, and Luigi Zingales. 2014. "How Stereotypes Impair Women's Careers in Science." *Proceedings of the National Academy of Sciences* 111: 4403–8.

Riccucci, Norma M., and Judith R. Saidel. 1997. "The Representativeness of State-Level Bureaucratic Leaders: A Missing Piece of the Representative Bureaucracy Puzzle." *Public Administration Review* 57: 423–30.

Richardson, Lilliard E., and Patricia K. Freeman. 1995. "Gender Differences in Constituency Service among State Legislators." *Political Research Quarterly* 48: 169–79.

Ridgeway, Cecilia L., and Shelley J. Correll. 2004. "Unpacking the Gender System: A Theoretical Perspective on Gender Beliefs and Social Relations." *Gender & Society* 18: 510–31.

Rivers, Douglas, and Morris Fiorina. 1989. "Constituency Service, Reputation, and the Incumbency Advantage." In *Homestyle and Washington Work: Studies of Congressional Politics*, ed. Morris Fiorina and David Rohde, 17–46. Ann Arbor: University of Michigan Press.

Rocca, Michael S., and Stacy B. Gordon. 2010. "The Position-Taking Value of Bill Sponsorship in Congress." *Political Research Quarterly* 63: 387–97.

Rocca, Michael S., and Stacy B. Gordon. 2013. "Earmarks as a Means and an End: The Link Between Earmarks and Campaign Contributions in the US House of Representatives." *Journal of Politics* 75: 241–53.

Rocca, Michael S., Gabriel Sanchez, and Joseph Uscinski. 2008. "Personal Attributes and Latino Voting Behavior in Congress." *Social Science Quarterly* 89:392–405.

Rogers, Mary Beth. 1998. *Barbara Jordan: American Hero.* New York, NY: Bantam Books.

Roig-Franzia, Manuel. 2013. "Kyrsten Sinema: A Success Story Like Nobody Else's." *Washington Post*, January 2.

Romano, Lois. 2016. "The Women Who Blazed a Long, Frustrating Trail in Politics." *Washington Post*, July 22.

Romero, David W. 2006. "What They Do *Does* Matter: Incumbent Resource Allocations and the Individual House Vote." *Political Behavior* 28: 241–58.

Roper, Eric. 2010. "Audio: Sen. Arlen Specter Tells Bachmann to 'Act Like a Lady.'" *Star Tribune*, January 21.

Rosenthal, Cindy Simon. 1995. "The Role of Gender in Descriptive Representation." *Political Research Quarterly* 48: 599–611.

Rosenwasser, Shirley M., and Jana Seale. 1988. "Attitudes Toward A Hypothetical Male or Female Presidential Candidate: A Research Note." *Political Psychology* 9: 591–98.

Rosenwasser, Shirley M., and Norma G. Dean. 1989. "Gender Role and Political Office: Effects of Perceived Masculinity/Femininity of Candidate and Political Office." *Psychology of Women Quarterly* 13: 77–85.

Rosenwasser, Shirley M., Robyn R. Rogers, Sheila Fling, Kayla Silvers-Pickens, and John Butemeyer. 1987. "Attitudes Toward Women and Men in Politics: Perceived Male and Female Candidate Competencies and Participant Personality Characteristics." *Political Psychology* 8: 191–200.

Roybal-Allard, Lucille. 2010. "Transportation Bill Passes House." July 29. http://roybal-allard.house.gov/News/DocumentSingle.aspx?DocumentID=201619. Accessed October 22, 2010.

Rundquist, Barry S. 1978. "On Testing a Military Industrial Complex Theory." *American Politics Quarterly* 6: 29–53.

Saint Germain, Michelle A. 1989. "Does Their Difference Make a Difference? The Impact of Women on Public Policy in the Arizona Legislature." *Social Science Quarterly* 70: 956–68.

Sanbonmatsu, Kira. 2002. *Democrats, Republicans, and the Politics of Women's Place*. Ann Arbor: University of Michigan Press.

Sanbonmatsu, Kira. 2006. *Where Women Run: Gender and Party in the American States*. Ann Arbor: University of Michigan Press.

Sanbonmatsu, Kira, and Kathleen Dolan. 2009. "Do Gender Stereotypes Transcend Party?" *Political Research Quarterly* 62: 485–94.

Sanbonmatsu, Kira, Susan J. Carroll, and Debbie Walsh. 2009. *Poised to Run: Women's Pathways to the State Legislatures*. Center for American Women and Policy, Eagleton Institute of Politics, Rutgers, the State University of New Jersey.

Sanchez, Linda, and Loretta Sanchez. 2008. *Dream in Color: How the Sanchez Sisters Are Making History in Congress*. Grand Central Publishing.

Sapiro, Virginia. 1981a. "If U.S. Senator Baker Were A Woman: An Experimental Study of Candidate Images." *Political Psychology* 3: 61–83.

Sapiro, Virginia. 1981b. "When Are Interests Interesting?" *American Political Science Review* 75: 701–16.

Savage, James D. 1991. "Saints and Cardinals in Appropriations Committees and the Fight against Distributive Politics." *Legislative Studies Quarterly* 16: 329–47.

Schiff, Steven H., and Steven S. Smith. 1983. "Generational Change and the Allocation of Staff in the U.S. Congress." *Legislative Studies Quarterly* 8: 457–67.

Schiller, Wendy J. 1995. "Senators as Political Entrepreneurs: Using Bill Sponsorship to Shape Legislative Agendas." *American Journal of Political Science* 39: 186–203.

Schiller, Wendy J. 2000. *Partners and Rivals: Representation in U.S. Senate Delegations*. Princeton: Princeton University Press.

Schlozman, Kay, and Jane Mansbridge. 1979. "Gender and the Power Differential? How Much? How Come? Who Cares?" *Harvard Educational Review* 49: 554–56.

Schnall, Marianne. 2015. "Interview with Senator Kirsten Gillibrand." December 10. https://www.politicalparity.org/interview-senator-gillibrand/

Schneider, Monica C., and Angela L. Bos. 2014. "Measuring Stereotypes of Female Politicians." *Political Psychology* 35: 245–66.

Schroeder, Patricia. 1999. *24 Years of House Work . . . and the Place Is Still a Mess*. Kansas City, MO: Andrews McMeel Publishing.

Schumach, Murray. 1977. "Metropolitan Baedeker: Astoria, the Largest Greek City Outside Greece." *New York Times*, October 7. Accessed September 27, 2010.

Sellers, Patrick J. 1997. "Fiscal Consistency and Federal District Spending in Congressional Elections." *American Journal of Political Science* 41:1024–41.

Serra, George, and Albert Cover. 1992. "The Electoral Consequences of Perquisite Use: The Casework Case." *Legislative Studies Quarterly* 17: 233–46.

Serra, George, and David Moon. 1994. "Casework, Issue Positions, and Voting in Congressional Elections: A District Analysis." *Journal of Politics* 56: 200–13.

Serra, George, and Neil Pinny. 2004. "Casework, Issues, and Voting in State Legislative Elections: A District Analysis." *Journal of Legislative Studies* 10: 32–46.

Sidman, Andrew H., and Maxwell H. H. Mak. 2006. "Pork, Awareness, and Ideological Consistency: The Effects of Distributive Benefits on Vote Choice." Paper delivered at the 2006 Annual Meeting of the Midwest Political Science Association, Chicago, April 20-23.

Sigelman, Lee, Carol K. Sigelman, and Christopher Fowler. 1987. "A Bird of a Different Feather? An Experimental Investigation of Physical Attractiveness and the Electability of Female Candidates." *Social Psychology Quarterly* 50: 32–43.

Sinclair, Barbara. 1989. *The Transformation of the U.S. Senate*. Baltimore: Johns Hopkins University Press.

Skenazy, Lenore. 2008. "Slacking Hillary." *New York Sun*, June 3.

Smith, Eric R.A.N., and Richard L. Fox. 2001. "The Electoral Fortunes of Women Candidate for Congress." *Political Research Quarterly* 54: 205–21.

Smith, Kevin B. 1997. "When All's Fair: Signs of Parity in Media Coverage of Female Candidates." *Political Communication* 14: 71–82.

Snowe, Olympia. 2013. *Fighting for Common Ground: How We Can Fix the Stalemate in Congress*. New York: Weinstein Publishing.

Sonmez, Felicia. 2011. "Female House Democrats Want Rebuke of West for Insults to Wasserman Schultz." *Washington Post*, July 20.

Steffensmeier, Darrell, and Chris Hebert. 1999. "Women and Men Policymakers: Does the Judge's Gender Affect the Sentencing of Criminal Defendants?" *Social Forces* 77: 1163–96.

Stein, Robert M., and Kenneth Bickers. 1994. "Congressional Elections and the Pork Barrel." *Journal of Politics* 56: 377–99.

Stout, Christopher T., and Reuben Kline. 2011. "I'm Not Voting For Her: Polling Discrepancies and Female Candidates." *Political Behavior* 33: 479–503.

Sulkin, Tracy. 2005. *Issue Politics in Congress*. Cambridge: Cambridge University Press.

Sullivan, Margaret. 2014. "On Campaign Trail, Missteps on Gender." *New York Times*, February 23, SR12.

Sussman, Glen, and Jonathan P. West. 1995. "Gender Differences in Legislators' Activities: Political Linkage with Constituents and Decision-Making Sources." Presented at the Southern Political Science Association Annual Meeting, January 3–6.

Swers, Michele L. 1998. "Are Congresswomen More Likely to Vote for Women's Issues Bills Than Their Male Colleagues?" *Legislative Studies Quarterly* 23: 435–48.

Swers, Michele L. 2001. "Understanding the Policy Impact of Electing Women: Evidence from Research on Congress and State Legislatures." *PS: Political Science and Politics* 34: 217–20.

Swers, Michele L. 2002. *The Difference Women Make: The Policy Impact of Women in Congress*. Chicago: University of Chicago Press.

Swers, Michele L. 2005. "Connecting Descriptive and Substantive Representation: An Analysis of Sex Differences in Cosponsorship Activity." *Legislative Studies Quarterly* 30: 407–33.

Swers, Michele L. 2013. *Women in the Club: Gender and Policy Making in the Senate*. Chicago: University of Chicago Press.

Tamari, Jonathan. 2014. "PA, NJ Women Face Obstacles in Political Races." *Philadelphia Inquirer*, June 9.

Tamerius, Karin L. 1995. "Sex, Gender, and Leadership in the Representation of Women." In *Gender Power, Leadership, and Governance*, ed. Georgia Duerst-Lahti and Rita Mae Kelly. Ann Arbor: University of Michigan Press.

Tatalovich, Raymond, and David Schier. 1993. "The Persistence of Ideological Cleavage in Voting on Abortion Legislation in the House of Representatives, 1973–1988." *American Politics Quarterly* 21: 125–39.

Terkel, Amanda. 2016. "How Women Became a Powerful Political Force in the Democratic Party." *Huffington Post*, July 28.

Thomas, Robert. 1996. "Coya Knutson, 82, Legislator; Husband Sought Her Defeat."

New York Times, October 12. http://www.nytimes.com/1996/10/12/us/coya-knutson-82-legislator-husband-sought-her-defeat.html. Accessed March 4, 2017.

Thomas, Sue. 1991. "The Impact of Women on State Legislative Policies." *Journal of Politics* 53: 958–76.

Thomas, Sue. 1992. "The Effects of Race and Gender on Constituency Service." *Western Political Quarterly* 45: 161–80.

Thomas, Sue. 1994. *How Women Legislate*. New York: Oxford University Press.

Thomas, Sue. 1997. "Why Gender Matters: The Perceptions of Officeholders." *Journal of Women, Politics and Policy* 17: 27–53.

Thomas, Sue. 2002. "The Personal Is The Political: Antecedents of Gendered Choices of Elected Representatives." *Sex Roles* 47: 343–53.

Thomas, Sue, and Clyde Wilcox. 2014. *Women and Elective Office: Past, Present and Future*. New York: Oxford University Press.

Thomas, Sue, and Susan Welch. 1991. "The Impact of Gender on Activities and Priorities of State Legislators." *Western Political Quarterly* 44 (2): 445–56.

Tomz, Michael, Jason Wittenberg, and Gary King. 2003. "CLARIFY: Software for

Interpreting and Presenting Statistical Results." Journal of Statistical Software, Vol. 8. http://gking.harvard.edu/stats.shtml.

Torregrosa, Luisita Lopez. 2012. "Evaluating Challenges Women Face." *International Herald Tribune*, March 7.

Van Vugt, Mark, David De Cremer, and Dirk P. Janssen. 2007. "Gender Differences in Cooperation and Competition: The Male-Warrior Hypothesis." *Psychological Science* 18: 19–23.

Vega, Arturo, and Juanita M. Firestone. 1995. "The Effects of Gender on Congressional Behavior and the Substantive Representation of Women." *Legislative Studies Quarterly* 20: 213–22.

Vennochi, Joan. 2012. "Warren Must Sell Substance Over Flash." *Boston Globe*, September 13.

Volden, Craig, Alan E. Wiseman, and Dana E. Wittmer. 2013. "When Are Women More Effective Lawmakers Than Men?" *American Journal of Political Science* 57: 326–41.

Vucanovich, Barbara, and Patricia D. Cafferata. 2005. *From Nevada to Congress, and Back Again.* Reno: University of Nevada Press.

Walsh, Katherine Cramer. 2002. "Enlarging Representation: Women Bringing Marginalized Perspectives to Floor Debate in the House of Representatives." In *Women Transforming Congress*, ed. Cindy Simon Rosenthal. Norman: University of Oklahoma Press.

Washington Post. 2011. "First Women to Wear Pants on House Floor, Rep, Charlotte Reid." *Washington Post.* https://www.washingtonpost.com/blogs/reliable-source/post/update-first-woman-to-wear-pants-on-house-floor-rep-charlotte-reid/2011/12/21/gIQAVLD99O_blog.html?utm_term=.6917ad9d7415. Accessed March 5, 2017.

Wawro, Gregory J. 2000. *Legislative Entrepreneurship in the U.S. House of Representatives.* Ann Arbor: University of Michigan Press.

Wehr-Flowers, Erin. 2006. "Differences Between Male and Female Students' Confidence, Anxiety, and Attitude Toward Learning Jazz Improvisation." *Journal of Research in Music Education* 54: 337–49.

Weisman, Jonathan, and Jennifer Steinhauer. 2013. "Senate Women Lead in Effort to Find Accord." *New York Times*, October 15, A1.

Welch, Susan. 1985. "Are Women More Liberal Than Men in the U.S. Congress?" *Legislative Studies Quarterly* 10: 125–34.

Williams, John E., and Deborah L. Best. 1990. *Measuring Sex Stereotypes: A Multination Study*. Beverly Hills, CA: Sage.

Williams, Melissa S. 1998. *Voice, Trust and Memory: Marginalized Groups and the Failings of Liberal Representation.* Princeton: Princeton University Press.

Wilson, Rick K., and Cheryl D. Young. 1993. "Cosponsorship in the U.S. Congress." *Legislative Studies Quarterly* 22: 25–41.

Witt, Linda, Karen M. Paget, and Glenna Matthews. 1994. *Running As A Woman: Gender and Power in American Politics*. New York: Simon and Schuster.

Wolbrecht, Christina. 2002. "Female Legislators and the Women's Rights Agenda: From Feminine Mystique to Feminist Era." In *Women Transforming Congress*, ed. Cindy Simon Rosenthal. Norman: University of Oklahoma Press.

Wong, Andrea. 2010. *Secrets of Powerful Women: Leading Change for a New Generation*. New York: Hachette Books.

Woolsey, Lynn. 2004. "Constituent Update." http://woolsey.house.gov/SupportingFiles/documents/Woolsey_NL_2004.pdf. Accessed October 22, 2010.

Woolsey, Lynn. 2008. "Constituent Update." http://woolsey.house.gov/SupportingFiles/documents/Woolsey_NL_2008.pdf. Accessed October 22, 2010.

Woolsey, Lynn. 2010. "Constituent Update." http://woolsey.house.gov/SupportingFiles/documents/Woolsey_NL_2010.pdf. Accessed October 22, 2010.

Woon, Jonathan. 2009. "Issue Attention in the U.S. Senate." *Legislative Studies Quarterly* 34: 29–54.

Yiannakis, Diana. 1981. "The Grateful Electorate: Casework and Congressional Elections." *American Journal of Political Science* 25: 568–80.

Index